Excessive Force

Excessive Force

TORONTO'S FIGHT TO REFORM CITY
POLICING

Alok Mukherjee *with* Tim Harper

Douglas & McIntyre

Douglas and McIntyre (2013) Ltd.
P.O. Box 219, Madeira Park, BC, V0N 2H0
www.douglas-mcintyre.com

Edited by Silas White
Copyedited by Amanda Growe
Cover design by Sari Naworynski
Text design by Shed Simas / Onça Design
Printed and bound in Canada

Canada Council   Conseil des arts
for the Arts   du Canada

BRITISH COLUMBIA
ARTS COUNCIL
An agency of the Province of British Columbia

Douglas and McIntyre (2013) Ltd. acknowledges the support of the Canada
Council for the Arts, which last year invested $153 million to bring the arts to
Canadians throughout the country. We also gratefully acknowledge financial
support from the Government of Canada and from the Province of British
Columbia through the BC Arts Council and the Book Publishing Tax Credit.

Library and Archives Canada Cataloguing in Publication

Mukherjee, Alok, author
    Excessive force : Toronto's fight to reform city policing / Alok Mukherjee
with Tim Harper.

Includes index.
Issued in print and electronic formats.
ISBN 978-1-77162-183-0 (softcover).--ISBN 978-1-77162-184-7 (HTML)

    1. Police--Ontario--Toronto. 2. Police brutality--Ontario--Toronto.
3. Police misconduct--Ontario--Toronto. I. Harper, Tim, 1955-, author
II. Title.

HV8160.T6M85 2018   363.2'32   C2017-907501-2
                                                     C2017-907502-0

Table of Contents

Acknowledgements

I COULD NOT have told these stories without the help of Tim Harper, my collaborator. Tim is a seasoned reporter, columnist and editor who has done tours of duty in some of the major capitals of the world. Policing was not his beat. However, as he heard my story of a decade with the Toronto police he was fascinated, and a partnership was born. I am forever grateful to Kirk Makin, another respected journalist, for bringing the two of us together.

Tim and I would like to say a sincere thank you to our partners, Tanya Talaga and Arun Mukherjee, for believing in our project, giving us their unstinting support and encouragement, and cheerfully putting up with our absences.

We are thankful to many journalists for their important work on policing. We would like to mention two in particular: Jim Rankin and Wendy Gillis of the *Toronto Star*. Rankin's consistent and probing examination of police interactions with Black and other racialized residents of Toronto dating back to the late 1990s has been groundbreaking. Gillis joined him some years ago and has contributed critically to public awareness of systemic issues that affect public trust and confidence in our system of policing.

I am grateful, also, to Toronto's weekly *NOW* magazine and editor Enzo DiMatteo for giving me space to explore emerging policing issues on a regular basis since I stepped down from the Toronto Police Services Board. This has helped me greatly to clarify my thinking and develop the analysis you see in this book.

I would be remiss if I did not express my gratitude to Ryerson University for its strong and generous support. Ryerson invited me to take up an appointment as a distinguished visiting professor after I left the police board in August 2015 and thus provided me with the academic, intellectual and physical environment necessary for writing this book.

Finally, Tim and I are grateful to Silas White and Amanda Growe, our editors, and Howard White, our publisher, at Douglas & McIntyre. Howard believed that the stories here were worth telling. And with their meticulous editing, Silas and Amanda helped make them much better. A special thank you as well to Drew Hayden Taylor, the Indigenous writer and a friend, who suggested that we consider approaching Douglas & McIntyre.

If this book resonates with you, much credit is due to Tim. Any errors or infelicities are, of course, mine.

Alok Mukherjee

Abbreviations

AMO   Association of Municipalities of Ontario; provincial organization representing the interests of municipal governments

CACP   Canadian Association of Chiefs of Police; the collective voice of Canada's police chiefs

CAPG   Canadian Association of Police Governance; a voluntary national organization representing and promoting the interests of Canada's police boards and commissions

CCLA   Canadian Civil Liberties Association

CPA   Canadian Police Association; the collective voice of Canada's police associations

FCM   Federation of Canadian Municipalities; national organization representing the interests of Canada's municipal governments

MCSCS   Ministry of Community Safety and Correctional Services; the Ontario provincial ministry responsible for the PSA and its regulations, and for setting and enforcing adequacy standards

OACP   Ontario Association of Chiefs of Police; the collective voice of Ontario's police chiefs

OAPSB   Ontario Association of Police Services Boards; a voluntary organization representing and promoting the interests of the province's police services boards

OCPC   Ontario Civilian Police Commission; the provincial agency that ensures the delivery of adequate and effective policing, oversees the conduct of members of a police board or the whole board, and adjudicates appeals of penalties imposed on a police officer by a police service due to misconduct under the PSA

OHRC   Ontario Human Rights Commission

OIPRD   Office of the Independent Police Review Director; the provincial agency responsible for the investigation of public complaints against a police officer or a police service related to officer conduct, officer service or policy

OPP   Ontario Provincial Police

PACER   Police and Community Engagement Review; a project of TPS to address public concern about the stopping and carding of people who are not the subject of a police investigation, their personal details being entered in the police database

PAO   Police Association of Ontario; the collective voice of Ontario's police associations

PSA   *Police Services Act*; the provincial statute in Ontario governing the provision of adequate and effective policing services

RCMP   Royal Canadian Mounted Police

SIU   Special Investigations Unit; an arm's-length Ontario provincial agency reporting to the Attorney General that is responsible for investigations of lethal use of force and serious injuries caused during police interactions with the public, as well as allegations of sexual assault against police officers

TPA   Toronto Police Association; organization representing the members of TPS, also their bargaining agent

TPS   Toronto Police Service; Canada's largest municipal police force

TPSB   Toronto Police Services Board; TPS's civilian governing and oversight body

Introduction

FORCE IS NOT just what comes out of the barrel of a police officer's gun. It certainly is that, but it also takes many other forms: intimidation; arbitrary actions that criminalize or harass ordinary people, especially if they are Black, brown, Indigenous or poor; use of the collective power of unions and professional associations to resist local and provincial efforts to change or modernize policing; ability to escape or avoid accountability when there has been wrongdoing... The list goes on.

This book is about the ways in which excessive force has been used by members of police forces in Toronto—and elsewhere in North America—to challenge and even undermine attempts to transform the model of policing we have today. They represent all ranks, from the chief on down. We examine over a decade of this fight in Toronto, which has Canada's largest municipal police service. But the fight is not occurring in Toronto only; it is happening in many cities in Canada and indeed throughout North America.

So, what's the matter with our police? Policing in North America is not merely at a crossroads. When it comes to maintaining the confidence and trust that they need for their legitimacy, our police organizations are teetering at the edge of a cliff. Here are some recent examples.

On July 15, 2017, Minnesota police officer Mohamed Noor shoots and kills Justine Damond, a white woman with an Australian background, who called 911 for assistance. Mayor Betsy Hodges loses no time in demanding and obtaining the resignation of the police chief.

That shooting came one year after the killing of Philando Castile, a Black thirty-two-year-old cafeteria worker, who was shot several times at point blank range by Minnesota officer Jeronimo Yanez. The aftermath of the shooting was livestreamed on Facebook by his girlfriend who was in the car with her then four-year-old daughter. The officer was cleared of all charges and the chief kept his job.

On December 28, 2016, in Whitby, Ontario, off-duty Toronto police officer Michael Theriault and his civilian brother Christian Theriault allegedly assault Dafonte Miller, a Black teenager, so badly with an iron pole that, according to reports, he would lose an eye and pieces of his skin are stuck to the hood of the car he is pinned down on. The province's oversight agency, the Special Investigations Unit (SIU), is not even informed of the incident by the local police department. Miller's lawyer Julian Falconer does so months later. Theriault is criminally charged and the matter becomes public more than a year after the incident. But Theriault's chief, Mark Saunders, evades taking responsibility in a case that has all the signs of a cover-up, and Toronto mayor John Tory, who is a member of the police services board, does a song and dance about being "troubled" by the alleged incident.

It turns out that Theriault's father, John, is a veteran police officer, a detective sergeant in the Toronto Police Service's professional standards unit. This is the unit that investigates police officer conduct, and it neither asked questions when the incident happened nor called in the SIU (as required by law).

In July 2017, Toronto's police association embarked on a public campaign to derail the police board's plans to modernize the force by scaring the public: *Your safety is at serious risk due to the irresponsible actions of the police board.* Sure enough, it didn't even take a month for the police board to backtrack on one of the most significant elements of its much-vaunted plan of transformation: a three-year freeze on hirings and promotions, a necessary pause until the implementation of its plan was complete and a new model of policing was in place. The board agreed with the police union to open the tap and allow the hiring of eighty new police officers, costing upwards of $10 million and significantly affecting the plan to reduce the cost of policing by an estimated $100 million over three years. Quite improbably, the mayor claimed that the implementation remained on track.

The quid pro quo trumpeted by the police board and the association in a joint statement was the association's proclamation of support for the board's plan, its decision to sit at the implementation table (which it had previously refused to do), and further confirmation that it would discuss a couple of potential savings that it had already agreed to discuss as part of the 2015 collective agreement. The association's motto is, "We protect those who protect others." Some might say the association does a good job of it, even when this is detrimental to the public interest. These are just the latest signs of a slew of challenges that have beset policing.

If we are to move forward to match a new way of policing to the changing needs of our communities, it is time to toss out the duct tape and the Band-Aids that have always been used to give the illusion of change by police chiefs and police union leaders. Tweaks have to give way to true transformation. And our political leaders have to make some tough decisions, even if police chiefs and police union leaders do not like it. Society pays those chiefs and union leaders well for their professional services and expert advice; it does not pay them to dictate public policy. Here are seven challenges that must be overcome if our forces are to be equipped for the future:

1. Police shootings and the use of lethal force.
2. Police handling of people in mental health crisis.
3. Relationships with racialized and Indigenous communities.
4. Lack of confidence and trust from *all* members of the public, whom police are sworn to protect.

5. The ever-ballooning costs of policing.
6. National security and anti-terrorism policing at the local level, and our drift into the surveillance state.
7. Police chiefs and police union/association leaders crossing into the political realm to try to influence public policy.

These challenges stem from government decisions based on political, economic and social considerations driven by a neoliberal agenda; an amorphous and difficult-to-define police culture; societal, systemic and individual discriminatory ideas and practices (conscious and unconscious); and an ineffective system of accountability that is more symbolic than substantive. What we are left with is a model of policing that is obsolete and out of sync with today's reality. Let's take a look at the challenges one by one.

Police shootings

THIS BOOK CHRONICLES some of the Black and other minority people who have been killed by Toronto police over nearly four decades. None of them was carrying a firearm. And in none of these killings did a police officer make a genuine attempt to de-escalate a tense situation. Time and again, officers barked orders at a person in distress, orders that cannot be properly comprehended by an agitated person.

The numbers in the United States are bracing. Two news organizations, *The Guardian* and *The Washington Post*, keep running totals of Americans killed in encounters with police and have compared rates for Blacks and whites in different age categories. According to *The Guardian*, 1,091 Americans were killed in police encounters in 2016, 169 of them unarmed.[1] It found that Black males aged fifteen to thirty-four were nine times more likely to be killed by police than the population in general, and at any age were more than twice as likely to die at the hands of police than whites. *The Guardian* also found that more than twice as many Indigenous Americans (twenty-four) were killed by police that year than the year before. While the number may be small, the jump is shocking.

The Washington Post logged a slightly smaller number in 2016: 963 deaths by police. But think of it as almost three deaths at the hands of police every day of the year.[2] The Post also found that Blacks were three times more likely than whites to be killed by police and found that 34 percent of Blacks killed by police were unarmed. One in four of those killed by police were dealing with mental illness, The Post database found. We know more about these killings than we have in the past because they are being captured on video. But despite all the attention that the shooting of an unarmed Michael Brown in Ferguson, Missouri, placed on police-minority interaction in the US, the rate of police killings has not abated there.

The proliferation of guns in that country means any police interaction with a citizen can suddenly turn deadly, amping up the temperature. And the July 7, 2016, revenge ambush of Dallas cops, in which five died and nine were wounded, put police on even sharper tenterhooks. Why do Canadians need to be concerned about what happens in the US? For one simple reason: there is considerable contact between police leaders in Canada and the US, and policing techniques are shared at forums where they meet regularly, like the Big City Chiefs, the International Association of Chiefs of Police (IACP) and the Police Education Research Forum (PERF). An observer will find that they even speak the same "language." Policing strategies, tactics, training and equipment in the two countries are significantly integrated.

People in mental health crisis

THE TORONTO KILLINGS of Albert Johnson, Lester Donaldson, Albert Moses, Tommy Barnett, Wayne Williams, Edmund Yu, O'Brien Christopher-Reid, Byron Debassige, Reyal Jardine-Douglas, Michael Eligon, Sammy Yatim and Andrew Loku are all evidence of the police mindset—officers aggressively shout out orders, orders that will likely not be properly processed or understood; this heightens, rather than de-escalates the situation and makes police safety, not public safety, the priority. These are officers who have inadequate training in identifying or dealing with mental illness or are influenced by police folklore about what constitutes a threat (such as the so-called twenty-one-foot rule), some of whom are too quick to stigmatize the people they encounter as crazy, violent, drunk or on drugs. They are seen as threats, not people in distress; there is no understanding that in their heightened state of anxiety, somebody pointing a gun at them will only increase their agitation.

Racialized and Indigenous communities

AS THE NAMES above imply, in Canada too it is people from racialized and Indigenous communities who disproportionately bear the brunt of this rush to violent force. A York University study of Ottawa police found Middle Eastern and Black drivers, particularly young Black men, were most likely to be pulled over by officers. The York research team examined 81,902 traffic stops involving Ottawa residents between 2013 and 2015 and found those perceived to be from the Middle East were stopped 10,066 times, 12.3 percent of total stops. They represent less than 4 percent of Ottawa's driving population, meaning they are stopped 3.3 times more often than their population would suggest. Black drivers were stopped 7,238 times, or 8.8 percent of the time, 2.3 times more often than what would be expected based on their population.[3]

In 2015, then–RCMP commissioner Bob Paulson stood before a special First Nations Assembly and was confronted by British Columbia Grand Chief Doug Kelly on the question of racism.[4] "We encounter racism every single day. Some of the worst racists carry a gun and they carry a badge, authorized by you, Commissioner Paulson...We need you to confront racism in the ranks," Kelly told him. Paulson responded: "I hear what you say. I understand there are racists in my police force. I don't want them to be in my police force."

I have exhaustively chronicled the practices of carding and racial profiling, which have dogged Toronto police over the years. They sever the trust between police and a community and establish a rigid "us versus them" barrier. Much of this, I believe, can be traced to systemic and individual bias, both conscious and unconscious, and the manner in which society—as well as those who are armed and are there to protect us—deal with the "other."

Andrew Loku was described as a gentle giant by those in his apartment block who knew him. On the night he was killed, police were told to prepare for a big, violent "African" man threatening a neighbour with a hammer. The words *African* and *Black* are not found in the siu or Toronto police reports, but officers Andrew Doyle and Haim "Jimmy" Queroub, who responded to the 911 call, heard this description from the dispatcher. How did this influence their judgment and their decisions? Was Loku a victim of bias, deliberate or unconscious? Coroners' inquests must start dealing with these questions; the inquest into Loku's death did, due to considerable community pressure. In many cases, as I will argue, these killings are nothing more than a state-sanctioned culling of the "other," and this must stop. The Toronto police treatment of Blacks and other racialized communities had become so troubling, the Ontario Human Rights Commission announced in late November 2017 that it was launching a public interest investigation of racial profiling and discrimination at the Toronto Police Service.

Police oversight

THERE IS LITTLE public confidence that complaints about the police are properly and thoroughly investigated. North Americans perceive that penalties for wrongdoing are less severe than they would be had an offence been committed by someone without a badge. Consider how many police officers in the us and Canada have gotten off scotfree even after being charged. And when charges are not laid, much of internal police discipline amounts to little more than a time out, a stint in the corner, the docking of pay that can be recovered in a single overtime shift. Why would the public believe in a system when even those who have overseen Ontario's Special Investigations Unit believe that their investigators are being undermined by police union lawyers who get to the scene of a shooting before they do, that officers routinely collude in polishing their notes until they have the narrative they need or do not answer routine questions from siu investigators? Why would the public believe in a system when police chiefs do not report incidents promptly to the siu, as they are required to, and do not respond to concerns raised by siu investigations, because they are not required to do so?[5]

Following the crackdown on protesters of the 2010 G20 summit in Toronto, the only criminal charge laid against a Toronto police officer who used excessive force came as a result of media pressure and resulted in no jail time. Officers who removed their name tags were initially given the most superficial of penalties. Only a tiny portion of those facing potential charges are ever charged by the siu, and we don't know whether or not this is justified because of the penchant for secrecy and confidentiality surrounding the reports. Collusion has been proven in court, whether it was creating an inaccurate version of an incident in northern Ontario by Ontario Provincial Police officers or of the fatal Tasering of Robert Dziekanski at the Vancouver airport by RCMP officers. Police misconduct, if not condoned, is usually met with a shrug by internal investigators and the unmistakable message from the chief—"I've got your back."

There are also recurring problems within police ranks. Paulson issued a historic apology to the more than a thousand female RCMP officers who had been sexually harassed, yet in announcing his retirement in March 2017 he admitted that harassment persisted under his watch. In February 2017, the Calgary Police Service was hit with fourteen formal complaints of workplace bullying and harassment, a number that is expected to grow. In Montreal, two senior officers alleged that information was fabricated to discredit them because they were about to go to internal affairs to blow the whistle on corruption in the force. In Halifax, there is evidence that police did not properly investigate a 2012 sexual assault allegation against cab driver Bassam Al-Rawi, the same man whose acquittal on a 2015 sexual assault charge led to protests in March 2017.

A groundbreaking series by *The Globe and Mail*'s Robyn Doolittle, entitled "Unfounded," has sparked a public debate about the way police investigate sex crime complaints brought by women. It has led to thousands of cases being reviewed across the country, but the untold story is how many women in this country don't even seek charges because of police bias. We go back to the age-old question: *Quis custodiet ipsos custodes?* Who watches the watchers?

Costs of policing

IF POLICING IS to move ahead, costs must be contained because there is too much money being wasted on paid duty, shift scheduling, and the heavy-arms race because... Well, because that's the way it's always been done.

Let's go back to 1957, a year when Canada's largest city was known as "Toronto the Bland." That year, Elvis Presley played Maple Leaf Gardens and the *Toronto Star* critic immediately declared him "strikingly devoid of talent." The old *Toronto Telegram* established a Sunday edition and was threatened with legal action by the provincial Attorney General for breaching the Lord's Day Act. When a young Queen Elizabeth made her first trip to Canada, she didn't even bother to visit the country's largest city.

That was also the year an amalgamated police organization was created by the Metropolitan Toronto police commission and given an annual budget of $12,659,813 for policing the newly named municipality of Metropolitan Toronto. By 2011, that police budget had hit $1 billion. The population of Toronto had gone from 1.3 million to 2.6 million in those fifty-four years, while the police service had increased from 2,291 to almost 10,000 uniformed and civilian members. While the population had doubled, the size of the police force had grown disproportionately—by three-and-a-half times. During the same period of time the budget had increased exponentially, rising from $12.6 million to over $1 billion annually.

An interesting factor with regards to population is that Toronto's demographic composition changed dramatically during those years. Toronto now has one of the most racially and ethnically diverse populations in the world. It has a large Indigenous population. There are a large number of people who are poor or homeless. Is there a connection between the changing population and the growth of the police force—were policing needs deemed by the powers that be to have changed, and risks to public safety to have increased? While the increase in the size of the force may be related to the changing population, it is not the only reason policing costs have evolved the way they have.

By 2017, the Toronto police budget was $1.1 billion, essentially remaining the same as the previous year. Still, Mayor John Tory crowed about a "historic" $2 million budget cut. The police budget has been the ever more bloated number on the municipal ledger, and taming it has been one of the overarching challenges for police boards for years. Listen to Judge C.O. Bick, in his 1977—and last—report as chair of the police board after twenty-one years at the helm:

Crime costs to the community cannot...be estimated. The very real, very present danger is that the continued escalation of costs for police services will seriously weaken the financial ability of Metropolitan Toronto to contain the growth of crime. In its assessment of the future financing of police services, the Ontario Task Force on Policing stated that there is "a very real potential crisis in financing municipal police services. This crisis could result in the imposition of constraints to growth." For us it is not a "potential" crisis, it has arrived...What should be recognized is that most citizens realize what a vital part an efficient and effective police force means to their enjoyment of life, but there are limits to financial support which can be given...One determination which will have to be made is what form of "community service" should the police be reasonably expected to provide. There are services now given which are not essentially police related, but which the public expects.

Four decades later his points are still well taken. The system sometimes appears crafted to line officers' pockets—and here I must pay grudging compliments to a strong union, which has grandfathered and fiercely protected a series of perks. The shift scheduling, for example, essentially means that the police service pays for a twenty-eight-hour day. This happens due to a one-hour overlap between shifts, meaning that when members of one platoon relieve those from another, both the outgoing and the incoming platoons are getting paid for an overlapping hour. Neither the chief nor the union has ever disputed the twenty-eight-hour reality. But they've argued that it is needed—and it has never changed.

Securitization

SINCE THE TERRORIST attacks of September 11, 2001, on New York's World Trade Center, the role of municipal police has changed, even in Canada. Police are expected to collect national security intelligence as part of a loosely co-ordinated team that also includes provincial and federal police. They are expected to assess threats to critical infrastructure, from bridges to travel hubs, power plants to oil fields. If their cities are on water, ports or waterways, extra vigilance is demanded. Local police have become an integral part of the federal anti-terror strategy, but they have received little and in some cases no federal funding to take on these new roles or purchase the equipment needed to deal with new threats—perceived or real.

In the post–9/11 period, Canadians were suddenly made aware of potential sleeper cells, the perils of our immigration system (a debate that continues to this day), potential terror targets, a sieve-like border with our American neighbours and a national naïveté because we believed we couldn't be next. No matter how serious or well founded these concerns actually are, they've served advocates of the security state extremely well. Predictably, police roles were overhauled and police spending spiked. Christopher Murphy, a Dalhousie University specialist in crime and criminal justice, has written about "security creep," a phenomenon that "breaks down the boundaries between risk and crime, between terrorist and conventional crime and between probable and possible events."[6]

This development also changed so-called community policing because suddenly the ethnic enclave was no longer a cherished part of the city's diversity. Rather, it was seen as possibly harbouring the enemy within and as Murphy puts it, there was a sea change from "communities *at* risk to communities *of* risk." Police-community relations were ruptured and goodwill was supplanted by suspicion as municipal police officers became crucial links in a national security effort.

But while local police moved away from what should be their core police functions and morphed into national security sleuths, Ottawa has provided very little for this shift. Some police chiefs loved it because they now got to play in the big pond. But the local community was left holding the bag. We got carding and profiling. Further, we undermined civilian oversight because national security is excluded from the jurisdiction of the local police board or commission.

This is part of the mismatch between the reality of policing today and the current model of policing. Only 30 percent of police work deals with crime as we popularly define it. The vast majority of officers will go an entire career without ever drawing their firearms. Yet much of the police budget is spent on aggressive hardware and use-of-force equipment, and more training is focused on the use of firearms than on other aspects of policing.

The arms race shows no signs of abating. Militarization does not involve equipment only, but also policing tactics and even uniforms. In Toronto, during demonstrations at the provincial legislature or outside the US consulate, the police typically put up all their heavy "assets," creating a militaristic atmosphere. The doctrine, I was told, is that you let people see everything you've got—the implication being that you are willing to use it, if necessary. It creates a mood of coercion and fear.

The same effect is achieved by the uniforms police officers in Canada wear. Gone are the days when they wore a light blue outfit. Now, it is all dark—a foreboding colour—with a belt full of hardware, complete with a Kevlar vest. The vest is worn regardless of the weather. And now, we have seen efforts to replace the highly visible white or yellow police car with a virtually invisible grey vehicle. What is the message being given to the public, and what is the effect on the officers' mindset? How do they view the community they are assigned to? These are all components of militarization.

Political lobbying

IT HAS HAPPENED gradually and stealthily, but the country's police chiefs and police unions have waded deeply into political activity aimed at influencing public policy. They have become quite adept at influencing and intimidating local police boards, lobbying city politicians and flexing their muscles as organized voices through their national associations. The national police association hosts an open house at Ottawa's Château Laurier after every federal election, and the free food and booze are a magnet for the politicians who flock to the event.

You can see the fruits of this lobbying everywhere. Prime Minister Justin Trudeau was going to legalize marijuana, but after he appointed former Toronto police chief and new MP Bill Blair to quarterback the file, the emphasis shifted to regulation, which happens to be the position of the chiefs. The Stephen Harper government moved to ticket marijuana sellers, which was backed by the chiefs. Harper also wanted to provide police with more access to cellphone data, a position the chiefs were lobbying for and continue to promote.

Current Toronto police chief Mark Saunders is known to glad-hand Toronto city councillors at budget time. Police associations donate to political campaigns, but chiefs lobby in different ways. Politicians love to have their picture taken with a chief in full uniform to send the message to voters that they are strong supporters of law and order. In 2003, John Tory accepted the endorsement of the police union when he ran for mayor. He conceded that this was wrong—*after* he lost the election. The chiefs and unions might engage in this practice, but politicians are equally culpable for legitimizing it. There is a history of legislation and policies being written—or not written—to suit the preference of the police. Never mind that the public interest has suffered as a result.

This collusion—or to put it charitably, lack of will—on the part of our political leaders has added to the inability or failure of local police governing bodies—the Police Services Boards and commissions—to bring about the transformation that our system of policing so sorely and urgently needs. The analysis and conclusions in this book were developed over the more than ten years I spent as a citizen member of the Toronto Police Services Board. I joined the board in September 2004, when it was in upheaval due to various issues including whether to extend the tenure of the then–chief of police, Julian Fantino. I was immediately appointed vice-chair.

The chair, city councillor Pam McConnell, and I shared with our board the belief that while changes were needed, they could be achieved incrementally, working as a team with a new police chief and the police association. We chose Bill Blair, who was regarded as a reformer, as the new chief and appointed a new leadership team. With McConnell's guidance, we took up some of the issues at hand, such as police investigation of sexual assault and alternatives to the use of lethal force. We also took up the issue of police accountability. Working with a co-operative police chief, we won improvements, bringing in mandatory name badges, ordering the installation of cameras in all police cars, severely restricting the use of Tasers and emphasizing greater diversity at all levels of the force as a key component of community-based policing.

I succeeded McConnell as chair in 2005. As results of the board's efforts began to come in, it became clear that the approach of incremental change wouldn't work. With greater understanding of the issues—including police culture and knowledge of what was happening in the world of policing in Canada and beyond—I came to the conclusion that transformation rather than incremental change was necessary, and that the interests of the board and the police were not always identical. In other words, the board needed to more firmly exercise its role as the governing body of the force, working in the public interest to provide the type of policing the community needed. I also began to analyze the influence of police culture on the one hand, and of political and ideological factors on the other. The chapters in this book draw on my experiences between 2004 and 2015, when I served on the board, as well as developments I've observed from outside the board through 2017, to chronicle what went on in relation to the seven challenges I've identified; to offer an analysis of the factors underlying them; and to propose solutions for moving forward.

Into the Viper's Nest

IT WAS AFTER 9 p.m. in late August of 2004. My local Toronto city councillor, Joe Mihevc, was calling. Tonight, he was phoning as chair of council's Nominations Committee. I had gone through rigorous interviews with the committee for a vacancy on the Toronto Police Services Board created by the resignation of the chair, Alan Heisey, during a very controversial period. The press had labelled the police board "dysfunctional." Heisey himself had described his experience on the board as being "in the viper's nest." The metaphor has stayed with me. The stories told here are about many vipers—not just people, but institutional, systemic, cultural and political vipers as well.

Mihevc told me the committee had decided to recommend my name to council. He wanted to alert me so I would be prepared for calls from the media. Technically my name was to stay confidential until it appeared on the council agenda, but this seldom happens. City council approved my appointment on September 29, 2004. The vote was split thirty-nine for and twelve against. Mayor David Miller described my credentials as "incredibly impressive," fuelling accusations that he had influenced the committee's recommendation. The *Toronto Sun* described me as a former consultant to the mayor, implying that I had worked for him for money. Press reports also mentioned a financial contribution I had made to Miller's election campaign.

I acknowledged that like many others, my wife and I had contributed to the campaign, and clarified that I had served on the mayor's non-partisan transition task force but had never been a consultant to him. But there were reasons behind the media's curiosity, as well as the twelve votes that were cast against my appointment. The city was in an uproar, the police board was in disarray and the battle lines were drawn within council over the fate of Julian Fantino, the chief of police whose five-year term was coming to an end. Fantino was a controversial figure, admired in conservative circles as a tough, no-nonsense law-and-order man and loathed by the left wing as a bully.

One side was pressing for him to continue on as chief, while the other was campaigning for his departure. Miller was considered to be anti-Fantino, so my connection to him mattered to both sides. With Heisey gone, the remaining six members were split down the middle over Fantino's future, unable to come to a decision. My appointment could break this stalemate among them, and there was much speculation in the media about which side I would support. I became vice-chair immediately and then acting chair in July 2005, assuming the position as the regular chair in September. Thus began a journey that lasted just over a decade until I chose to step down as chair and leave the board altogether on August 1, 2015.

Only one chair has served longer than I did: Judge C.O. Bick, from 1956 to 1977. I was an eleven-year-old Grade 7 student in my hometown of Kanpur, India, when he became chair. Within the transition from Charles Otter Bick, a scion of the establishment closely tied to the movers and shakers of the city, to Alok Mukherjee—a "new Canadian" immigrant of colour known as a human rights advocate and a community activist—is the fifty-plus-year story of this city. When I had my first contact with the press in 2004, reporters wanted to know how to pronounce my name. I asked them to turn off their microphones and cameras, spelled it slowly and had them practise the pronunciation with me.

My journey from the northern Indian city of Kanpur to become civilian overseer of Canada's largest police service can be traced to a social activist who was shaking up the status quo before I was even born. This was Indubala, my grandmother, a woman who was married off before she was ten years old to a doctor almost twenty years her senior. She was expected to take over the domestic management of her house at a very young age. She learned to manage the finances and run a household—but she also developed a deeply ingrained sense of social justice and activism, and she spent her life indefatigably trying to right wrongs. I inherited my grandmother's sense of social justice and it has guided me through a life spent fighting racism, promoting diversity and giving voice to the marginalized and the oppressed.

We were Brahmans, an upper caste family with a well-honed interest in the arts, music, literature and culture, but when Muslims were persecuted after the partition of India and the creation of Pakistan in 1947, my grandmother hid Muslims in her house in Varanasi at great peril to her and her family. In her eyes, these people were neighbours. They were innocent. It was an act of bravery, but consistent with her sense of justice and her need to provide support to those under siege. Meanwhile, my mother fell seriously ill at the same time, two years after I was born. She was bedridden and needed constant attention the rest of her life.

Her side of the family paid for her medications but my father gave up his merchandising business to be her full-time caregiver. The result was a descent into poverty for the family, but our basic needs were never denied. My grandmother gave me my activism and sense of social equality, but my mother gave me my love of books and culture. When I went to college in 1961 for my BA, my maternal uncle paid the annual fee of about 100 rupees. I didn't leave home until 1964, when my mother died. I graduated from university with my MA in 1966.

It was during my master's program that I met Arun, who would become my wife of fifty years. After graduation, I began teaching in Delhi, but Arun and I decided it would be a good idea to go somewhere else for three years to finish our PhDs and then return.

After five years of teaching in Delhi, I could get a three-year sabbatical at half my salary. But where to go? Arun was accepted at the University of Toronto and selected for a Commonwealth Scholarship. Indians had a generally favourable view of Canada due to a visit by Prime Minister John Diefenbaker during which he spoke about Canada's Bill of Rights, the precursor to today's Charter of Rights and Freedoms. And we were also familiar with the Massey Ferguson tractor, the ubiquitous farm machine used to plow land in India. So, knowing the name of a prime minister and a tractor from Canada, we left on August 15, 1971, India's Independence Day, with high hopes but uncertain what awaited us.

Toronto was a sleepy city in those years, and it was not particularly friendly. We encountered racism—some of it subtle, but much of it disturbingly blatant. When Arun rightly questioned a surprising English department requirement for her to complete four undergraduate courses, the program director said, "I guess if you don't like it, you'll have to think about going back to where you came from." Later, we received notes slid under our door on campus saying, "Pigs, go back home." White students mocked our accents, made racist jokes and called us "Pakis." After a year in Toronto, no one had extended a helping hand or invited us into their circle. Indeed, the city was still very inward looking, stuck in an earlier era with a Victorian mindset.

After commuting to the University of Waterloo for two years, I moved to the University of Toronto in 1974. It was there that I gravitated to political involvement, becoming active with the Graduate Students' Union and the Indian Students Association, mainly with a goal of combatting racism. I also connected with activists and leaders in the broader South Asian community who were seeking better treatment and social programs. The key community organization dealing with these issues was the Indian Immigrant Aid Services (IIAS), based in a rented space in a church basement where volunteers welcomed, counselled and supported new immigrants.

One day I attended a community meeting hosted by IIAS out of curiosity. The president, Audi Dharmalingam, and co-ordinator

Ratan Panda introduced themselves and later recruited me to help prepare the report from the first-ever conference about "Indians in Toronto." I became president of IIAS in the 1980s, which led to other leadership roles nationally and locally. Dharmalingam—or "Dharma," as he was popularly known—and Panda became my mentors. Dharma, a straight-talking activist of the utmost integrity, was a highly respected social worker, head of the University Settlement, president of the Urban Alliance on Race Relations and a vocal, early champion of racial equality and inclusion.

This is how I cut my teeth on activism and social justice work. But it was one event—unplanned but illuminating—that really sparked a career combatting systemic racism in Canada. Friends had asked us to come to their daughters' school in Georgetown, just west of Toronto, to speak to students in Grades 4 and 5 who had never seen Indians before. When we arrived, the children were surprised. They had expected members of Canada's Indigenous peoples, wearing leather skirts, moccasins and headdresses. I arrived in a suit and tie; Arun wore her best silk and gold jewellery. This started a lively discussion, including questions about food scarcity in parts of India. One young man offered a novel solution—all those cows wandering the streets of India, why don't you just eat them? I had to wonder, what were these children learning in school? We asked to see their textbooks and were taken aback by what they contained.

I found the portrayal of South Asians in these textbooks offensive. I proposed a project to give these kids a chance to learn about India, as well as a content analysis of the representation of the Indian subcontinent in secondary school textbooks. Further, I wanted to provide information about everyday life of the Indian diaspora in Canada, about where we work, how we contribute to community and how we raise our children. I applied for and received federal funding for the project and hired a dozen young people for the summer to do the study, with enough money remaining to publish our findings.

When the book *East Indians, Myths and Reality* was published in 1978, the Toronto Board of Education held a press conference to have me talk about the findings of our content analysis. It was well covered. The *Toronto Sun*, of course, editorialized in celebration of the British taming of India, headlining the article "Curried History." The provincial government established a task force to look for bias in the curriculum, and several of the books we had identified as particularly offensive were removed. In addition, provincial guidelines were developed to ensure that textbooks were free of bias related to race, religion and culture. Before any new textbook was approved, an external review had to take place using these guidelines, which is the policy to this day.

Ultimately, I was hired as a school community-relations worker—my first real job. My mandate was the South Asian community, known then as the East Indian community. I was given a tiny office in the East End at the corner of Broadview and Dundas. At that time, nearby Gerrard Street was in transition; a long-time WASP bastion, it was becoming Toronto's Little India. The transition was rocky, marked by racism and tension between the old-guard residents and new businesses.

The Sikh community bought an old church nearby, at the corner of Queen and Pape, and established the first Sikh temple in Toronto. It became a magnet not only for Sikhs but also for Punjabi Hindus, who were now coming to this part of Toronto. Then a prominent member of the community, Gyan Naaz, bought an old movie theatre on Gerrard Street and established the city's first Indian cinema, calling it the Naaz. The two buildings lured the crowds, and small merchants such as grocers began renting out storefronts. People came to pray, buy groceries and watch a movie. The grocers led to restaurants. The influx led to a typical 1970s-style problem: there was not enough parking, so residents' driveways were often blocked. This irritant was ramped up with the rumour that an Indian nightclub was coming. Racism now had a material context—parking and a potential nightclub. It had found a new justification in the perceived inconvenience.

I felt the school in the neighbourhood had a responsibility to the community. We got the school board to open the lot at Pape Avenue

School for free parking after school on Friday and on weekends; that dialled down some of the pressure. The nightclub never materialized. People started talking to each other. But the Ku Klux Klan believed conditions in this part of the city were ripe for its virulent racism, and it established a branch there, marching down Gerrard Street in a threatening manner. The nascent Riverdale Intercultural Council, established in 1977 by Father Jim Robson and run by Tim McCaskell, started a campaign to drive the KKK out, and I was part of it. Our efforts succeeded, but just as importantly, our combined anti-KKK effort brought the community together. Long-time residents knew that the South Asian invaders were certainly not the menace that the KKK posed.

In 1984, I became the race relations adviser for the Toronto Board of Education. It was a very progressive board in those days—it focused on issues of diversity and poverty and had a more expansive view of where education and inclusiveness was headed at that time in the mid-80s. It had started with a policy on multiculturalism, then followed it up with a separate policy on race relations. Five years after the race relations policy was implemented the board moved to a more preventative, proactive anti-racism program, embracing the knowledge that racism—both one-on-one and systemic racism—is a major barrier to educational success. I was appointed to implement this new policy of anti-racism.

East Indians, as we were called then, were the primary target of racism, in the education system and the city as a whole. The school board developed training programs for teachers, principals and superintendents and we tried to build a "team of champions" because we could not train every teacher throughout the system overnight. The director of education, Ned McKeown, provided incredible support. Anti-racism was always one of his top priorities and he wanted it in the "sinews of our system." We had to convert the skeptics and the opponents. And when it came to inequality and discrimination, we learned some things—we began to understand the difference between focusing on the individual "bad apple" and systemic racism.

Institutional practices are often based on assumptions, norms and beliefs that are not universal but are class, race and gender specific. Here is an example from a different sector, namely policing—specifically, police recruitment. There was a time when, to be hired as a cop in Toronto, you had to be at least six feet tall and weigh two hundred pounds. This wasn't decided by looking at the question of who or what makes a good cop through any scientific or evidence-based lens, but because the first cops were Irish and they fit that profile. With such specific requirements, others were excluded. Anti-racism and affirmative action meant looking at things people had always taken for granted, rather than adopting a McCarthy-style search for the racist under every bed. It was a very progressive era in this country, and it was exciting.

We were beginning to think about a major new way to attain equality and what Pierre Trudeau had christened the "Just Society." I was travelling across the country as this rolled out, writing about it and explaining it to other school boards. While I was doing this, David Peterson became Liberal premier of Ontario and his education minister, Sean Conway, embraced the concept of anti-racism. Conway created a working group, which I was part of, to develop a mandatory provincial policy of anti-racism and ethnocultural equity. We created a full guide on how to implement this policy. The policy survived Bob Rae's NDP government, but not the Progressive Conservative rule of Mike Harris.

Our work was groundbreaking. Instead of doing another study showing that Blacks, South Asians and other racialized people were not getting key jobs, we undertook a study we called *Who Seeks the Work?* We collected all the applications for the teaching jobs that had been filled in the previous year. We then sent questionnaires to the applicants' homes to ask how they heard about the job, whether they had been interviewed and whether they had been shortlisted. We showed that there was no shortage of qualified applicants. We showed that the non-white applicant often had a higher level of education than the successful applicant.

But about one-third of the jobs were going to people who had heard by word of mouth. Who hears by word of mouth? Someone's child. A friend. A neighbour. "Someone I know." It was a systemic practice. So were those related to promotion. In the school district, it was known as the "tap on the shoulder." It worked very simply: Toronto superintendents and principals had cottages in the same area so if you wanted to get in their good books, that's where you went. It was all figured out in Muskoka. Or at the curling club. Every year, the high school principals of each of Toronto's four school districts came together for a big meeting, and they would bring the applications of everyone who had applied for a senior job. A principal would say he had an application from John Doe, and someone else would pipe up, "Oh, I know John. He's in our curling club. He's a good guy."

So, the director of education put me in the room. Principals didn't like this because they were now being watched and could not promote their friends or favourites. I told people committed to equality and anti-racism that they would not be able to make the necessary institutional change at the board unless they had power. I began identifying such individuals, training them and coaching them to go after principals' positions. And we succeeded in putting some fabulous people in principals' offices. In five years, we made a big difference, and I loved it. The message was coming from the provincial government by that point as well, and that showed we had made an impact.

The year 1988 marked a decade of the Toronto Board of Education doing this type of work and it had been quite successful. We thought we should take a year to celebrate our achievement, to share it nationally and use it as an opportunity to build support for the next phase of work that needed to be done. Major change was also ahead and we had to do this right. But the director of education, Ned McKeown, was retiring. Two of the three qualified candidates to replace him were Black. All three were well qualified and of comparable experience having held numerous senior positions. Joan Green, the only white candidate, got the job. The announcement was made on the night before the start of the national anti-racism education conference we were hosting in downtown Toronto.

In response to the decision, I gathered a small group of people who worked on the board and were my strongest allies at 5 a.m. in my house to discuss what this meant and how we should respond. The conference was to start at 8 a.m. We quickly agreed to turn it into an accountability session for the board. We came up with a plan. Talk of the appointment dominated every workshop and plenary session; no one wanted to talk about anything else. McKeown wouldn't even look at me. I became an untouchable. On the final day of the conference, Tony Silipo, chair of the school board, finally showed up at the conference and pledged to establish an employment equity program within six months. We had succeeded.

However, when Green set up the employment equity committee in December 1989, she made someone else the chair but seemingly wanted me to do all the work. The day before the winter holidays began, I submitted my letter of resignation, effective January 1, 1990. I moved on to private consulting and it went very well. My business partner, Gail Posen, had been the school board's affirmative action adviser, responsible for work related to gender equity. We made a strong team. We got our first contract three months after we started, from Ontario's deputy solicitor-general, Stien Lal.

Lal was modernizing policing. He had a human rights background and a solid commitment to addressing workplace discrimination and harassment. His ministry's policy ultimately became a provincial government policy. I trained people from his ministry and the Ontario Provincial Police on conducting proper workplace harassment investigations. Our co-trainer from the OPP was Gwen Boniface, a young inspector who would later become the first female commissioner of the provincial police. Thus, my first contract dealt with policing. It was our breakthrough, and contracts began to flow in from across the country.

In 1992, Bob Rae's NDP government appointed me to the province's human rights commission. A mentor from my school board days, Fran Endicott, had a hand in it. Endicott was one of the finest anti-racism educators I had known. She was a visionary and the first Black woman to be elected to public office in our province. After leaving the school board, Endicott had been appointed to the commission and was its vice-chair, designated to become the chair after the term of the current one, Catherine Frazee, expired. She wanted me to be her vice-chair. The human rights commission was lacking in credibility because of a backlog of thousands of cases, lost files and bad decisions. We were going to shake up the place.

But Endicott died of cancer a few short months after taking the post, and I served as the acting chief commissioner for the next two years. Under Frazee's leadership, the commission had developed a new strategic plan that was waiting to be implemented. It fell on me to take the work forward. We also came up with a new system that would deal with all complaints within six months. Working to re-establish our credibility on LGBT issues, we took the Rae government to the tribunal, forcing it to provide benefits to same-sex couples. We fought systemic racism in hospitals against nurses of colour and threatened the Toronto firefighters with an investigation because they weren't hiring women, people of colour and Indigenous people.

When it came to formalizing my appointment as chief commissioner, however, Rae decided to instead bring in Rosemary Brown from Vancouver. I received a call from the premier's office conveying his decision, telling me how much Rae appreciated my work and inviting me to serve as vice-chair, working closely with Brown. I had already heard about the choice of Brown. The province's minister of citizenship, Elaine Ziemba, to whom I'd reported, had called me immediately after the cabinet's decision. She told me she had lost the fight at the cabinet table despite strong support from her colleagues, and Rae had prevailed.

I never learned why Rae wanted to bring in Brown, who had little familiarity with Ontario. I can only guess that, with issues related to anti-Black racism coming to the surface, he may have felt that Brown, the first Black woman to be elected to a provincial legislature, would be a reassuring presence. As it happened, the relationship with Brown did not work out and other commission members began conveying to me their concerns about the new leadership. But I felt that the premier had made his choice and Brown had a right to establish her own approach.

So a few months later, I told Rae's office I was ready to move on. I was appointed to the Ontario Civilian Police Commission at the end of 1994. The appointment ended in 1997 when Mike Harris's Progressive Conservatives decided to appoint people of their choosing. But it had been valuable work. We had conducted disciplinary appeals from police members and had assessed decisions by municipalities to reduce or disband their police forces (and merge or contract out to the OPP) after reviewing their proposed alternative plans.

When that appointment ended, just over twenty-five years after my arrival in Canada, I finally went back to York University to finish my PhD and to teach. Then Alan Heisey resigned his post as chair of the Toronto Police Board. Some senior community activists decided that policing in Toronto needed a shakeup and that it was going to come from either me or Avvy Go of the Toronto Chinese and Southeast Asian Legal Clinic. Avvy and I applied and were both shortlisted to join the board. After two interviews, I received the memorable phone call from Joe Mihevc. "You are either mad or hopelessly idealistic," he said. "Why would you want to sit on the police board? But that's your decision and we are recommending you go forward."

So, for the first time since 1997, when I completed my term at the Ontario police commission, I would be taking up a public appointment. I had spent the intervening years at York University, getting my PhD, teaching and writing. I had also continued to do a limited amount of consulting work.

My first police board meeting was in October 2004, and I was immediately named vice-chair. I had been urged by activists whose advice I valued to seek the post to shake up the status quo, something my grandmother had done more than six decades earlier. My ascension to the police board took my thoughts back many years to a conference on diversity in the media, where I had sat next to Wilson Head, who was a distinguished academic and scholar and a revered community elder. At the conference, people from the CBC were talking about what the public broadcaster was doing to address issues of diversity. "It does not matter what face or accent you put behind the camera or the mic unless you change the lens through which you see the world," I said as an aside. He turned to me and said, "You know, you're a PSD."

"A PSD?" I asked.

"A professional shit disturber." Of all the awards and recognitions I have received, I hold this one closest as a badge of honour. My grandmother would have been thrilled to be called the same.

One of the senior members of the police board approached me soon after my appointment and said, "Do you know who you are here to serve? You're here to serve the police."

I fixed him in my gaze. "No," I told him. "My grandmother taught me I am here to serve the community."

So what is a police services board? Who does it serve? What does it do, who are its members and who is it accountable to?

I am asked these questions often. One of the most significant features of municipal policing in Canada is the system of civilian oversight and governance. With a few exceptions, municipal policing in Canada is overseen by a civilian board or commission. The composition, role, responsibilities and authority of the board or commission as well as the separation of powers between the board and the chief of police are delineated in the police service act for each province.

In Ontario, a board's composition and legislated duties are set out in the *Police Services Act*. The Police Services Board of Toronto, a large city, is composed of seven members. They include the mayor, two city councillors chosen by council, and four citizen members—one appointed by city council and three by the province on the recommendation of the minister of community safety and correction-al services. If the mayor decides not to take his or her seat, the council appoints another councillor, usually hand-picked by the mayor.

Neither the board nor the police service is an agency of the municipal or provincial governments. The police chief is an employee of the board and is answerable only to it. The sole body that can hold the board and its members accountable is the Ontario Civilian Police Commission (OCPC). It has the authority to investigate the conduct of a board or a member and the power to order the dismissal of the entire board or a member. The purpose behind this arrangement is to ensure that policing is free of any real or perceived political inter-ference. It is supposed to allow chiefs and officers to carry out their duties without fear or favour. This expectation came under scrutiny in 2013 when the Toronto police under Bill Blair began investigating allegations against the city's mayor, Rob Ford, who the service had initially been suspected of shielding.

In general terms, the legislated mandate of a police services board in Ontario can be summarized as general management and the establishment of policing policy. In effect, the board's role in shaping the structure of policing is very broad, as the board "is re-sponsible for the provision of adequate and effective police services." The *Act* gives the board certain specific responsibilities, including the following:

(a) appoint the members of the municipal police force;
(b) generally determine, after consultation with the chief of police, objectives and priorities with respect to police services in the municipality;
(c) establish policies for the effective management of the police force;
(d) recruit and appoint the chief of police and any deputy chief of police, and annually determine their remuneration and working conditions;
(e) direct the chief of police and monitor his or her performance;

(f) establish guidelines with respect to the indemnification of members of the police force for legal costs;

(g) establish guidelines for dealing with complaints; and

(h) review the chief of police's administration of the complaints system and receive regular reports from the chief of police on his or her administration of the complaints system.

The board is the employer, and as such has a key role in labour relations including negotiating collective agreements with police associations. The board is also a legal entity that enters into contracts and takes legal action. And it is the board that submits operating and capital budget estimates to city council each year and defends the amounts requested. As explored in the following chapters, the provisions in the *Police Services Act* have significant implications for the board's ability to uphold the public interest and bring about change.

When I joined the police services board, it was too divided to make a decision on the extension of Chief Julian Fantino's employment. The chair at the time, Heisey, had resigned amid a controversy in which he was smeared in a leaked memo questioning his views on child pornography. A senior judge, brought in by the board to look into the allegation, found it to be baseless. But Heisey had had enough. Amid the board gridlock, Fantino served out his term with no extension.

Fantino's future was decided by default. For several months before my appointment, the remaining six members of the board had failed to even approve the minutes of the meeting at which Fantino's term had last been discussed. However, when the minutes came up for approval after I had joined the board, I abstained. I had taken legal advice on the propriety of my voting on such an important matter when I had not been privy to its consideration. Therefore, the motion to approve the minutes failed. This happened during the same month that Fantino's employment with the board expired. Contrary to a widely held view, his employment was never terminated; he served out his term.

With this matter dealt with, the board agreed on the process for beginning the search for his successor. It decided to avoid making a hasty decision and to engage in an extensive community consultation. This breathing room would also allow the board to get to know people in the police service who had the attributes we were looking for. As a stopgap measure, popular former deputy chief Mike Boyd was brought out of retirement to serve as the interim chief.

FROM CHARLES OTTER Bick to Alok Mukherjee—the world has changed. Our names are not the only differences between us. We signify different eras, different cities, and different cultural, social and political environments—as well as different expectations, needs, interests and worries. It has been a journey through a time in which the state has embraced neoliberalism, with its profound inequalities and shrinking social safety net, and a time in which the state has been consumed by concerns about terrorism and national security, resulting in a greater willingness to empower the criminal justice system—especially the police—to maintain social order.

It has also been a journey to a present day when sections of our communities are restive, no longer prepared to silently accept their unequal status, their marginalization, their denial of access to opportunities for a better future, and their experience of oppressive treatment by those who exercise power. To many, policing embodies the coercive component of this power. The stories this book tells are about the exercise of, and resistance to, this power.

During my decade-long engagement with policing in Toronto, I met many amazing people in the community, in our public institutions, in the media and in the police service—people who wanted to get it right and were willing to work for it. I met numerous police officers who took up the profession because they wanted to serve the community—especially the most vulnerable—and who genuinely believed in public service. I met people from the community who were committed to social justice and were willing to give their time to fight for it—whether on committees, through briefs and deputations, or on the street protesting and agitating. I also met journalists, lawyers, academics, civil servants and politicians who agreed with this fight for a just and fair society in which discrimination and inequality will not prevail, where racism and other forms of oppression will not be permitted, where innocent people will not be killed or criminalized, and where the vulnerable will receive the support they need. They believed that policing could play a very important part in achieving such a vision—or not.

The stories in this book are about the people who were involved, but they are also about the institutional, systemic, political and cultural factors that help or hinder us in achieving our collective vision of a just society. They are about the resulting struggles, successes and failures. These stories describe a society that has come a long way from the days of Bick. They are about efforts to ensure that the powerful and expensive apparatus of policing functions in step with the needs and expectations of today's society, and that it serves the best interests of our whole society in a way that is transparent and accountable. As chair of the police services board, I lived through these stories, and sometimes found myself at the centre of them. However, they are about our collective struggle for the kind of policing that we want as a community.

Carding the Letter Carrier

RON PHIPPS WORKED as a letter carrier for Canada Post. He was Black and had moved to Canada from Jamaica with his family as a boy. On March 9, 2005, Phipps was delivering mail on Vernham Avenue in the northeast of Toronto. Vernham Avenue is part of the affluent and predominantly white neighbourhood known as the Bridle Path. On that day, Phipps was filling in for the regular letter carrier. He did not know the area and was criss-crossing the street, delivering mail sequentially. Occasionally, he would go back to a house to make sure that he had delivered mail to the correct address. Phipps was dressed in the Canada Post uniform and there were two mailbags slung over his shoulder.

Michael Shaw was a veteran constable of the Toronto Police Service. On March 9, he was on patrol in that neighbourhood. With him was a young probationary constable. Shaw was his "coach officer," showing him how policing is done. There was an alert that someone was cutting and stealing copper wires from that area. The suspect was described as "white, middle-aged, East European." Officers on patrol had been asked to be on the lookout. In the front yard of one of the houses on Vernham, a white, middle-aged man was tending to the plants. Constable Shaw had patrolled the area before and was apparently familiar with the regular letter carrier.

He didn't recognize Phipps. He noticed how Phipps was delivering mail, criss-crossing the street. Once, retracing his steps, he had gone back to a house and rung the bell to speak to the resident. Shaw found Phipps's actions unusual. He knew letter carriers generally went down one side of the street and then up the other. Shaw decided he had a reasonable basis for stopping Phipps and questioning him. Phipps identified himself, explained that he was filling in, that he did not know the street and that he had spoken to the resident to check if he had mistakenly delivered mail to the wrong address. Shaw and Phipps then went their separate ways. Except on the next street, Shaw spoke to the letter carrier who delivered mail there. He wanted to verify Phipps's identity. Phipps later found out. He had no objection to Shaw stopping and questioning him. But he had strong objections to what the police officer had done on the next street over. The matter would end up being ruled on by the Human Rights Tribunal of Ontario more than four years later.

In the meantime, less than two months after the Phipps incident, the Toronto Police Services Board ended intense speculation on April 26, 2005, by announcing the city's new chief of police. At a crowded press conference in our spacious boardroom on the seventh floor of police headquarters, the then–chair of the board, Toronto city councillor Pam McConnell, and I as the vice-chair, introduced Bill Blair. Other board members were there to show he was our unanimous choice. After a long period of public acrimony between those who wanted outgoing chief Julian Fantino to stay on and those who wanted him gone, the board was signalling that we were united.

Almost the very first question Blair was asked concerned his position on racial profiling by members of the Toronto Police Service, particularly of Black residents of the city. Board chair McConnell and I weren't surprised. When we'd taken Blair to meet the mayor, David Miller, the City Hall press had asked the same question during the scrum outside the mayor's office. The issue of how our police officers engaged with members of the city's impoverished, racialized and Indigenous communities, and the specific question of whether they treated Black Torontonians differently, had dogged the service and the board ever since October 19, 2002, when the *Toronto Star* had published data suggesting that police stopped Black people more often than anyone else.

The phenomenon had come to be known as "racial profiling." The front-page report by Jim Rankin, titled "Singled Out," had started a firestorm of controversy.[1] And the response from Chief Fantino had worsened the climate. He was furious with the *Star* study and retained Ed Harvey, a well-known senior academic from the Ontario Institute for Studies in Education (OISE) at the University of Toronto, to assess it.

Harvey was paid well and based on his conclusions, Fantino had called the claim of racial profiling "junk science." He categorically rejected the idea that this was a systemic issue, saying instead that there may be some "bad apples" in the service. However, the matter was not limited to Toronto. The police chief in Kingston, for example, had engaged University of Toronto criminology professor Scot Wortley to do a study of police stops in his community. Wortley's report, released in May 2005, had added fuel to the fire.[2] In deciding how to respond to Wortley's Kingston study, the Kingston Police Association had sought the opinion of a professor from the University of Ottawa, Ron Melchers. He, too, had been devastatingly critical.

On March 31, 2005, the *Star* had headlined its front page, "Racial Profiling Exists; Promises of Internal Probe Fell Flat," reporting that Toronto's Black police officers were claiming that racial profiling was a fact within the organization itself.[3] The report was based on the results of focus groups conducted with Black members of the police service. Three Black senior officers—Keith Forde, Peter Sloly and David McLeod—had gone on record supporting their account, directly contradicting Fantino's position.

When we had embarked on a city-wide consultation with the community about selecting a replacement for Fantino, one message that came through loud and clear was that the new chief must be a champion of diversity and as a priority, must work to ensure that the police service is truly reflective of the community. Clearly, the issue of profiling—the different treatment of different communities by Toronto police—was top of mind for residents.

It was not a surprise, then, that the first question put to Blair at his first appearance before the media as chief was about this issue. In fact, he was already mired in it. Before becoming chief, he had been a staff superintendent and an acting deputy chief. He had sided with the Black officers, agreeing that racial profiling was a fact inside the organization. As if to underscore this, in 2004 McLeod, an inspector, had become embroiled in a highly publicized conflict with the police association about his claim that a constable, Alex Chung, had treated him differently because he was Black.

One evening while off duty, McLeod was driving his unmarked service-issue car. Needing gas, he had pulled into a police station and as he was filling his car, Constable Chung, a new recruit, had challenged him and asked to see his identification. Chung would not take McLeod at his word that he was a senior officer driving a police car. An incensed McLeod asked if the constable would have acted the same way if he had been white. McLeod took no further action, but the constable reported the incident to his sergeant. The matter exploded. The sergeant, Ron Wretham, a well-connected veteran, took up the cudgels on behalf of Chung.

With interim chief Boyd's permission, Blair, a staff superintendent at the time, brought the parties together to find a mediated resolution. He declared this a success, with the constable and the inspector ending their dispute by shaking hands. In fact, the matter had not quite ended there. Sergeant Wretham and the police association were not satisfied. The newly elected president of the association, Dave Wilson, also a sergeant, accused Blair of coercing the young constable. Blair already had his foretaste of an issue that would dog him and the board during his and my entire tenures, with serious consequences for the police service, the police services board and the community. It would also have a profound impact on our personal relationship.

An important reason for my appointment to the board was my background in anti-racism and human rights–based organizational change. Since the 1980s, I had been involved in both areas as an educator, a trainer and a consultant. As the race relations adviser to the Toronto Board of Education and the vice-chair and acting chief commissioner of the Ontario Human Rights Commission, I had developed policies, provided training and sought remedies through the human rights complaints process and advocated for equitable and inclusive practices.

Among my first actions after joining the board had been to propose a new Race and Ethnocultural Equity Policy to replace the old Race Relations Policy, which dated back to the 1990s. I recommended that the board direct the chief to undertake reviews to identify and remove barriers to the employment and promotion of women and men from a variety of backgrounds within the police service. Many, myself included, thought we had found an ally in Blair. "In the police service I now lead, racial profiling will not be tolerated," Blair told the *Star* the day he was introduced as the new chief. "I want to make that statement as strongly and as unequivocally as possible. It will not be tolerated in the way in which we deal with the public and it will not be tolerated in the way in which we deal with each other."[4]

In his inaugural speech as chief, Blair spoke openly and emotionally about the reality and impact of racism. He acknowledged without reservation that the police service was not exempt from a phenomenon that was present in society. His words were warmly welcomed by employees of colour. For them, this was a complete reversal of the position taken by his predecessor. In the community as well, Blair received full support for his forthright message.

As if to signal that this was indeed a new era, the board, working closely with Blair as he built a new leadership team, gave Keith Forde, as one of the newly appointed deputy chiefs, responsibility for human resources including recruitment, promotion and training. At the same time, Blair selected Peter Sloly for one of the staff superintendent positions, the third-highest rank, with major involvement in developing a new model of engagement with the community. Sloly would later join Forde as a deputy chief in 2009.

It appeared we were well on our way to dealing strongly and effectively with an issue that had long bedevilled relations between the police and the community. Our approach was twofold: on one hand, aggressively recruit new, highly educated police officers from various ethnic, racial and language backgrounds; improve training in diversity, human rights and anti-racism; and proactively consider equity objectives during the promotion processes. On the other hand, we had to reform the system for deployment of officers in police divisions, taking into account the actual demands of different parts of the city to strengthen community-based policing based on our newly introduced model of community mobilization. This two-part approach was based on our view that we needed systemic change to deal with the issue of discriminatory and differential policing.

To emphasize this point, Blair and I invited Barbara Hall, chief commissioner of the Ontario Human Rights Commission at the time, to join us in a project that would examine all aspects of the organization—both as an employer and as a service provider—from a human rights perspective to identify areas, policies and practices that should be changed. This was a major change in direction. Historically, the relationship between the board and service and the human rights agency had been adversarial. The commission had relied on individual complaints to force changes, and the board and the service had gone to great lengths, involving significant legal costs, to fight back.

A major turning point had occurred in 2005, when the board, disregarding Chief Fantino's objections, had opted to settle a long-standing human rights complaint by members of the LGBTQ community arising out of the police raids on a bathhouse known as "Pussy Palace." It had fallen on me as vice-chair to work with the board's legal counsel to negotiate the settlement, since McConnell had a perceived conflict of interest. She had donated to the legal defence of the complainants when they were charged as a result of the raid. This was a far-reaching settlement, with the board agreeing to significant changes in areas that were traditionally considered to be operational and, thus, outside its purview. However, this settlement had marked the beginning of an era of co-operation that was to last several years, one when the board and the service preferred collaboration over rigid separation of roles.

The human rights project was the high point of that era. Blair, Hall and I sat down and personally drafted a Human Rights Charter, causing consternation among our staff and lawyers. Co-operation with the old adversary was unheard of and unthinkable. Safeguarding of information, a characteristic of police culture, was evidently not confined to the men and women in blue. In 2007, the charter, signed by the three of us, launched a unique three-year initiative in policing to bring the police service in line with the requirements of Ontario human rights legislation. Representing our respective organizations, we became the project sponsors and assigned a large team comprising representatives of the commission, the board and the service to implement the charter. We were in it together, motivated by a lofty shared goal of bringing about progressive policing based on respect for human rights and the dignity of every person.

The human rights charter project was not the only undertaking marked by this spirit of collaboration. Another initiative of the board was even more remarkable for the openness and participation of Blair and the police service: the Saving Lives Implementation Group (SLIG). It was exceptional for several reasons. First, Blair co-chaired the group with an old adversary and trenchant critic of the police, criminal lawyer Julian Falconer. Falconer was well known nationally for challenging police actions in court. It would have been unimaginable in prior years that the two would be engaged in a shared endeavour. Second, the membership of SLIG included other community activists and lawyers with whom the police service had a history of friction. And finally, Blair gave members of SLIG access to the police service procedures and other relevant confidential materials to enable them to do their work. He trusted that they would not use this information for other purposes, such as litigation.

SLIG was formed to assist the board and the police service in fully implementing the recommendations from a groundbreaking conference held in late 1999 called "Saving Lives: Alternatives to the Use of Lethal Force by Police." It remains a controversial issue to this day and is the subject of extensive discussion elsewhere in this book. The reason for this conference was community concern over police killings of people with mental health issues, many of whom were Black or of other non-white backgrounds. Leaders from the community had wanted to make one more serious effort at addressing this issue through dialogue rather than confrontation and protest. The conference ended with a signed joint commitment by Black leaders, Fantino and police services board chair Norm Gardner to act on its recommendations.

But the solemn promise to implement the recommendations had not been kept. Hence SLIG was born and, in the first flush of a new vision of leadership, it received the personal attention and participation of the newly minted chief. Yet when people like Sammy Yatim, Byron Debassige and Andrew Loku were killed, questions about police culture would arise all over again. Is it immutable and unchanging, with this resistance to change inherent in its conservative DNA? Or is it just very good at, on one hand, devoting significant human and material resources to areas of change—sometimes even with the involvement of the community—and, on the other, successfully tailoring the implementation of results to keep the status quo, such that a reformist approach to change proves time and again to be futile? The work of SLIG and its impact are very much relevant to this discussion of racial profiling. For the community members of this group, the police record of using lethal force against non-whites certainly raised the issue of racial profiling. In other words, the subjects of use of force and racially biased policing were interconnected.

This brings me back to the work of the human rights charter project. It had two purposes. First was to scrutinize and review policies, procedures and practices related to the provision of policing

services to the community and recruitment, employment and promotion practices within the organization. Second was to make recommendations for actions to ensure that, both as a service provider
and as an employer, the police service treated everyone equally, re-
spectfully and without discrimination. As with SLIG, there were early
signs of unprecedented co-operation and goodwill. I believed that
this systemic, systematic and organization-wide approach was our
best shot at slaying the dragon of discriminatory and biased policing
that had so seriously wounded relations between the police and the
community for so long.

But Blair's response to the Human Rights Tribunal's Phipps
letter-carrier decision turned out to be a serious deviation from the
direction I thought we were heading. Adjudicator Kaye Joachim
found that Constable Shaw had engaged in racial profiling, and
underlying his actions was unconscious racial bias. Her decision
came more than four years after the incident, on June 18, 2009.[5]
Many in the Toronto Police Service, led by Chief Blair, fulminated
against the decision. In the upper echelons, there was a lively debate,
with Blair's two Black deputy chiefs, Forde and Sloly, supporting the
tribunal's finding. A few months later, in February 2010, when Blair
and I were touring India at the invitation of the Indian government,
I took the opportunity to discuss the matter with him.

Blair told me it was a hugely problematic decision for him.
Officers would be very hesitant to do their job, he said, not knowing
when they might be accused of having unconscious bias. He felt the
decision gave him no guidance because he thought the adjudicator
had not clearly spelled out how she had arrived at her conclusion.
He believed he had no alternative but to appeal to the divisional
court for a judicial review. I said the board would not be a party to
the appeal. Blair's appeal was unsuccessful. The court found that
Joachim had made a proper decision, taking into consideration all
the evidence, and had provided clear reasons. In the court's view,
there were no procedural or legal defects in the decision, so there
was no reason to overturn it.

During the same month as the visit to India, February 2010, *Star* reporter Rankin published an analysis of data on police-community interactions—entitled "Race Matters"—to follow up the *Star* report that had so enraged former chief Fantino.[6] Rankin had brought the analysis to me and Blair for any explanation we might have had for the fact that there had been no change in the frequency of police stops of Black and other non-white residents of Toronto. In fact, it appeared the situation had worsened. I speculated that this might have been a result of the enhanced police response to public concern about gun violence, sparked by the downtown Toronto shooting of a young white woman, Jane Creba, on Boxing Day in 2005.

The public reaction had been so intense that city council had supported our proposal to add 250 officers to the police force. At the same time, I told him about my high hopes for our recently launched human rights charter project. I told him the results of the project would take a few years to be implemented and bear fruit. I pleaded for some time for the project to make a difference, telling him that he should see improvement before his next update. In the meantime, the mere existence of the project bore immediate fruit for the board and the police service in terms of managing risk and liability. Our response to every complaint about discrimination brought to the provincial Human Rights Tribunal would include a statement about the charter project and our new Race and Ethnocultural Equity Policy. Every tribunal would accept these as evidence that the board and the service were already addressing the issue. They wouldn't need to order further systemic remedies.

But what was happening in reality? Our own review and analysis went extremely well. Based on that, the board established a new human rights policy with a dedicated section on racial profiling. However, as an independent evaluation of the project by the Diversity Institute of Ryerson University found, at best there had been inadequate implementation of the recommendations by the police service. Yes, training on diversity had been augmented: there was a mandatory module, with training being provided on a different subject each year. Yes, more men and women from various racial, ethnic and linguistic backgrounds were being hired and even promoted. Yes, there was a greater focus on recognizing and supporting LGBTQ employees. But was the police service workplace truly safe and inclusive for everyone? Was the treatment by police of those from racialized backgrounds any different? Were services bias-free and non-discriminatory? Was the Toronto Police Service a different organization, as we had hoped for when Blair, Hall and I signed on to the human rights charter?

Wendy Cukier, director of Ryerson's Diversity Institute and the lead project evaluator, told me her team did not have the documentary evidence to answer those questions. Police service staff could not provide concrete data in response to the evaluation team's requests. They could not produce a paper trail showing any operational decisions that had been based on the recommendations. They could not demonstrate what real difference the recommendations had made in terms of changed practices, supervision, monitoring and accountability. Cukier and her team felt considerable pressure to write a favourable report, with representatives of the police service rewriting draft versions. The previous spirit of co-operation was gone and police service staff took it upon themselves to produce a glossy report, one that the board had commissioned and paid for. Gone even was adequate mention of the board's role in the project. When the board staff showed me one of the drafts, I rejected it. I met with Cukier and made it clear the board was looking for an objective and independent evaluation.

By this time, the issue of racial profiling—specifically, the phenomenon that would come to be known as carding—had turned into a matter of great public controversy. I told Cukier it would be odd if an evaluation report on policing and human rights did not deal with this issue. Indeed, it would kill the credibility of the evaluation itself. The report finally came in 2014. In a presentation to the board on March 13, 2014, Cukier acknowledged that there had been progress in several areas. However, in very guarded language, she also noted the gaps, including a lack of internal tools to measure quality and effectiveness of promotional processes, a need for streamlining data collection and reporting to ensure accountability, and a need for further focus on racially biased policing and training on mental health issues. She concluded that inconsistencies in the data meant a "rigorous analysis of changes over time" was not possible. And she quoted a male leader of the police service, who told the evaluation team, "Anything that tends to challenge our culture, there's resistance."

We had been up against yet another aspect of the police culture: papering over difficult matters and making it appear that everything was fine and dandy. If there were any issues, they were isolated, related to the behaviour or actions of individuals and not the organization. It was as if the leadership believed the line it repeated at every opportunity: "We are the best police service in the world." This aspect of the police culture is an integral part of the preoccupation with damage control and risk avoidance. More recently, we have seen the important role it played in how the fallout from the 2013 killing of Yatim was managed.

During this back and forth on the evaluation report, solid evidence that the Toronto Police Service had not dealt with racial profiling through the human rights project presented itself. It came in the form of another follow-up report by Rankin and his colleague Patty Winsa in the *Toronto Star*, published as a series called *Known to Police*, which ran during the spring of 2012.[7] As with the 2010 *Star* report on racial profiling, before publication Rankin shared the data, methodology and findings with me and Blair. We were given an opportunity to review the material, respond and explain. Blair's office shared its analysis with me. The contention of his staff was that the *Star*'s methodology was wrong, the use of census demographic data to compare police interactions with the populations of different neighbourhoods was erroneous, and thus the conclusions were questionable.

I couldn't follow this script. As far as I was concerned, the human rights charter project had failed to achieve the hoped-for results. Its recommendations had not been implemented with the necessary diligence or seriousness. The project had simply become a part of the police service's obsession with risk management and liability mitigation. Rankin and his team had painted a devastating picture. This time, not only had the reporters updated their findings since the 2010 report, they had compiled the data for the last eight years to show the year-on-year trend.

The first conclusion drawn by the reporters was that the police had stopped Black and other non-white people more frequently than white people, and young men more often than women or people from other age groups. Their second conclusion was that Black youth had been stopped so often that virtually every Black youth in Toronto had been the subject of police attention. And their third conclusion was that during the very same time we were working on the human rights charter project, these stops had increased—so much, in fact, that the total number of stops under Blair was more than double the number of stops under Fantino.

The *Star* analysis of Toronto police-stop data from 2008 to mid-2011 showed that the number of young Black and brown males aged fifteen to twenty-four who were documented by police in each of the city's seventy-two patrol zones was greater than the actual number of young men of colour living in those areas. Overall in Toronto, between 2008 and mid-2011, young Black men were carded at a rate that was 3.4 times higher than the rate for the young white male population.

I felt let down. I felt used. For me, the era of gentle persuasion and dialogue had ended. It may have yielded some very good policies enacted by the board, but the changes on the ground had been largely cosmetic. Clearly, a new and more aggressive approach was needed to confront the issue of biased policing.

"Devastating. Unacceptable: Toronto police board chair appalled by *Star* findings that show a stubborn rise in the number of citizens stopped and documented by our police officers—with black males heavily overrepresented," read the front-page headline of the *Toronto*

Star on September 28, 2013—in large, bold type. The controversy over racial profiling erupted in a charged environment. The fight against it had escalated because the *Star* series had revealed something else that was to become a flashpoint for community anger.

The *Star* hadn't just pointed out that Black and other visible minority youth had been stopped by the police disproportionately, with some being stopped multiple times, but also that police officers were filling out what was called a "contact card" for each interaction. It came out that data from these contact cards were being stored in the Toronto police database. Some people had been "carded" and their information stored in the database as many as forty times. Knia Singh, a young law student from York University's Osgoode Hall Law School and a former radio DJ originally from Guyana, became the poster boy for this practice. Never accused of or charged with a crime, Singh had been carded multiple times and the information about him in the police database was thoroughly inconsistent. His race was described differently, as was his physical appearance and even his height. It turned out that virtually all stops in which he was involved were related to him, a young Black man, driving a car that drew the police officers' attention.

Following the *Star* reports, the police services board became the battleground. Month after month, individuals and representatives of community-based human rights and civil liberties organizations appeared before the board urging action. Their one common demand—stop carding. In response, the board created a subcommittee of three members—committee chair Marie Moliner, Michael Thompson and Andy Pringle—to consult with the community and the police service, and come back to the board with recommendations. In a sign of the political turmoil engulfing the board at this time, I was excluded—but not for long.

When Thompson resigned from the subcommittee, frustrated by what he felt was inaction and a lack of focus, Moliner requested my participation. She had been organizing numerous public sessions to hear from the community. She wanted all these submissions to be posted on the board's website. People like Barbara Hall, chief commissioner of the human rights commission, Howard Morton, a former director of the province's Special Investigations Unit (SIU) and a member of the Law Union of Ontario, Noa Mendelsohn Aviv of the Canadian Civil Liberties Association, Singh of the Osgoode Society Against Institutional Injustices and a target of carding many times over, Kingsley Gilliam of the Black Action Defence Committee, John Sewell of the Toronto Police Accountability Coalition, Jennifer Chambers of the Empowerment Council and countless others appeared before the board time and again, repeating their experiences, demands and proposals, urging the board to act. Prominent journalists took up the cause. Royson James of the *Toronto Star* and Arnold Auguste, the highly regarded editor of the Black community newspaper *Share*, repeatedly pressed for strong action to end racially biased policing.

Under pressure, Blair established his own review of police and community engagement, known as PACER. Once this process began, Blair found that board members were spending too much time directing the work of PACER, rather than doing their real job of developing board policy. He bluntly told them so at one of the meetings of the committee. But led by Deputy Chief Sloly, the PACER committee came up with significant ideas. For once, it seemed that there was a strong and muscular response to the whole phenomenon of racial profiling by the police service.

The report addressed for the first time the vexing issue of unconscious, or implicit, bias. The chief approved bringing in experts from the US such as Lorie Fridell, an expert on fair and impartial policing from the University of South Florida, to develop a mandatory training program for all members of the police service from the chief on down. An advisory committee had been established, co-chaired by community representative Audrey Campbell, onetime president of the Jamaican Canadian Association, and David McLeod, a well-respected, plain-speaking veteran of anti-racism battles within the police service. It included representatives of the human rights commission, the privacy commission, the civil liberties association and others from the community and the service.

But from the board, no sign of a policy. Yet its nose was out of joint because Blair was upstaging it. His PACER report was ready. In a memo, I asked the chief to delay release of the report to allow the board to develop its policy. Blair agreed. The board had passed one related motion, based on a suggestion by Sewell, a former Toronto mayor, that a receipt be given to any person stopped by a police officer. Within a month, on December 7, 2012, Blair advised the board that the receipts had been prepared and printed, and were ready to be distributed.

But then the board insisted that the final receipt would need to be approved by the subcommittee first, which meant further delay. The receipt was only intended to be an interim measure pending the introduction of board policy and a comprehensive action plan. Apparently, the board wanted these to be in place before the summer, when the risk of carding was the greatest. But now, with the board preoccupied by the receipt, completion of work on these measures would be delayed. Blair shared his frustration with me and said that he was not willing to wait any longer and would move forward with the PACER recommendations. I told him I could not object; he had already complied with my request for delay. Blair was concerned that he needed lead time to prepare his people through the necessary communication, procedures and training to implement PACER. So he began the training on unconscious bias and other administrative preparations in anticipation of full implementation while continuing to go back and forth with the board on the details of the receipt. In the meantime, he held off on formally presenting the PACER report to the board publicly.

When almost a full year had passed since the initial receipt direction, I gave up hope that the subcommittee would ever bring forward a policy. And so I took a few days to write my own report for the board's November 2013 meeting, recommending a policy on racial profiling. This was to be the meeting at which the chief would present his PACER report. I wanted to make sure that in keeping with our practice, there would at least be a draft policy for consideration alongside the operational plan, namely PACER. On the morning of November 18, 2013, which was the day of the board meeting, I shared my report, "Police Carding and the Issue of Profiling," privately with my colleagues and announced that it would be on the agenda of the public board meeting that afternoon. Board members were given some time to review it and discuss it with me. A copy was sent to Blair as well.

I had prepared a thorough report that reviewed historical efforts to deal with racially biased or discriminatory policing, and recommended measures to address the vexing issues related to police stopping and carding people who were not engaged in or suspected of any crime, nor under investigation. This was the problem with police stops—they criminalized people, especially young Blacks and others of colour, who were not criminals. My recommendations also addressed the collection, storage and use of data about people who were stopped.

I pointed out that the community had been raising concerns since the 1980s, and that successive boards and chiefs had attempted to respond. My analysis of these responses suggested their focus had always been on rewriting policies, providing more or different training to front-line officers, and introducing initiatives to enhance relations between the police and the community. Yet clearly these measures had not eliminated the problem. I concluded that for the most part, the engagement between police and the public is influenced by policing strategies developed by senior brass.

Despite the discretionary powers of an individual officer, front-line police officers are guided by the orders of their superiors. Yet board policies had not dealt with questions related to the accountability of the brass, had not articulated expectations in terms of supervision and monitoring, and had not required that police strategies be consistent with the goal of bias-free policing. In short, there were no consequences for the senior ranks. Virtually all attention had been focused on modifying and controlling the actions of front-line officers through more training and education.

Thus, police officers were directed to enforce the much-vaunted Toronto Anti-Violence Intervention Strategy (TAVIS) created by Blair and funded by the provincial government. Whatever the original objectives, over time TAVIS had turned into a muscular policing response to violence, with a centralized unit going into neighbourhoods, breaking down doors of people's residences, arbitrarily stopping and questioning young people. The strategy may have reduced gun violence, but was the result good value considering the damage to relationships with the community? The province eventually stopped funding TAVIS and the strategy has since been dismantled.

Similarly, as the police association would point out, carding had become a tool for measuring productivity. Supervisors were measuring police officers' daily productivity by the number of cards they were writing. In my view, police *leadership* had to be held accountable for discriminatory or biased policing, which my report's eighteen recommendations reflected. I called for a policy that would eliminate "conscious or unconscious" profiling of individuals while supporting the legitimate collection and retention of information for bona fide investigations. I also recommended that only information on an individual's background that was demonstrably relevant to specific police investigations should be retained.

However, all hell broke loose that morning at the informal private meeting of board members. Even before reading my report and asking me questions, some board members demanded that the chief be asked to give his reaction. Blair came in and embarked on a diatribe against my report. He claimed that I had gone too far with my recommendations, waded into operational areas that were exclusively his responsibility and proposed tying the hands of police officers. He left, having sliced and diced both me and my report. A livid Pringle turned to me and asked, "Who the fuck gave you the right to write this report?"

I explained that this was not the first time when as chair, I had taken the initiative to prepare reports on matters before the board. In this case, I had felt compelled to do this because the subcommittee had failed to do its job. Finally, I got emotional and addressing Pringle directly, I said that this was an issue that mattered to me as a person of colour, and that as a father and a friend of parents of Black and other racialized children, I was not prepared to tolerate this state of affairs any longer. I added that this was something he could not appreciate. I told him that if he or any other board member did not like what I had done, they could remove me as board chair at the public meeting.

Two board members spoke up to support me: vice-chair Thompson and city councillor Mike Del Grande. Pringle backed off and became conciliatory. He talked about how much he appreciated my passion for the issue, how I knew a whole lot more about it, and how I had given leadership to the board in dealing with it. Later, when we ran into each other in the washroom, he said that he was very upset and offended by my imputation that as a rich, old white guy he could not understand the issue. He claimed that he had agreed to join the subcommittee and spent a great deal of his time precisely because he did care and wanted to help deal with it.

I responded that I could not help it if he was offended, but that I very much wanted him to be an ally and a supporter in dealing with this tough issue. This episode vividly and dramatically illustrates the complexity in providing bias-free and inclusive policing, respecting the diversity of our community, and not allowing actions that destroy the life chances of young people simply because of who they are. And it shows how it affects us personally in our skin. In the end, Pringle contributed a great deal of time and attention to how we dealt with this difficult issue. My report did make it to that day's public board meeting. However, the board, intimidated by Blair's outburst, simply received my report and decided to retain a criminal lawyer well versed in policing to write a board policy.

Thus, Frank Addario, a leading and highly respected member of the criminal defence bar, entered the picture. Addario's involvement in this protracted saga did not start auspiciously for me. He didn't know me, but he knew committee chair Marie Moliner, a senior federal bureaucrat, lawyer and the spouse of a judge who apparently moved in the same social circles. Initially, Addario would only communicate with Moliner and take instructions from her. But when Moliner was called upon to provide direction, she felt compelled to bring me in, and the three of us became a team.

Addario's first task was to provide the board with a legal opinion on its powers to craft policy to deal with the various aspects of racial profiling. The opinion would also set the scope of our policy. This was necessary because Blair had insisted that his approach through PACER was legally sound, based on independent legal advice from three senior lawyers. However, the lawyers had identified certain legal risks from "the manner in which personal data is collected from individuals" during carding.[8] To mitigate these risks, it was important that 1) collection of data was a neutral and bias-free activity not guided by race; and 2) it was voluntary, meaning that individuals could freely choose whether or not to respond to questions posed by officers unless legally detained or under arrest. Addario's own legal opinion given to the board reiterated these areas of concern. Clearly, the board policy needed to establish clarity on this matter.

Addario's task now was to propose a draft policy. He closely considered the voluminous amount of material from numerous community consultations and deputations at board meetings containing legal advice, narrated personal experiences and recommended options. He even held his own meetings with members of the community and embarked on serious discussions with members of the police service, including Blair and the police association. He felt an atmosphere of transparency and consultation was critical if we were to have any hope of obtaining organizational buy-in.

The early signs were good. Blair had a long, frank, cordial meeting with Addario, who was provided with all the documents he had requested. Addario and I met with police association president Mike McCormack in my office with no pushback. Blair designated Sloly as the senior management point person, given his lead role on the PACER file. Of course, Sloly rarely met with Addario alone. The chief's executive officer, Inspector Stu Eley, in-house legal counsel Marianne Wright, and others were almost always in the room, but Addario understood Sloly to be speaking for the chief.

Addario brought forward the first draft of the policy on February 13, 2014. I was exceedingly pleased and felt vindicated that Addario had incorporated much of what I had proposed in my board report. When we met with Blair in my office to review the draft policy, Addario went through it word by word, clause by clause. Blair actively participated in the discussion and even proposed adding some strong clauses banning discriminatory practices based on race or ethnicity. We felt we had the chief on side and were good to go.

But when Addario presented the draft policy to the board at a closed meeting, Blair expressed concern about the proposed requirement that people be advised by any officer stopping them that they have the right to leave and the right to refuse to answer questions; and second, that they would automatically receive a receipt including the date, time and place of the interaction and the officer's name, badge number and phone number. These concerns were consistent with Blair's long-held view that a board policy was about *what* was to be done, whereas the chief made operational decisions about *how* it would be done. However, he was aware of other existing policies that prescribed specific operational details, and he had not outright objected to their provisions.

The final version of the draft policy was presented at the public board meeting of April 24, 2014. At a press conference preceding it, Addario and I characterized the policy as "rights based": members of the public had the right to equal treatment "before and under the law," in the words of the Charter, and the right of freedom from discrimination. These rights are enshrined in the Canadian Charter of Rights and Freedoms as well as provincial human rights legislation. The provisions that had caused Blair concern were the cornerstones of a rights-based approach.

In addition, the policy sought to provide a clear definition of what constituted a valid "public safety purpose" for which a police officer can stop an individual when not engaged in a criminal investigation. This was our attempt to eliminate arbitrary stops and stops where the appearance of detention, known as "psychological detention," is used to embark on a kind of fishing expedition. Psychological detention is a legal term describing how police, by use of their body and speech, make it clear that a person is not free to leave. The policy also provided direction on the collection, retention and use of information gathered from such informal interactions. And finally, the policy prohibited the use of carding as a measure of the productivity of police officers.

When the policy was released to the public, there was some muted criticism that it did not ban the practice of carding altogether. The overwhelming response, however, was favourable. People applauded its rights-based approach, accountability mechanisms, safeguards— and its clear definition of a legitimate reason for stopping someone. In other words, the proposed policy acknowledged that in certain limited circumstances, this was a valid policing technique.

But the definition of public safety was one of the major speed bumps ahead. We had agreed with Addario that the definition was an operational matter and should come from the service. Sloly had undertaken this task. To us this was reassuring. He had, after all, played a strong leadership role in the PACER project, after taking it over from Mark Saunders, Toronto's current police chief and then a superintendent. To Sloly's dismay, Saunders's report had justified carding and it was never made public.[9] We were confident that Sloly would provide a satisfactory definition, consistent with the rest of the policy. But the definition that came from him after much waiting, literally at the eleventh hour, was so vague and broad as to be meaningless. If accepted, it would undermine the entire policy. Some on the board wondered if Sloly was so committed to the PACER report that he had little interest in the board's policy. Others were of the view that this was the doing of Wright, the chief's in-house legal counsel and a disciple of old-school policing, and other senior officials who did not want to give up carding.

Addario made a last-ditch effort to engage Sloly to do better. This did not happen. Whether Sloly's hands were tied, whether he was powerless in the face of Wright running interference for Blair, we would never know. In the end, Addario had to develop a definition of valid public safety purpose as a placeholder. We hoped that this would give the chief time to provide a useful and workable definition. With this placeholder and small changes based on public feedback, the final policy was approved by the board unanimously. In response, Blair publicly announced his inability to implement the policy, claiming that it breached the *Police Services Act* by infringing on operational matters. Months later, he would even claim that the provincial government had advised me of this, which was blatantly untrue.

As a matter of fact, it was Blair who had approached minister of community safety Yasir Naqvi and deputy minister Matt Torigian, a former Waterloo Region police chief. During a brief conversation while we were waiting in line to be marched into a graduation ceremony at the Toronto Police College, he had told them he was concerned about the board policy and might need their intervention. But from what he told the board, it appeared he had made a formal complaint and that the province was very concerned. So I met with Torigian, who assured me the province had no intention of intervening because this was an internal matter and the law was clear. It was in this meeting that I also learned about the limited nature of Blair's interaction with Naqvi and Torigian on this matter.

Blair declared that the requirements that members of the public must be proactively informed of their rights during informal interactions and provided with a receipt were unworkable—they tied the hands of police officers. At various times, he went so far as to claim that violent crime had increased because police officers were no longer sure what they could or could not do, and so they were not acting on their own initiative to avoid getting in trouble. He was essentially suggesting that the board was jeopardizing public safety. This was a different man from the one who had spoken so loftily about eradicating racial profiling when he became the chief in 2005. Board members were understandably apoplectic. They asked if police officers were not doing their job, what was Blair doing about it? Wasn't this neglect of duty, a breach of their oath of office and serious misconduct? Blair quickly backtracked and tried to clarify: officers were very much on the job, but working by the book and not going above and beyond it.

To try to resolve the impasse, Addario and Pringle worked with Blair's office to revise the policy, which Addario presented to the board on December 16, 2014. It essentially gutted the policy the board had already approved, removing all the "rights-based" features. There was no way the board could accept the chief's alternative version. Blair complained that he had not been consulted during the development of the original policy and had not been given an opportunity to review the draft before it was published, which again was plainly untrue.

What had caused this hardening of position on Blair's part? For someone who had taken pride in being a modern chief who embraced and celebrated diversity, who believed in the rule of law, who championed progressive policing, this was a stunning *U*-turn. Pringle assured me that Blair was legitimately trying to address the negative effect on public safety that had occurred due to the rank and file working by the book, doing the minimum the law required. It was difficult for me to accept this explanation. A lot of cops do not like change, period. However, another feature of police culture is that once a rule is made and the directions are clear, they comply. If there was confusion this time, it was being caused by the drawn-out and constantly changing process. Once the dust had settled and everyone knew what was expected of them, they would fall in line.

As well, cops are not a homogeneous lot. By this time Toronto had a very diverse police service. Officers who themselves were members of minorities and worried about the safety of their own children had told me they supported the policy. Could it be, then, that some in the leadership of the police service and the police association were using supposed discontent in the rank and file to hide their own opposition to the policy? Carding would remain an issue in Toronto throughout Bill Blair's term as chief and would carry over to the next board and chief after my eventual departure.

The View from the G20 Command Centre

TAKE THE ELEVATOR up to the tenth floor of Toronto police head-quarters and there in front of you is Bill Blair's baby. Blair oversaw the renovations and upgrades that turned the room into a state-of-the-art military-style command centre. On the day of the most challenging security operation in Toronto police history, the G20 summit of world leaders in June 2010, Deputy Chief Keith Forde took me up from the seventh-floor boardroom to see the command cen-tre in action. Everyone had their designated posts. People watched the police feeds on giant wall-mounted monitors, while others communicated with the headquarters of the RCMP-led Integrated Security Unit (ISU) in Barrie, the inter-service group responsible for the overall security of the G20. We would learn much later about the ISU and its role. There were recorders on one side, a phalanx of note-takers on the other and they were all in their places that day as order on the streets of Toronto began to break down.

Everyone except Bill Blair. I spotted him tucked into an ante-room, watching events not through police cameras or any official communications channel, but on Toronto TV station CP24. Forde hadn't seen any reason why I shouldn't be there. He had thought that as the board chair I was allowed anywhere in the building. I greeted Blair, but he barely acknowledged me. Then he quickly turned to the deputy chief and barked, "Get the chair out of here!" His reaction spoke volumes. It dawned on me many months later—Blair had deceived me and his board during the period the police service and the police service board had spent planning the G20 police operations. He knew the jig was up when I saw him that day and saw the setup on the tenth floor.

WE KNOW WHAT happened that weekend, perhaps the darkest chapter in Toronto police history. Officers—as many as a hundred—removed their identity badges during confrontations with protesters, in clear violation of police board policy requiring every uniformed member of the police service to wear their name badge. As many as 1,140 protesters, peaceful and otherwise, were arrested. To this day the numbers remain speculative, because processing of those arrested on that weekend was so slipshod that the numbers provided by the prisoner processing centre, the RCMP and Toronto police do not align. The detention of these people and the time they spent in an overcrowded, chaotic centre represent the worst breach of civil rights in the history of peacetime policing, not only in this city, but in Canada.

A previously little-known—and discredited—police tactic known as "kettling," rarely used in Canada, detained innocent citizens for hours during a torrential downpour. It turned out that the geniuses who enforced this tactic did not know how to disengage from it or what to do with the hundreds of people they had kettled—literally contained inside a solid circle of cops. The vast majority of these detainees were ordinary residents of the neighbourhood on their way home or out for a walk and had nothing to do with the protest.

An even more draconian practice was implemented as police assumed the extraordinary power to search people outside a security fence that had been erected to protect the venue of the summit, the Metro Toronto Convention Centre. Police believed they were authorized to do so by the provincial government under an arcane piece of legislation, the *Public Works Protection Act* (PWPA). The government had given its approval hastily and in secret. But the regulation passed by the cabinet gave police no such powers. Neither the fact that the regulation had been enacted nor that it was wrongly interpreted was ever properly communicated to the public. Eventually, the act itself was repealed under intense public pressure.

Regarding the removal of name badges by about a hundred Toronto police officers deployed during the summit, the police association had fought a 2005 board directive that an officer's name be visible on a badge, arguing it would endanger officer safety. Blair wanted to make the badges optional, phase in the change, ensure officers were comfortable, then weed out the laggards. But the board won its case to make name badges mandatory at the Ontario Labour Relations Board. Still, without support for this initiative from management and the police association, many officers evidently felt they could remove their badges when accountability mattered most at the G20 summit (and to this day you can find officers not wearing their badges).

The 21,000 security personnel on Toronto streets during the summit included 6,200 Toronto officers, 5,000 from the RCMP, 3,000 from the Canadian Armed Forces, 3,000 from the Ontario Provincial Police and 740 from Peel region as well as contributions from Halton, York, Ottawa, Hamilton, London, Niagara Falls, Peterborough, Durham, Sudbury, Waterloo, Barrie, Newfoundland and Labrador, Winnipeg, Montreal, Edmonton and Calgary. Collectively, the police response was one of confusion, communication breakdowns and overreaction.

Some of this would have been comical had it not been so damaging to the image of the city and policing in the twenty-first century. At one point, as protesters stayed many steps ahead of slow-footed police during Saturday's day of damage, one out-of-town police unit purchased a street map from a subway kiosk to find out where they were supposed to be headed. There certainly was enough blame to go around and I have taken my fair share, but it is important to know how the board's hands were tied ahead of that June weekend.

As that fateful Saturday dawned, I honestly felt we were ready. On the morning of June 26, 2010, I decided to take an early morning walk around the security perimeter put in place as part of this unprecedented operation. I saw police dealing with people in the friendliest of ways, offering help with directions, calm and smiling. Later that morning, my wife was part of a march organized by the labour movement, and she texted me afterward to tell me it had been peaceful, with police chanting along with the demonstrators. Yes, we were ready.

I headed to my office at police headquarters after my walk and flipped on a local news station, CP24. Deputy Chief Forde spotted me and invited me up to the boardroom, where he was watching the events with other senior officials from the RCMP and Ontario Provincial Police. Perhaps a half-dozen of us sat and watched. Marchers were heading west on Queen Street when suddenly I saw a plume of smoke. There had been no disturbances, so it couldn't be tear gas. Had someone tossed a firecracker? "That's a signal," Forde told me.

And indeed, within seconds a bunch of people in identical black clothing appeared on the street. It was a carefully planned diversionary tactic, a call to arms by "black bloc" protesters scattered throughout the march. The black bloc has become a ubiquitous presence at every international summit protest since the 1980s. Many members are self-described anarchists. They wear black clothing, black bandanas, gas masks or goggles, and are organized with military precision, darting out of crowds to vandalize targets that they say represent capitalism or oppression. Almost as soon as they break from the protesters, they are back amongst them, quickly changing out of their black garb to avoid detection. According to accounts in the *Star*, the flare we had noticed and shouts of "Umbrella!" were signals for the bloc to break to the front lines.

Soon, I saw the police cars burning. I saw the image of the protester on top of the car hitting it with a baseball bat. I saw all that. But there were thousands of people protesting and thousands of officers guarding the city. It seemed to me that those were isolated incidents.

In the run-up to the summit, we had carefully studied what had happened during the so-called Battle of Seattle in 1999, the World Trade Organization protests during which police rained tear gas, rubber bullets and concussion bombs on demonstrators. The City of Seattle ultimately had to pay out about US$1.3 million to those who had been mistreated, and the police response cost the chief his job.[1] We had studied the 2001 Summit of the Americas in Quebec City, in which the building of a three-metre-tall fence around the summit site was seen as a provocation and the RCMP was ultimately found to have acted irresponsibly in its use of tear gas and rubber bullets against protesters.

More recently, and closer to home, we had the experience of handling the huge Toronto Tamil protests of 2009. During these, Blair allowed peaceful demonstrations along Toronto's busy University Avenue, but he made sure protesters saw his heavy armaments parked around the corner from the protest site. He even allowed a shutdown of one of the city's major commuter routes, the Gardiner Expressway, showing respect for the protesters by allowing them to temporarily take over a vital thoroughfare. People complained—sometimes vehemently—about the inconvenience, but we proved that large, diverse cities have room for peaceful dissent. I have nothing but praise for the chief's handling of that potentially incendiary situation.

But what was happening on our streets on that G20 Saturday was different; it didn't look like the pitched battles of Quebec City or the chaos of Seattle. Here it is worth mentioning that seven years after the lessons of Toronto, international summits in major cities *still* sometimes devolve into chaos. At the G20 summit in Hamburg in July 2017, violent clashes between police and protesters left 476 officers injured, more than 400 protesters jailed or detained, and untold damage and looting to businesses in the city centre. At the Toronto G20, some twenty thousand police officers engaged in three days of pitched battles against the black bloc and thousands of other protesters who took to the streets.

At the end of that June weekend in 2010, I looked back and assessed things this way: the entire crowd had not turned violent and the police had not turned en masse on the protesters. Two police cars burning looked dramatic, but they looked more dramatic because those two isolated images were broadcast nearly non-stop on cable news networks. I believed I was looking at things in context. All the speculation about whether police had set fire to the cars themselves and whether the trouble was instigated by police provocateurs dressed in black came later. I don't buy either theory. As I digested the events, all I believed I had seen was two burning cars, a kettling and a bunch of windows being kicked in (though the kettling puzzled me—and everyone else—that night).

Board members were calling me and asking what was going on, but none of us knew anything more than what we were seeing on television. I couldn't reach Blair by phone but I reached Deputy Chief Sloly. He was not able to provide any insight. To his credit, Chief Blair finally did order everyone released, even as his underlings sought to arrest everyone, innocent or not, caught up in the traps during monsoon-like rains. In the hours and days after the summit, neither I nor Toronto City Council had any objective basis for believing that police had been out of control. No one had died and the streets had not become a war zone. But I quickly learned not everyone saw it this way.

The following Monday, Blair and I had a brief chat. We did not make a big deal about the kettling. We did talk about the black bloc and about a couple of cars burning. The view we shared was, given how bad things could have been, the summit had gone reasonably well. A few days later there was a board meeting, and on behalf of the board I publicly expressed appreciation for how well it had been managed. Toronto City Council passed a similar motion unanimously expressing its appreciation for the work of our police.

We didn't know much of what had happened at Queen's Park—not the scope or the depth. The kettling fiasco had not been fully brought to light yet and we were still learning how disastrous the

detention centre had been. We knew police had detained several hundred people and then the chief had come in and directed
the front-line people to let them go. We didn't know at that time
that there had been a dispute between the service's top brass and
Superintendent Mark Fenton, the front-line commander who was
insisting on giving people tickets or sending them to the detention
centre, completely misreading the chief's direction.

I did know there had been a few incidents at the detention
centre, east of downtown. Pam McConnell—the city councillor and
former police board chair—had called me on Saturday night and
told me she had heard from a journalist who couldn't find his son.
I had said his son was probably at the detention centre, and if that
was the case, he would be out in a couple of hours. It didn't work
out that way.

But in the immediate aftermath of the summit, Blair and I felt
we had survived an operation imposed on us by Stephen Harper.
That's why I had no problem speaking on behalf of the board to
thank the officers for their hard work. But then came the pushback.
Charles Pascal, a senior academic and former provincial deputy
minister of education, responded to my statement with an email
saying I was too close to this and that I should resign. In response, I
wrote that I was sure that during his time as deputy minister he had
given his people difficult projects. And I asked, did he wait until he
was positive there was no risk to him because of any as yet unknown
problems with their work before he thanked them? We had put these
people in a tough spot. I expected there would be discipline for some
police overreaction. But I did not anticipate the fire-hose magnitude
of the revelations that were just ahead.

Within a few days, the *Toronto Star* and others began to publish
photos of violent takedowns that had occurred. They published
first-person accounts of mistreatment and police heavy-handedness.
We learned of the removal of badges at Queen's Park and the conduct of "Officer Bubbles," Constable Adam Josephs, now the star
of a YouTube video in which he threatened to charge a twenty-one-

year-old female protester with assault if one of the bubbles she was blowing touched him. The video received worldwide, embarrassing attention. A York Region officer was caught on video telling a citizen, "This ain't Canada right now."

The cooling of relations between me and Blair began as more and more of this information was revealed, a drip-drip-drip of damaging front-page revelations. Blair retreated into a denying, resisting stance, refusing to acknowledge the severity of the damage that had been done. He never emerged from the police-culture cocoon to acknowledge that things had gone wrong.

THINGS HAD STARTED to go wrong during the planning process. The story of the lead-up to the G20 is the story of a prime minister dumping a major event with significant security implications on a city on short notice, utterly disregarding advice from local politicians. It's a tale of a police chief who kept crucial information to himself and a board that did not push him hard enough.[2] Harper publicly announced in December 2009 that the G20 summit would be held in Toronto the following June. Blair had been told by the RCMP that the G20 would be coming to Toronto as early as the previous month. He advised the board and the mayor at that time that this would be the biggest security challenge Toronto had ever faced, and he pledged to come to us when more details were available and before it became public.

Even if the summit remained north of the city in Huntsville—where the earlier G8 meeting would be held—nobody was going to head up there to protest, Blair said. They would do so in Toronto. Even the Canadian government would be setting up its media centre in the city. There were always protests during these summits, so we had to be ready regardless. The board told Blair that not a penny of Toronto money should be spent on the summit because this was not a Toronto event. He was told to make sure Ottawa covered the entire cost. Blair told the board about a conversation he had had with the mayor during which Mayor Miller had said, "Chief, I hope this turns out well." Blair had apparently replied, "Mr. Mayor, you can be assured these things don't turn out well." His message to the mayor and the board was blunt and unvarnished. No matter how much you plan, you cannot anticipate every possibility.

On January 26, 2010, Miller and I met with foreign journalists on a pre-summit visit for them to get to know Toronto. It was part orientation, part promotion. We assured them that our values were based on the principles of democracy and people's right to express lawful, peaceful dissent. We said that not only would we allow this, our police would facilitate it. Afterward, Miller and I discussed the danger of heading into this without any commitment of direct funding from the federal government beyond policing costs. Blair had informally signalled to us that he was going to need a lot of money for this summit. He said he needed immediate approval of approximately $14 million from the city to be able to order critical communications equipment.

I asked Tony Veneziano, Blair's chief administrative officer, why they couldn't lease or rent this equipment. We were in the middle of a major capital expenditure, modernizing our emergency communications, and this purchase would skewer our plans. From Veneziano's response, I gathered that we were essentially at the mercy of the sole multinational corporation that could provide the equipment needed for the summit. I told him, "We will not make any commitment without something in writing from the feds, even if it jeopardizes the summit planning."

The next day, Toronto city manager Joseph Pennachetti wrote to Wayne Wouters, clerk of the federal Privy Council. Blair had already written to Ward Elcock, the Privy Council office co-ordinator of G8/G20 security, seeking federal assurance that Toronto security costs would be covered. The city's overarching concerns ran deeper, with worries about potential financial impacts on city programs and services, city businesses and residents, and its ability to get a funding request to city council in February. "Of some concern at this time is the city's ability to deploy the required resources in a timely manner,"

Pennachetti wrote. "The City of Toronto and the Government of Canada have a long history of working collaboratively and effectively together on matters of shared interest." Pennachetti told Wouters that by working as partners, Toronto and Ottawa could deliver a memorable G20 summit.

Ottawa responded on February 8, 2010, leading to negotiations about the federal government's contribution. Ottawa agreed to pick up all direct costs related to items like equipment, salaries and any overtime for front-line officers and non-supervisory civilians in accordance with contractual agreements in place at the time. What the government would not do was indemnify the city, the board and the police service against any legal action resulting from the G20 policing. Based on the February 8 response, the funds for the purchase of communications equipment were approved by city council. There was some debate as to whether the convention centre was the best venue, but Harper's people were adamant that was where it would be held.

We asked Blair for a briefing on his plans. We did not seek operational details because Blair had told us that he had been given the highest security clearance to receive sensitive classified information, but that he couldn't share that information even with the board. It would have been easier to secure the Canadian National Exhibition grounds, given that Lake Ontario provided a natural security barrier; plunking the summit down in the middle of the city made security planning much more challenging. Blair mentioned a fence but provided no details about which streets would be blocked. There would be a fence. That was all. Period. Full stop.

But Adam Vaughan, a city councillor whose ward included the summit site (and who later, like Blair, became a Liberal MP), sent a newsletter to his constituents telling them he had attended a confidential briefing, and he provided them with a map of the area that was to be fenced. How was it that Vaughan knew more about this fence than the Toronto Police Board? We confronted Blair about what other confidential briefings he had provided to Vaughan. Blair denied he had provided any briefings and claimed Vaughan had provided his constituents with incorrect information. But I was then approached by Blair's executive officer, Stu Eley, and told we had a problem because the RCMP wanted to know why the chief was giving confidential briefings—something Blair denied a second time.

We clearly wanted operational details from Blair but the chief had always maintained that operations were his purview, not the board's, and our legal counsel had backed his position. When we were travelling together in India at the invitation of the Indian government in February 2010, I spoke to Blair about the board's need to receive more information on a regular basis about the G20 planning. Based on our conversation, I advised board staff about the matters on which the board could ask for a regular update from the chief.

In the weeks following the fiasco on the streets of Canada's largest city, there were calls for an inquiry from multiple voices. Our board appointed John Morden, a retired Ontario Court of Appeal judge, to independently review the conduct of the police and our board. But when Morden talked to Blair, the chief said he had no recollection of our discussion in India. Morden issued his report in June 2012. In his review he was critical of the board's role, but police chiefs, police boards and their legal counsels across the province were following the same separation of roles the Toronto board was following.

However, Morden did find that we were kept in the dark about police operational matters related to the G20 and were effectively reduced to bystanders. He acknowledged at the beginning of his report that the board, "in many of its decisions, was applying the former 'operations' and 'policies' distinction that held sway before the *Police Services Act* and it is clear that it acted conscientiously in doing so." Indeed, Blair would later demonstrate, during the carding controversy, how chiefs clung to what Morden called an outdated definition of powers. Morden had a different interpretation of the powers of the Toronto Police Board than our lawyers did. "Perhaps in its desire not to be seen as treading on the territory of the chief of police, the board has, wrongly, limited its consultative mandate such that it has come to view it was improper to engage in a discussion that involves the board asking questions about, commenting on, or making recommendations concerning operational matters," Morden wrote.[3]

In responding to Morden on July 19, 2012, I did not delve into the different interpretations of our mandate, but I accepted my responsibility as chair and publicly apologized to "innocent people who had their rights abridged, their liberty interfered with and their physical safety jeopardized. This is contrary to everything I have worked to achieve as a member of this board." I was the only public official to apologize. Neither Prime Minister Harper nor Ontario Premier Dalton McGuinty felt the need to acknowledge how their decisions had affected what happened in Toronto that weekend. Nor did the RCMP, which had been in charge of the policing strategy. Blair spoke to me about how the RCMP brass had run for cover, but being a loyal soldier he did not break rank and make public the RCMP's overall responsibility for what had happened.

In any event, Blair would have fought the board had we pushed for anything more than answers on planning or communication because police always want an ironclad distinction between policy and operations. But when the operational plans were being finalized, we wanted—needed—a regular report to the board; thus, we asked for a confidential monthly update. I'm still not sure that was the right thing to do. But I thought offering confidentiality would give Blair more latitude and allow him to be more forthcoming. My relationship with him was good and there was trust between him and the board. The board was realistic enough to understand that there were always things the chief would not tell us, but there was an acceptance that he would always have good reasons for doing so—even when we suspected he was merely protecting his fiefdom, his authority.

Things became complicated when Blair told us about the fence and a so-called five-metre rule. Blair believed the provincial *Public*

Works Protection Act, enacted in 1939, would allow officers to stop and search anyone coming within five metres of the fence. Initially, there had been a request to Ottawa asking for enhanced powers for Toronto police around the fence under the *Foreign Missions and International Organizations Act*. But Ottawa had inexplicably rejected the request; it was the feds' event but they didn't want to be tied directly to its policing.

So, on the advice of the Integrated Security Unit, on May 12, 2010, Blair asked the province to make a regulation under the PWPA. He told the board after he had already done this. The board did not ask more questions because we had not seen the letter. We only had the chief's word, and he made it sound like a routine matter. He painted it strictly as a security move—that people would not be able to approach the security fence because there was a fear that they would try to breach it.

During its own probe of police actions that weekend, the Office of the Independent Police Review Director (OIPRD) reported that Deputy Chief Tony Warr felt the extra authority from the PWPA was needed. Warr was in charge of special operations at the police service, which included intelligence and security functions, and was Toronto's highest-ranking designate to the Integrated Security Unit headed by the RCMP and responsible for planning the operations. As reported by the OIPRD, Blair went along with his request, saying it was probably "not necessary, but it couldn't hurt."

The board was under the clear impression that the chief of Toronto police was solely or primarily responsible for security operations during the G20. Blair had not told us about the security hierarchy—the extent of the RCMP and OPP involvement, or where he stood in the planning or operational structure. Therefore, the board assumed the chief had written the letter on May 12 because he was in charge of security. He had actually written the letter at the behest of the inter-services committee chaired by the RCMP. The OIPRD review said the existence of the *Public Works Protection Act*, created to protect public buildings during World War II, its application during the summit, and the communication around the move were a "public relations disaster."

A month before the beginning of the summit, we told Blair that the public needed assurances from him. So we put the G20 on our public agenda and had the chief speak to it. We specifically asked that all policies of the Toronto Police Board be followed. He assured us unequivocally and on the public record that they would be. He did not qualify that those assurances only applied to certain circumstances and that he had no authority over other ones. At this point, the board had not been made aware of the federal legislation that covered the G20. We did not know of the planning and operations process that typically occurred in these circumstances, but were correct in assuming that we would need to bring in officers from neighbouring jurisdictions.

We made it clear to Blair that officers from other forces would need to undergo training to learn our board's approach to policing. They were to be appointed by me to act as officers in Toronto and the agreement for them to do so was to be between police boards, not police chiefs. This was such a cumbersome process that I was deputizing and signing papers up until the day of the G20. But it was important for a couple of reasons. We wanted clarity that the officers were acting under the authority of the Toronto police and operating under Toronto police rules. Our concern was that if any of them were to cause harm to or mistreat a citizen, they could avoid investigation unless they were appointed by Toronto. In this way, Toronto would at least do the initial investigation.

We had faith in Toronto police and the culture of community-based policing we had been working on establishing here. But there was no way to provide proper training to others. The officers, who came from across the country, received a very short classroom orientation but it wasn't enough. Because of time constraints, they couldn't receive the training needed to build them into one integrated functioning team. The OIPRD probe said online, video and interactive training elements lasted a mere two-and-a-half hours, and in-person training a scant two hours. According to the OIPRD report, the online training did not adequately cover Charter rights, and the in-person training dealt with justifying police actions and preparing for violent battles. It did not tell officers how to deal with peaceful assembly and how it should be facilitated.

I knew where the officers were coming from but I didn't realize they were not under Blair's control. This became clear only when, two days before the summit, *Toronto Star* columnist Haroon Siddiqui called me requesting help. He was concerned that he wouldn't be able to get into the Fairmont Royal York hotel the next morning to interview the president of Turkey, Recep Tayyip Erdoğan, who had invited him to breakfast. No one was allowed to enter the hotel, where heads of state were staying, without prior security clearance. I called Blair, who said he would do what he could, but that he wasn't in charge of security for the Royal York. I thought it strange that the chief of Toronto police was not in charge of the landmark Royal York. I suppose I interpreted this to mean that the RCMP was in charge of security for foreign leaders.

The chief asserted the need for a temporary detention centre and arranged a board tour of it just before the summit to allay any concerns we might have had. The centre's superintendent told us about the research they had done, how they had come up with the size and layout of the centre, and what they foresaw happening. They had conceptualized a flow-through centre where people would be in and out in a couple of hours. They had even provided an area large enough for demonstrations when people exited the centre. I felt reassured that those who were detained would be treated in a reasonable, humane manner. The superintendent told me they had looked at previous summits and the largest number of people ever arrested was 750 in Copenhagen, so they had built one that would comfortably accommodate up to a thousand. They also told us that no more than five or six people would be held in each cell. We left with the impression that people would be processed in an efficient way and would have access to legal assistance.

The reality couldn't have been more different. If we had had an inkling of the mess that would arise, we might have asked more questions. The summit included twenty of the world's leaders, a number of whom—including the host—were not popular in their home country. With conflicts going on in many of these countries, there was at least a reasonable expectation of rallies, marches and demonstrations. There was an understandable worry on the part of the police that something drastic could be attempted by unknown elements. Therefore, the board was willing to accept the high level of security. The five-metre rule, the detention centre, the level of police visibility in the city—people would inevitably be inconvenienced when you put on an event like the G20 in the heart of the city. But Blair assured us there were plans to allow people to flow through the downtown core and minimize inconvenience.

Here's what actually happened. The Prisoner Processing Centre was a former film studio on Toronto's Eastern Avenue, about five kilometres from the epicentre of the summit and the protests. Contrary to claims that the facility could accommodate up to a thousand detainees, the OIPRD review found that Toronto Police Services had planned for five hundred.[4] Except they hadn't been clear whether that meant five hundred at one time or five hundred over the course of the weekend. OIPRD interviews with officers who had been in charge (who had received little or no training in the processing of prisoners) revealed they had assumed the cells could hold about twenty people, not five or six.[5]

The processing centre turned out to be a complete failure of planning. Nothing appeared to have been enshrined in writing, the numbers anticipated and the numbers accommodated per cell were arbitrary, and there were no contingency plans for the much larger number of people who were brought to the facility. When the building flooded and part of the roof caved in following heavy rain, there was no emergency plan to fall back on. When mass arrests were ordered on the Saturday evening, the processing centre was given no more than twenty to thirty minutes' notice before protesters began arriving. Predictably, all hell broke loose.

Young people were held in cells with adult prisoners. There was a lack of privacy in some toilet facilities. Others were denied access to toilets for hours. More importantly, Charter rights, including access to phones and lawyers, were denied. Charter rights limiting the length of detention on minor charges were grossly breached. According to the OIPRD review, only thirty-three of 269 prisoners facing criminal charges at the processing centre were given access to a lawyer. Close to eight hundred people were held on minor, non-criminal breach-of-peace charges and only thirty-two were given access to duty counsel. While many did not ask to see a lawyer, 513 did, according to the review. Of that number, 448 were denied that basic right or were simply ignored.[6]

Contrary to Canadian law, at least fourteen of those charged with breach of peace—and likely many more—were held longer than the twenty-four-hour maximum stipulated for that charge. Sloppy paperwork meant the exact number could not be determined, but the OIPRD found one prisoner was held for thirty-five hours and another for more than one hundred hours. Neither was facing criminal charges.[7] Many of those who ended up at the processing centre were scooped up at Queen's Park, part of which had been designated a "free speech" area. Instead, when protesters ended their march and began returning to Queen's Park around 5 p.m. on Saturday, they were inadvertently walking into a cauldron of anger because of mounting frustration from police, from Blair on down, over the events of the day. There was essentially an order for police to "take back the streets."

Fenton, one of the senior Toronto police officers responsible for overseeing on-the-ground crowd management, told OIPRD investigators that Blair was "angry and frustrated" at a meeting of the brass, and when Fenton asked why police were not arresting the "terrorists," Blair turned to him and said, "That is a very good question, Mark."[8] Fenton then ordered mass arrests. At 5:46 p.m. the

Long Range Acoustic Device was deployed at Queen's Park to warn of impending arrests, once in English and once in French.[9] There was no discernible reaction from the crowd, which police estimated at one to two thousand by 7 p.m.

One protester, during testimony to the OIPRD, described the scene this way: "Police started to push people sitting and standing on the grass close to College Street. We turned to attempt escape but we were both jumped on by police. Before they even had us on the ground they were yelling, 'Stop resisting arrest, stop resisting arrest.' We were dragged over to the pavement on the west side of the road. They started beating my sides and buttocks."[10] The OIPRD could not substantiate a large number of complaints of police mistreatment because the officers were not wearing name badges.

Later that year, Blair dealt with the question in an appearance before the parliamentary Standing Committee on Public Safety and National Security. "I have a rule at the Toronto Police Service. It's my rule and it's in accordance with the policy of the Toronto Police Services Board, that our officers will wear their names displayed on their uniforms. It is a rule that they wear it. If an individual officer chose not to wear it, he's breaking a rule. What I have stated is, if they have made a choice to engage in misconduct by disobeying a rule of the service, they will be held accountable and disciplined."

An estimated one hundred Toronto police officers had removed their name badges, a clear violation of board policy and the chief's direct order. It made a mockery of Blair's commitment that all board policies would be enforced. What punishment did they receive? They got a day off—voluntary leave. They went to their commanders and admitted to a breach of policy and got one unpaid day off. Blair felt his punishment of one day was proportionate, even significant. Under the law, the board could not direct him on the punishment, only express our disagreement. We could not tell him to do anything differently. His message to the uniformed officer was clear—the chief has your back. We have seen this time and time again. It is part of police culture.

At the board table, we had a heated discussion about this. I felt strongly that the board had to take action. When these third- and fourth-class officers came before the board for reclassification, I withheld their reclassification, essentially their promotion and the pay hike that goes with it, for six months. Of course, because of this, arbitration was brought by the police association. I refused to budge. Ultimately, they lost three months, not six. The officers had to accept the board was right in withholding their promotion on the basis that their failure to follow a board policy had eroded public confidence and demonstrated that they were not yet ready to be promoted. Reclassification is usually a routine matter. My refusal to accept that convention in the face of misconduct likely set a precedent. Nearly one hundred officers were affected. I had to individually address each officer's file and give a specific reason why he or she was not ready to be reclassified.

YES, IN THE run-up to the G20, the members of the board put a lot of faith in the Toronto Police Service. When your chief is telling you in unambiguous language that all your policies will be followed, you tend to believe him. When all of the questioning began after the summit about what went wrong, Blair finally said, "I was not even in charge that day and the chair saw me sitting by myself." He then explained the integrated command structure and his limited role in it. One day while he was under attack—the *Toronto Star* had called for his resignation—he confessed to me and fellow board member Hamlin Grange that he wasn't even a member of the command structure. In fact, it was Warr who was on the planning committee. Grange almost fell off his chair as he said to me, "Why the hell didn't he tell us this before?"

Blair's personal standing in the eyes of the public took a big hit, and it took a long time to even partially repair the damage. A large number of police officers paid a price for their actions that weekend. A few careers were affected as a result, such as that of Mark Fenton of kettling fame. Fenton was convicted by a police disciplinary tribunal in 2015 of three counts of unnecessary and unlawful use of authority. He was reprimanded and docked thirty days' vacation. He appealed, and those who were kettled cross-appealed, saying his penalty was too lenient. The Ontario Civilian Police Commission heard the appeals in April 2017 and in November of that year, the commission upheld his conviction but dismissed a cross-appeal seeking his dismissal from the police service.

The commission, in fact, upped his penalty, docking Fenton sixty days' vacation.

The police board spent more than $1 million on Morden's review. It lost credibility and received severe criticism, as did I. What the policing of the G20 did to ordinary people who were exercising their democratic right to publicly express disagreement with their government has left a permanent emotional scar on me. Seven years later, the final bill is not yet in: two class-action suits representing several hundred victims, filed soon after the questions began, have been given court clearance to proceed. The police services board went all the way to the Supreme Court of Canada to try to block the suits. It lost and was assessed costs. To me, the board's appeal was inexplicable: it had itself initiated the Morden review of governance at considerable cost and accepted all of Morden's recommendations.

There has been no shortage of investigations; Morden's is only one of them. The Toronto Police Service and the RCMP conducted their own operational after-action reviews. The OIPRD conducted a comprehensive systemic review. The RCMP's Public Complaints Commission undertook a review of the RCMP's role. The Canadian Parliament's all-party Standing Committee on Public Safety and National Security did its study. The Canadian Civil Liberties Association, together with the National Union of Public and General Employees, carried out a citizens' inquiry into policing and governance related to the G20 summit.

A large number of police officers faced disciplinary hearings. And yet the board spent public money attempting to stop the class action when it was obvious that its policies had not been followed and there had been excessive use of force, unlawful detentions and extensive breaches of people's Charter and human rights. But the board is not the only entity whose actions make me wonder whether any lessons have been learned. What about the federal and provincial governments?

To be sure, the provincial government took advice from former Ontario Chief Justice Roy McMurtry and dismantled the antiquated *Public Works Protection Act* and developed regulations for the use of the infamous Long Range Acoustic Device. The minister of community safety at the time, Rick Bartolucci, became the scapegoat for the reviled order-in-council under the PWPA giving cops special powers—the regulatory change requested by Blair and misused by security personnel. Bartolucci lost his cabinet post and soon left politics. But all of this was political damage control. Beyond it, the provincial government made no effort to reflect on its degree of responsibility for major events taking place in local communities, or whether its laws and directions related to policing and national security need examining.

If the province was derelict in its response, the feds were worse. Harper took no responsibility for his last-minute decision to inflict his project on the heart of the city. And no one examined the legislation under which Harper had acted, in order to ascertain if there were any flaws or weaknesses that should be fixed to prevent a repeat. The *Foreign Missions and International Organizations Act* is the piece of federal legislation under which major international events hosted by Canada are administered. Once the prime minister has designated an event under this act, the primary responsibility for security arrangements falls to the RCMP. The act allows Ottawa to enter into arrangements with its provincial counterpart for assistance from provincial and municipal police forces. The act gives the RCMP extensive powers because it has the "primary responsibility" for ensuring security.

What transpired during the G20 ought to have served as a red flag. Nowhere in the act is any recognition of the governance of local or municipal policing. The arrangements are between the federal and provincial governments; yet neither order of government has day-to-day jurisdiction over the local police forces. That belongs to the police boards or commissions. But the act does not even mention their existence. How does the RCMP's "primary responsibility" for security arrangements align with the local focus on community-based policing, especially in a situation where the sole objective is the security of the event and safety of so-called internationally protected persons, and given concerns about terrorism and national security?

The foundation of community-based policing is engagement with the community in a transparent manner, with a shared object-ive of well-being and safety. Policing driven by national security and anti-terrorism operations, by contrast, treats the community—or segments of it—as "the other" and as a legitimate target of surveil-lance and intelligence gathering. The two objectives cannot be pursued simultaneously.

Let us be very clear: concerns about terrorism and national sec-urity may well be justified. In Ontario, the provincial government circulated a Provincial Counter-Terrorism Plan in May 2014. And on October 22, 2014, following the shooting on Parliament Hill, when Michael Zehaf-Bibeau fatally shot Corporal Nathan Cirillo at the National War Memorial before being shot dead in the Centre Block, the province's Ministry of Community Safety and Correctional Services issued a memorandum to police board chairs, police chiefs and the commissioner of the OPP, reminding them about this plan. The plan states that, while the RCMP has primary responsibil-ity for responding to domestic acts of terrorism, it is obvious that the first response to such an act will often come from municipal or provincial police.

It seems to me from this message that the same provincial gov-ernment that promotes community-based policing through its *Police Services Act* is also directing local police to engage in activities that run counter to this very model. Could it be that officers on duty during the G20 weekend were given a message and training that pumped them up on the basis that they were there to prevent acts of terrorism and threats to national security? Those of us who were around were certainly struck by the heavily militarized way in which the police officers were clothed and equipped. How did this preparation reinforce the message about the event and condition these men and women psychologically?

Securitization and militarization are manifested not only with uniforms and equipment, but also in terms of surveillance, information gathering, policing tactics, and relationships with communities marked by race, ethnicity, religion, political views and economic status. In his conversation with me and Grange, Blair said, "We were like rent-a-cops." In other words, we, the people of Toronto, had surrendered the control and direction of our police service for those days to another entity, the RCMP, whose "primary responsibilities" when it comes to national security do not align with those of the local police paid for by the local community and governed by its representatives. And yet at the federal level no one asked questions afterward—not even the opposition members of Parliament. So, we are no further ahead than we were before the G20. There is no guarantee that the same policing behaviour will not be repeated in another part of the country that finds itself saddled with another major international event.

The implications of making local police forces responsible for national security and anti-terrorism duties are worrisome. How would the resulting securitization and militarization affect methods of local policing, especially in responding to civil dissent in a less just, less fair and less equal socio-political environment? How would it be ensured that the government's willingness to extend greater surveillance powers to police forces—especially as they relate to areas like cellphone surveillance—would not result in a greater intrusion into ordinary people's lives? How do police agencies maintain public trust and confidence in community-based policing while also being involved in national security and anti-terrorism activities? Seven years after that tumultuous weekend, these questions remain unanswered.

The Boy on the Streetcar

THE CORNER OF Dundas Street West and Bellwoods Avenue is defiant in its working-class status. The pavement is cracked. Wrought-iron railings stand guard in front of narrow but sturdy brick homes. Graffiti covers the walls of the buildings. The corner shakes as the overcrowded 505 streetcar trundles along its track. Here you can buy lottery tickets and international phone cards at Pacho's Convenience or drop in at Victoria's Wellness Spa and Rehabilitation Centre, which promises the "synergy of mind, body and soul." What you can't find is any sign of that July night in 2013 when a young man named Sammy Yatim lay dying on the platform near the open front doors of the 505.

Yet a year before the police killing of Michael Brown in Ferguson, Missouri, roiled the continent and three years before the bleak American summer of police killings of Blacks, that night might have been the Canadian tipping point, when relentless demand for change in police culture and behaviour could no longer be ignored. There was the crack of nine shots—nine hollow-point bullets from a Glock that echoed through a neighbourhood and shook the city from its midsummer torpor.

While no sign of Yatim's death remains there, the video footage endures. And because of that video taken by a citizen, what transpired that night could not be hidden from the public. I remember sitting in stunned silence as I watched the scene on my computer screen. Like so many others in the city that night, I had been following live reports of the event. The video graphically showed us what had happened. Chief Blair came into my office at police headquarters the next morning. For a moment, we sat in silence. Then he asked, "Did you see it?"

"Yes, I did," I told him. We were both numb and were having trouble believing what we had seen. We talked, not as police board chair and police chief, but as human beings, as parents, as Torontonians who wanted our city to be a safe place, especially for our young people. We were among hundreds of thousands who had seen what looked like the deliberate killing of one human being by another—on a street we knew well, by someone who worked for us. I told Blair the killing looked cold-blooded.

THE BRIEF FOOTAGE on YouTube is both riveting and chilling. A streetcar stands still on a dark summer evening. The vehicle looks empty, with its lights on and doors open. It stands in the middle of a Toronto street. One solitary individual, a young man, can be seen standing at the top of the front steps. Scores of people are milling about on the sidewalk; scores of police officers are keeping them at bay. Two officers stand on either side of the front doors. Voices can be heard, but it is not clear who is saying what.

Later we would learn that Constable James Forcillo, a Toronto cop for six years, encountering a clearly troubled eighteen-year-old immigrant from Syria brandishing a knife, barked commands that were dismissed: "Drop the knife. Drop the knife. Drop the fucking knife." Yatim replied, "You're a pussy, you're a fucking pussy." Several more commands to drop the knife came from Forcillo but were met with silence.[1] Forcillo's partner, twenty-four-year veteran Iris Fleckeisen, tried to verbally engage Yatim but got no response. Still, there was no apparent sign of crisis or urgency. There was no physical interaction between the person in the streetcar and the police officers. Two officers stood on either side of the streetcar door and all of the passengers had been evacuated. The door to the streetcar could be closed from the outside, the crisis contained. Fleckeisen had holstered her weapon, although she would later testify that was so she could call for a Taser, not because Yatim represented no danger.

Forcillo would testify that he chose not to try to talk Yatim down in order to defuse the situation. If Yatim would not comply with orders when a gun was trained on him, why would he respond if Forcillo offered him a glass of water, the officer reasoned.[2] As Yatim took a step backward on the 505 car, Forcillo issued what proved to be the final warning: "If you take one step closer I will shoot you, I'm telling you right now." Suddenly, a sound like something popping pierced the night. It was followed in rapid succession by a few more. The person inside the streetcar fell to the ground. There was a brief quiet period lasting six seconds, followed by more of the same popping sound. The whole scene lasted less than a minute. Within four days, half a million viewers had seen the video.

We know what happened that night. But it is vital that we come to grips with *why* it happened and what it says about police use of lethal force. At the time, we didn't know why Forcillo had killed Yatim. We didn't know what Yatim was doing in the hours prior to his death on the streetcar. However, with the video in circulation, we could anticipate a strong public reaction. We didn't have to wait long.

There had been strong public outcries before when people suffering from mental health crises had died at the hands of Toronto police. For the most part, outrage over previous highly publicized deaths such as those of Edmund Yu, Lester Donaldson, Otto Vass and Jeffrey Reodica had come from the media and from community-based anti-racism and mental health organizations. It had taken the form of mental-health care providers and mental-health consumers'/survivors' advocacy groups demanding to participate at inquests and making editorial comments and deputations to the police services board. This time, the public reaction was intense, immediate and broad based. Clearly, the video evidence available to the public had humanized the killing like none before. The death had been inscribed indelibly in the public mind, and as more details emerged from tireless media digging, outrage grew. People had had enough.

That outrage eclipsed other concerns about police action that night. Rules had been broken. No one was in charge. A sergeant, Dan Pravica, Tasered Yatim as he lay dying, an action that is likely unprecedented. It is alleged that spent bullets were kicked out of the way by officers, which would have hampered any investigation. No member of the police service is allowed to touch or disturb the scene of a shooting; they are to wait for the arrival of officers from the Special Investigations Unit—better known as the SIU. In this case, given that a man had been shot and presumably killed there, every police officer should have known there would be an SIU investigation. They knew the rules: you don't disturb the scene.

There were many officers present as the scene unfolded. The video shows four officers standing in a line facing the streetcar. Forcillo was one of them. Two officers stood on either side of the door. There were officers keeping the crowd at bay, as well as managing the crowd on bicycles. Things appeared calm. It is standard police practice that, in the absence of a sergeant, the most senior officer is to take charge at the scene. It appeared to me from the video that no one was in charge and that Forcillo had acted alone. There was no sign of a co-ordinated strategy, no tactical plan, no leadership. A sergeant arrived after the shooting had already taken place.

This had been an issue in the February 2012 killing of Michael Eligon, a disturbed young man armed with scissors. There had been a phalanx of at least eight officers facing Eligon, who was taunting them, before an officer shot him dead. Supposedly they had been backing off, but two or three officers were backed up against a truck and could move no farther. Constable Louie Cerqua said he feared for his life when he shot Eligon three times, killing him. But again the question was who was in charge? If no one is in charge, ultimately no one is held accountable.

In the Yatim case, the streetcar was empty (although Forcillo testified he didn't know if there were people hiding on board). Everyone had left, even the driver. Yatim was alone. There was no sign that he was making any move to jump off the streetcar to attack anyone. There was a considerable distance between him and the officers. Being that there were two officers on either side of the door, why couldn't they have closed the door and contained him, and then brought in a negotiator, a psychologist? The streetcar doors could have been closed from the outside using a button on the side meant for that purpose.

There is an old folklore in police circles. It's known as the twenty-one-foot (6.4 metres) rule. More myth than science, it was first promoted by a Utah police firearms instructor in 1983. He postulated that anyone advancing with a knife or other edged weapon on an officer was a lethal threat starting at twenty-one feet, because at that distance, an officer with a holstered weapon would not have time to draw and accurately shoot his or her assailant. It had become a police rule of thumb across the continent—and was not removed from any policing curriculum until early 2016.[3] If Forcillo's actions were prompted by this now-discredited "rule," he had ignored one basic element: his weapon was already drawn, not holstered. The world over, there are policies that firearms are not to be drawn on someone armed with scissors, a knife or a machete. But here, alternative responses were ignored.

Public protests of the Sammy Yatim killing culminated on August 13 with a rally outside police headquarters in which hundreds of people participated. Yatim's family spoke passionately at the rally. It was the day the police board was holding its monthly meeting—our first public meeting since the killing. We invited the family to the meeting, and on behalf of the board I stated that we "share the pain of the Yatim family" and wanted to "express our condolences over the tragic death of a young person." To my knowledge, this was the first time the police board had publicly commented on an event of this kind. Chief Blair took the family into his office for a private meeting. Although he declined to state in public what was said at this meeting, he made sure the media knew the meeting had happened.

For its part, the board understood that it could not remain a silent bystander—it could not claim it had no role in operational matters or that it could not comment while various investigations were taking place. Almost immediately after we learned about Yatim's death, the board began to give directions to the police chief and to make its expectations clear. My personal reaction, immediately after the killing, was visceral. As an immigrant myself, I kept wondering about his parents, who had brought their children here from a violent and hopeless environment so they would be safe and would have a future. I could not get these thoughts out of my head, and I did something that police services board chairs and public officials in high positions tend not to do.

Late at night a few days after the shooting, unable to sleep, I sat down at my computer and wrote an article expressing my personal feelings and emotions. They were so overwhelming that words flowed out as if of their own accord. At around 2 a.m. I sent it to John Stackhouse, *The Globe and Mail*'s editor at the time. Within the hour, Stackhouse told me he would publish my thoughts. The op-ed piece, "Police board chair asks for answers in Sammy Yatim shooting," was published on August 3, a week after the shooting. In it, I imagined the hopes and fears of the Yatim family in the context of my own life as an immigrant who had worked for many years to ensure a better future for children like Sammy Yatim and our son. I wrote:

My wife and I came to Canada from India in 1971. We were in our twenties then. India was a very different country at that time, independent for not quite twenty-five years, trying to make its way in the world. We were allowed to bring with us $7 (US) each.

We grew fond of this place and decided to sink our roots here. It was a peaceful place, and despite the fact that it didn't really know how to facilitate the integration of people such as us, we liked it. Some old-timers took us into their homes and made us feel welcome. Now it is our home.

Our son was born here. In 1978 came my first publication, *East Indians, Myths and Reality* (yes, we were called East Indians then, not South Asians). The dedication on the book's first page says the work was for our son "and all other beautiful children with the hope that they will be permitted to grow without discrimination or persecution but with freedom and dignity."

I imagine that Sammy Yatim's family came here four years ago to pursue a similar objective for themselves and their children. The fate that befell the eighteen-year-old—who died after being shot by police on a Toronto streetcar—is not one that they could have expected or imagined. It is one that none of us can accept, whether we came here four or forty years ago or our family has been here for generations.

By publishing the article, I ran the risk that some would accuse me of prejudging before the facts were known, and question my role as board chair in the formal processes that were to come. There was further concern that my actions might create a legal liability for the organization through a suggestion of wrongdoing by one of our employees. But I felt strongly that publishing my thoughts was the right thing to do. So, in the op-ed piece, I went on to say:

Ever since that tragic night when the Yatims lost their son, I have been trying to put myself in their situation. Every time, that leads me to one question: How could this happen?

It leads me to this question because of all the effort that I and many other people of goodwill have made to realize a different vision of policing than we had been accustomed to. I can say in all honesty that it has been a significant effort, intended to bring about comprehensive change in the culture and practice of policing. Those efforts, to a very large degree, have been in response to earlier incidents, such as the deaths of Edmund Yu and Jeffrey Reodica in police shootings.

Tragedy such as the one that has befallen the Yatims causes profound soul-searching. I very much hope there will be a collective soul-searching on the part of all of us involved with policing, in whatever capacity.

I know there will be no letup on my part until we have an answer to the question, How could this happen? I have heard and read the pat, instant solutions that have been offered so far, and I find them wanting or off-base.

We had better get down to the task quickly and in all seriousness. We owe it to the memory of Sammy Yatim.

As police services board members and police chief, we had certain clear obligations in terms of the investigations required by law, questions of accountability and liability, the impact on the work we were doing with our community partners on how police officers dealt with people in mental health crisis, and responding to the public's need for information and explanation. For the management of all these obligations, there was no rule book or guidance. And no one could predict or anticipate repercussions.

As more information became available, it turned out that Forcillo had fired the additional shots because Yatim, already wounded and lying on the floor of the streetcar, still had a knife in his hand and was still alive. If the officers feared for their safety, certainly the firing of the extra shots should have alleviated their fear. But that wasn't all. Pravica, who had subsequently joined the group of constables, had discharged his Taser at Yatim—after he had taken eight of the nine bullets fired by Forcillo. Pravica would testify he was initially unaware Yatim had been shot.[4] Almost four years after Yatim's death, acting on a complaint from Yatim's father, Nabil, the Office of the Independent Police Review Director instructed the Toronto police to charge Pravica with misconduct under the *Police Services Act*, saying he used unnecessary force and acted in haste by climbing on the streetcar

and Tasering Yatim thirty-three seconds after the youth was shot. That
is an internal Toronto police charge, not a criminal charge.

Then there was the troubling scattering of the gun shells. Video
from the CCTV cameras inside the streetcar, which is posted on
YouTube, shows much of this activity on the part of the police officers at the scene. But the SIU designated only one officer, Forcillo,
as the subject of its investigation and excluded all others. Based on
this narrow investigation, the SIU held only Forcillo responsible for
Yatim's death and charged him.

In the course of the day-after conversations in my office, I expressed my concern that this shooting would deepen the public's
negative view of how police deal with mental health crises, coming as
it did while the joint inquest into the highly publicized deaths of three
individuals—Reyal Jardine-Douglas, Sylvia Klibingaitis and Eligon—
better known as the J-K-E inquest, was ongoing. Coincidentally,
edged weapons (that is, knives and scissors) were involved in those
three deaths as well. I was also afraid the shooting might destroy
the mental health subcommittee that the board had established
to engage mental health consumers, survivors, service providers,
advocates and the police service to improve and strengthen the way
in which our officers handle people in mental health crisis. Our goal
had been to restore the community's confidence in us and enable
our officers to resolve these crises peacefully.

Step one in the service's damage control, then, was to insist that
mental health had not played any role in the shooting of Yatim. In
response to my loud questioning of their insistence, senior officials
assured me there were no police records of prior contact with Yatim
related to mental health issues. Further, they claimed the police
officers responding to the incident on the streetcar could not have
known that they would be dealing with someone who was having
a mental health crisis. They encountered a young man travelling
on the streetcar who had been walking around inside the vehicle
exposing himself and at some point began brandishing a knife he
had taken out of his pocket.

I do not expect officers to be clinical psychologists, but they can be expected to take stock of a situation. I was completely taken aback by the claim that officers could not have known that this was a mental health–related situation. Surely they could tell that Yatim's behaviour was very much that of an emotionally disturbed person. I argued that common sense would have told them that. At that point, this line of explanation stopped.

The next step in damage control was a decision that the police chief would initiate an external, arm's-length review of the shooting. The chief could not initiate a review while the SIU investigation was going on. But as the idea developed, it was decided that this external review would be carried out within the chief's legal responsibility to undertake an administrative review of policies, procedures, training, equipment and officer conduct whenever there was an SIU investigation. The use of external expertise was not something new. There have been occasions when a chief considered it prudent and in the public interest to seek outside help. In most cases, though, such help was obtained from another police agency or the judiciary.

The most celebrated example of this, to my mind, came when the police chief at the time, Julian Fantino, asked the RCMP to conduct a massive investigation into allegations of corruption among members of one of his drug squads, the Central Field Command Drug Squad, which operated in downtown Toronto. On other occasions, former judges have been brought in to preside over disciplinary hearings concerning officers charged with misconduct. Chief Blair had, for instance, appointed judges to hear disciplinary charges against officers accused of misconduct during the policing of the G20 summit.

But to my knowledge, this would be the first time a chief's administrative review of a matter being investigated by the SIU would be handed over to an external party. This was a clear indication of the impact of the public outcry that had arisen from the killing of Yatim. Being a good tactician, Blair had found a way to respond to this outcry that had some big advantages for him—it was *his* review, overseen by his delegate, conducted away from the public gaze. It would not be a wide-open public inquiry. At the same time, it would be independent, removed from him. And for that reason, it would take its own time, for which he could not be blamed, while avoiding constant public questioning. As well, if conducted by a person of high reputation and credibility, it would reflect well on Blair's willingness to fix things.

Blair announced his choice to oversee the review within days—but it immediately misfired. Within hours of the planned announcement, concerns were raised that his choice, retired Ontario Judge Dennis O'Connor, was closely associated with Borden Ladner Gervais, a legal firm on retainer to defend all legal actions against the police. Blair didn't see the conflict, but O'Connor did.[5] Even though he had essentially only loaned his name to the firm, he knew his independence would be questioned, and he called Blair to tell him he would have to step aside.

· Before his plan suffered any damage, Blair identified a replacement in former Supreme Court Justice Frank Iacobucci, an appointment that was widely applauded. But because Blair was intent on moving quickly, the terms of reference for the review were not clear. Although officer conduct can be included within the scope of a chief's administrative review, Blair asked Iacobucci to look at policy, procedures, equipment and training in situations related to police interactions with people experiencing a mental health crisis. The question of the conduct of the officers at the Yatim scene was kept within the control of the police service, including the discharge of the Taser by Sergeant Pravica on someone who was already on the ground with several bullets in his body, the allegation about the scattering of the spent bullets, and the absence of a co-ordinated response with a leader.

Blair was now a staunch defender of the actions, or lack thereof, of his officers. He said that Pravica had done exactly the right thing in Tasering Yatim, who was still alive and holding the knife. According to Blair, Pravica had followed correct procedure and training. And so, when the results of the investigation by the police service's internal professional standards unit came to the board as a confidential report, everyone was found to have acted in compliance with procedures and training—and cleared. With the questions about officer conduct neatly and confidentially dispensed with, Iacobucci's report and Forcillo's trial became the subjects of discussion. No one else was held accountable, and little had changed in the police service in terms of the use of force. Wagons were circled and crisis management became the driving goal.

This is part of the police culture I spent ten years battling. Both the police association and senior leadership constantly send out a message to officers: "We've got your back." This deeply entrenched culture proved to be the biggest enemy I would face over my decade as chair of the Toronto Police Services Board. There is a very elaborate, expensive and busy machinery to deal with the conduct of individual police officers and supposedly hold them accountable for their actions. Yet when I think about the meagre results this machinery produced, I find myself asking whether its real purpose is symbolic rather than substantive.

The Yatim incident, at least, was video-recorded. The chief had officers' backs again in the matter of turning off their in-car cameras. This issue stemmed from the April 12, 2010, police takedown of a Toronto cook named Raymond Costain in front of the venerable King Edward Hotel. A judge subsequently found that Constable Christian Dobbs used excessive force in arresting Costain, calling it an "unlawful extrajudicial punishment that will shock the public."[6] Dobbs rained down twelve blows on a prone Costain and was subsequently charged with assault, but he was ultimately acquitted in 2016. More importantly, provincial court Justice Ford Clements found that two of Dobbs's fellow officers turned off their in-car cameras in a bid to cover up the beating. One of the officers initially said he turned off the camera to conserve energy.

In response, Blair ordered a random audit of officers' use of in-car cameras. Again, it was board policy to have these cameras installed and for them to be activated whenever the officers were engaged in a call. The camera would record actions both outside and inside the car. The audit found that 30 percent of officers were not turning on their cameras all the time. Blair asked his road sergeants to randomly check how many cameras were turned on, but then he learned from a report from his Audit and Quality Assurance Unit that the sergeants themselves were not turning on their cameras. So he had another audit done, and he found 30 to 35 percent of the road sergeants did not have their cameras on. He did not report this to the board. But he had not been a supporter of the board's order to install the cameras in the first place, and had only installed them because of the board's insistence.

The police association was not happy with the board directive to install the cameras, and the force had taken its sweet time—three to four years—to equip all cars with cameras. I only found out about the audit of camera usage by sergeants during a conversation with Blair and police association president Mike McCormack. Blair came up with a range of punishments and again he decided to be kind. According to him, people sometimes forget to turn on the camera, or there could be technical reasons for it not being on. If it appeared deliberate, they would get counselling from their supervisor. In other cases, they would be given a unit-level discipline, which didn't go into their records. The discipline was in the range of one to three days depending on the severity. In most cases, it was one day.

This is a serious business: you are turning off a camera so that there will be no evidence of what you are doing. In some cases, cameras are turned off because officers have had enough of troublesome suspects and they have decided to physically teach them a lesson. Knowing they will get nothing more than a slap on the wrist—as opposed to a more serious penalty if an assault was filmed—creates an incentive to turn off the camera. It all feeds into a police culture built on the use of force.

There is another feature of this police culture that has largely gone unnoticed: the strategic decisions of senior brass that get front-line officers in trouble with the public and the law. When I drew attention to this in a public report to the board some years ago, I found no takers—in the police service, on the police services board or even in the media. When things go wrong and there is a crisis, whether related to mental health or treatment of racialized people or the G20 summit, there is a flurry of activity. Policies and procedures are examined, training is reviewed, officer conduct is investigated. And always, the focus is on the actions of the individual police officer, not on the systems or strategies that guide him or her or the leadership that developed and implemented them.

Yet it is the senior leadership that can decide it is going to bring down gun violence in the city and can direct officers to implement some very vigorous measures. To address this, it creates units like the rapid deployment force, known as the Rapid Response Team. It brings in the Toronto Anti-Violence Intervention Strategy (TAVIS), the Guns and Gangs unit, the drug squad and so on. It is the senior leadership that empowers these units to operate in an aggressive way, breaking down doors and cornering people. It thus legitimizes and gives permission for a culture in which officers are expected to act in a muscular way. But this role of senior police leadership is not discussed.

What message does the leadership give to the rank and file, first through these types of strategies, for which it is not held account-able, and then by the kid-glove treatment it gives those who engage in the excessive use of force? The senior leadership escapes largely unscathed from decisions made in the name of operations. They are also shielded by a vague provision in the *Police Services Act* that is used as a firewall against questioning of operational decisions.

Take the example of carding, which had been condemned by the community, in particular the Black community, for years. Media analyses had documented how widespread it was and how it had grown exponentially under Blair's watch as TAVIS was implemented. The police board finally made a serious effort to respond to public criticism by introducing a policy to bring carding under strict control, and to ensure that policing services in Toronto were delivered in a manner consistent with people's Charter rights and human rights, as the law requires. It proved extremely difficult to implement the policy even though it received widespread public support. Why? Because police leadership decided that some of its key provisions infringed upon operational matters that were solely its preserve. Blair refused to enforce the policy—and presumably he had the loyalty of the rank and file because he had their backs.

What are the implications of these features of police culture on the use of force, in particular lethal force? We have a system of policing built on giving officers a large variety of force options, including a gun. And the law gives them the authority to use this force, including lethal force, at their discretion—as long as they can provide a lawful justification. Killing someone when an officer fears for his or her personal safety is a lawful justification.

Forcillo testified at his trial that he shot Yatim because he feared for his safety. He was convicted, but not for the first set of bullets that he aimed at Yatim. The jury found Forcillo was justified in firing the first three shots at Yatim. He was convicted for firing the subsequent six. Had he stopped at three he would not have been convicted. Officer safety now appears to have taken precedence over public safety. Consider the officer uniform. Throughout Canada, police officers and even civilian employees of the police service, such as parking officers and court officers, routinely wear Kevlar vests as part of their uniforms. What message does this give to the public and more importantly, to these men and women themselves? The message is that they work in a dangerous environment in which their personal safety is constantly at risk.

Each officer death anywhere in North America becomes the occasion for a highly ritualized gathering of police personnel from across the continent and a huge public funeral. Each year, provincial and national memorials are held to remember "our fallen comrades." These are attended by politicians from all levels and are covered extensively in the media. They reinforce the message that policing is a dangerous profession and that those engaged in it are at risk each day they come to work. This too is part of police culture and even Justice Edward Then, who presided over the Forcillo trial, alluded to it in his sentencing of the constable. According to Then, the shooting of Yatim by Forcillo showed the officer's "fundamental failure to understand his duty to preserve all life and not just his own."[7]

The data do not support this perception of constant danger. In fact, today policing is relatively safe compared to many other occupations. Policing in Canada and elsewhere has evolved significantly from its early days—so much so that in Ontario, government policy requires municipalities to develop a community safety and well-being plan, of which policing is one component. Within this broader framework, policing is not confined to the protection of person and property in a narrow sense; it is no longer limited to catching the violent criminal. Approximately two-thirds of police officers' work deals with helping people in crisis, domestic violence, sexual assault, assisting the elderly, keeping streets safe, school safety, cybercrime and so on.

Responding to what constitutes violent crime in the conventional sense makes up less than 30 percent of police work. As Justice Iacobucci said in his report, police officers are social workers. It is conceivable that a large segment of a police force will not need to draw a gun—ever. And yet, by law, we train every police officer to shoot to kill. This constitutes the largest component of the training provided to new officers. In many forces in Canada, every year each police officer from constable to chief is required to re-certify in use of force. There is no comparable emphasis on other policing skills. To me, this model of policing is the direct consequence of a North American model being grafted onto the British model of modern policing credited to Sir Robert Peel.

In Peel's model of professional policing, officers were but members of the public, with the exception that they performed their duties on a full-time basis and were given additional authority. However, their success and effectiveness—and indeed, legitimacy—depended on receiving and maintaining public consent at all times. This was obtained by treating all members of the public equally and without giving undue favour to any one segment. These concepts are widely considered to lie at the heart of community-based policing. In this framework, a police organization can never behave or be regarded as an occupying force.

Overlaid on this framework is the North American model of policing, the history of which lies in the use of an armed group to protect the interests of the privileged. In North America, policing is inextricably tied to the settlement of America, the onward push of the frontier and the resulting conflict with the Indigenous population. The gun-toting American sheriff, chosen by the wealthy and powerful members of a community, symbolized law and order. The early duties of police included "slave-catching," noted New York police chief Bill Bratton in a rare moment of candour during a 2015 speech at a Black church. "Since then, the stories of police and Black citizens have intertwined again and again...The unequal nature of that relationship cannot and must not be denied," he said.[8]

North of the border, the founding in 1873 of the North-West Mounted Police, precursor of today's Royal Canadian Mounted Police, was very specifically intended to provide armed support to expansion and deal with the restive "native." When local policing developed, it was a bit of a hodgepodge. We imported the constable from England in the nineteenth century, originally to have somebody in the community to protect and safeguard property. And we armed this person. In Toronto, for example, it was a group of five wealthy citizens—including the mayor and the magistrate—who created the first system of policing. In 1834, a full-time High Constable was appointed for the city of Toronto. According to Michael Sale's history of the Toronto Police Services Board, one year later, a full force was formed consisting of a High Constable, five constables and fourteen special constables.

This original police contingent was formed for the protection of property and the lives of the privileged. Its mandate has expanded since then, but the basic model of relying on authority, attained through the legal right to carry and use arms, has not changed. Policing remains heavily armed, dependent on the use of force, ill-equipped to deal with non-criminal social or personal situations without resorting to use-of-force options, and trained to use threats over empathy, negotiation and communication. This armed response to crises is more of a North American policing phenomenon, not one that is embraced worldwide. This is a model at odds with itself. On the one hand, it pays lip service to community-based policing. On the other, it trains police officers to be something akin to an occupation force. This contradictory model gets the individual officer into trouble. The consequence is that police do not receive the public legitimacy or consent they require.

What is needed is a serious examination of the model of using a uniformed police officer equipped with an arsenal of force options to deal with the policing needs of a community. We also need to question why every police officer is equipped with lethal force. What is needed is a consideration of the consequences of taking a militaristic approach to community safety, one that is based on maintaining and promoting the perception that every police officer is at mortal risk each of his or her days on the job.

As for Forcillo, in September 2017 he began an appeal of his six-year jail sentence. He has also filed an unprecedented second part of his appeal based on new evidence. This will be heard in 2018. In the meantime, he had spent but one night in jail—until November 2017, when he was found at his fiancee's apartment, an alleged breach of his bail. That was the end of his luck. He was remanded in custody.

Regardless of the outcome of Forcillo's appeal, if there is to be reform, it must go beyond the punishment of one officer. It must be a catalyst to reshape the culture of police and our definition of their role. Yatim is dead. Forcillo *will* be punished. But if there is to be reform, we must remember those who were killed before Sammy Yatim.

Cull of "the Other"

IT'S A MACABRE roll call stretching back more than three decades.

- Albert Johnson, a thirty-five-year-old Jamaican immigrant with mental health issues, shot and killed in his home by Toronto police in August 1979.
- Lester Donaldson, forty-five, who suffered from paranoid schizophrenia, produced a knife in a standoff with police, shot and killed in August 1988.
- Albert Moses, forty-one, with a history of mental illness, shot and killed by police in his rooming house in September 1994 after attacking an officer with a hammer.
- Tommy Barnett, twenty-two, shot and killed by police in January 1996 after threatening an officer with a sword. His family said he had a history of mental illness.
- Wayne Williams, a twenty-four-year-old with schizophrenia, shot and killed by Toronto police in June 1996 after he advanced, with two knives in his hands, on five officers who were confronting him.
- Edmund Yu, thirty-five, shot and killed by police in February 1997 as he waved a small hammer on an empty bus.

- Jeffrey Reodica, seventeen, allegedly brandishing a knife, shot three times in the back and killed by police responding to a report of a fight involving teenagers in May 2004.
- O'Brien Christopher-Reid, twenty-six, who had paranoid schizophrenia and was brandishing a knife in Edwards Gardens in June 2004, shot and killed by Toronto police.
- Byron Debassige, twenty-eight, shot and killed by Toronto police in February 2008, described by the 911 dispatcher as armed and dangerous when he took two lemons from a store and pulled a three-inch knife as he was chased by the store owner.
- Reyal Jardine-Douglas, twenty-five, shot and killed by a Toronto police officer on a streetcar after he charged at the officer with a knife in August 2010.
- Michael Eligon, twenty-nine, wearing a hospital gown and carrying two pairs of scissors, shot and killed by police in February 2012.
- Andrew Loku, forty-five, holding a hammer in the hallway of his apartment building, which housed people with mental health problems, shot and killed by Toronto police in July 2015.
- And, of course, Yatim in July 2013.

Each tragedy had the following in common:

- All were male.
- None of them was carrying a gun.
- All had mental health problems.
- None of them was white.
- No officer ever tried to de-escalate the confrontation.

And until James Forcillo, no police officer had been criminally convicted for any of these deaths.

This is the state-sanctioned culling of the inferior "other," particularly the other of colour. It is the often-deadly intersection of police who are ill-equipped to deal with those who have a mental illness re-acting to a perceived threat from someone who looks different. There have been more than forty fatal police shootings of people with mental illness in Ontario since 2000.[1] Coroners' inquests have returned more than 550 recommendations for improvement and change since 1989.[2] An Ontario government review of recommendations across the province between 1989 and 2011 counted 109 different calls for better police training, including better de-escalation techniques.[3]

In the summer of 2017, back-to-back inquests—dealing with the death of Loku and the Durham police incident involving Michael MacIsaac, forty-seven, shot while running naked through his Ajax, Ontario, neighbourhood on a frigid December morning in 2013—called once again for better de-escalation training for police. "I'm sure there have been lots of good recommendations from the inquests that have been had," MacIsaac's mother, Yvonne MacIsaac, told the *Toronto Star*. "My son would be alive if even a few of them had been followed."[4]

After the shooting of Yatim, retired Supreme Court Justice Frank Iacobucci looked into the question of police response to people in mental health crisis.[5] But his review did not include the broader issues related to the use of force by police, or policing and racial bias, especially anti-Black racism. The report was comprehensive, but it did not deal with the question of why so many of those with mental health problems killed by police were racialized people, particularly Black people. The question of what goes through a police officer's mind—what thoughts, ideas, stereotypes and prejudices an officer may have—when he or she is dealing with someone who is acting up and who is non-white was left unexamined. Justice Iacobucci stayed away from the question, although he was asked about it at the press conference where he released his report. His answer? "It was not in my terms of reference."

He did, however, acknowledge that it was an important question. The question of implicit, or unconscious, bias was raised at the Loku inquest. Nicholas Rule, an associate professor of psychology at the University of Toronto, told the inquest about a study he had done with two American academics that showed when photos of the faces of white and Black men with identical heights and weights were shown to subjects, the Black men were perceived to be taller, heavier, more muscular and more physically threatening than white men. People's stereotypes literally distort their vision, his study found. That perception held regardless of the race of the person who was asked to evaluate a set of photographs. "Black men tend to be stereotyped as threatening and, as a result, may be disproportionately targeted by police even when unarmed," he said.[6]

The study did not introduce the question of a person possessing a weapon, nor did it study police officers, but the inaccurate perception of the size of a Black assailant has been cited in a number of US police shootings. Tamir Rice, who was shot and killed on a Cleveland playground in 2014, was described by a police union spokesperson as menacing. "He's five-feet-seven, 191 pounds. He wasn't that little kid you're seeing in pictures. He's a twelve-year-old in an adult body," Steve Loomis, president of Cleveland's police union, told *Politico* magazine in 2015.[7] It bears repeating: Tamir Rice was *twelve*. Police shot him two seconds after their patrol car pulled up to the recreation centre playground after they had received a report about someone with a gun. The caller had told dispatch it was "probably fake." The officers were not charged.

There are two sets of complicating factors leading to these deaths. First, we have police dealing with people in mental health crisis; these officers may lack knowledge about how to handle these situations, and they may harbour stereotypes and prejudices about such people. And second, we have people who are Black, brown or Indigenous. What assumptions and ideas affect how officers respond to these people? Beyond these factors, there is the big question of why a medical or health issue has become a police issue.

Despite the deficiencies noted earlier, Iacobucci's report is one of the few comprehensive, systematic explorations of police engagement with people in mental health crisis. One of its strengths is Iacobucci's view on police culture and the kind of people police should be recruiting. He talks about attracting people with a high level of education and a compassionate bent. Most of all, however, I subscribe to his philosophy of doing no harm when dealing with people in crisis. As he says, even one death is too many. The report calls for a different way of thinking about and approaching these situations.

As Ontario ombudsman Paul Dubé concluded in his June 2016 report, *A Matter of Life and Death*, police officers receive a disproportionately large amount of training in the use of their firearms and very little training in the use of negotiation, reasoning, empathy and de-escalation. (Toronto police officers now receive bias-free training, but the course is only a day long. The Loku inquest recommended officers receive annual anti-racism training focusing on the equitable treatment of Blacks, but this has not yet been implemented.) They know how to use their guns, Dubé said. They must learn to use their mouths. Once their firearm is drawn, too often it becomes the only way to resolve the situation. This fact exacerbates an aspect of police culture that these days plays a prominent role in police interactions with the public–officer safety.

Today, it appears every encounter is seen through the prism of officer safety, not community safety. This is reinforced by the proclivity of investigators, be they from the SIU or the police service, to accept uncritically an officer's actions in the name of personal safety. Why did Forcillo shoot? According to his testimony, he was fearful for his own safety. He did not talk about danger to the public or the community, but about his own safety. What is the threshold of officer safety? I am not aware of any objective standard or measure to determine the validity of an officer's claim of imminent threat. It is subjective, residing in the officer's mind. In fact, I would argue that the threshold of officer safety has consistently been lowered over the years. When I look at incidents that involve police use of violence, I ask myself, "What was the risk to the officer?"

The shooting of Michael Eligon in 2012 is a case in point. One man holding two pairs of scissors; a sick man, faced by a bevy of officers. He was at a distance, but as officers backed away from him, one inadvertently backed into a parked pickup truck. Then Constable Louie Cerqua shot and killed Eligon. Two of the three rounds missed Eligon, endangering bystanders. Writing in *The Walrus*, journalist John Lorinc quoted a bystander who witnessed the encounter. Doug Pritchard, who was out for a jog, watched the scene. "It's a cold winter day," he would later recall. "The guy is standing there in a hospital gown, with bare legs. My first thought: this guy is in a mental health crisis."[8]

Eligon had spent two sleepless nights in the emergency room at Toronto East General. There were no beds available. He had been taken there by police after he became unable to take care of himself at a mental health facility. He stole two pairs of scissors from a convenience store after walking out of the hospital and gave the store owner a minor cut in a tussle (the owner did not even bother to attend to his cut until the end of the day, after Eligon was dead). None of the ten officers who confronted Eligon attempted to engage him verbally. There were conflicting strategies from the officers at the scene. At least one yelled at a colleague to fire, while another called on his fellow officers to back away from the troubled man. Again, who was in charge? And on what basis did the SIU and the police service investigators conclude that any of the officers had been in such mortal danger that killing Eligon was justified?

Look at the case of Otto Vass. He was a big man, and when officers scuffled with him, one put him in a chokehold and he died. An inquest jury determined Vass had died of a rare medical condition called "excited delirium."[9] Other experts believed he had died from a fat embolism released by blows delivered by the officers. Four officers were ultimately found not guilty of manslaughter. Did they use excessive force? Was anyone else at risk from Vass? When I questioned the circumstances of Vass's death, I was told by a senior officer working in the chief's office, "Chair, you don't understand how much demonic strength a person who is having a mental health crisis can gather." I will never forget his use of that term.

An SIU investigation absolved Andrew Doyle, the officer who shot Loku, on the basis that imminent threat to officer safety justified the use of lethal force. As with every SIU investigation, the scope was narrow and the troubling issues I've identified here were not examined. Nor did the investigation scrutinize the validity of the claim of imminent threat, which appears to be the pattern with SIU investigations. The police chief's mandatory internal administrative review did not consider it either, consistent with the pro forma nature of these reviews. "The threat that he presented to me was immediate grievous bodily harm or death," Doyle told the inquest. "I was afraid for my life."[10]

I am aware that it may seem like I am generalizing and discounting police danger. There are cases I can understand. Sylvia Klibingaitis, killed in 2011, was by every account on a rampage. She called police from her house and said she was going to kill her mother, whom she lived with. She told them, "Somebody come and stop me." When she lunged out the front door of her house, the police officers facing her had no room to move because they would have backed into a shrub. Constable Henry Tang was backpedalling as Klibingaitis charged at him with a butcher's knife, a chilling scene caught on the officer's dashboard camera. "I knew that she was trying to kill me," Tang told an inquest. "The ferocity of her attack and the speed that she was coming towards me, I knew I had no choice but to fire my firearm."[11]

However, I cannot understand the case of Byron Debassige, an Indigenous man killed in 2008. It is inconceivable to me that the two police officers involved could not have backed off. There was nothing behind them. They could have called for reinforcements. Again, they made the same argument: he came too close to us. He could have done us serious harm. I think about the icy condition of the path on which he approached them, and I think about a man who was very drunk. Maybe there was a misunderstanding: he was staggering and they thought he was being aggressive.

I discussed this with a retired police superintendent and he told me, "You don't let somebody get that close to you." He emphasized the importance of planning before entering a scene, having clear objectives, gathering information and taking one's time. He wondered why containment was not considered, with officers backing off and calling for reinforcements. "What was the hurry? Debassige was not going anywhere," he said. Instead, constables John Tanner and Bradley Coutts shot and killed Debassige, a twenty-eight-year-old schizophrenic man who also suffered from alcoholism and drug addiction, when he allegedly lunged at them in Oriole Park that February day.

Debassige had taken two lemons from a corner store. As he left, the owner gave chase while his daughter called 911 and reported a "robbery." To ward off the owner, Debassige brandished a pocket knife as he ran away. He was described as armed and dangerous by the call dispatcher. He was said to have charged at the officers from a distance of about six metres (19.5 feet). "I've never second-guessed anything I did that night," Tanner told an inquest.[12] Again, we are talking about officer safety above all else.

Even as I was tabulating this awful list and looking back on the circumstances, it happened again, this time in Ottawa. On the morning of July 24, 2016, police were called to deal with a man alleged to be groping a woman in a coffee shop just west of Parliament Hill. Abdirahman Abdi, a thirty-seven-year-old Somali-Canadian with mental health issues, tried to flee to his nearby apartment when he saw police. He didn't make it. Officers tackled him, pepper-sprayed him, beat him with a baton and punched him in the head, killing him. The events were witnessed and caught on smartphone camera amid screams for police to let him go. Abdi was armed with a piece of foam. In this case, the SIU charged Ottawa police constable Daniel Montsion with manslaughter, aggravated assault and assault with a weapon. The weapon, in this case, was allegedly reinforced gloves—that is, gloves with brass knuckles, worn by Montsion. In an example of how tone-deaf police culture can be, Ottawa officers began wearing black-and-blue wristbands in support of Montsion. The wristbands bore the words "United we stand" on the outside and "Divided we fall" on the inside, which also featured Montsion's badge number. Ottawa police chief Charles Bordeleau, citing the perception of the community and pushback from its leaders, refused to let officers wear the wristbands while on duty.

Mental health is a global societal issue. But why is it a policing issue? The fact is that people suffering from mental health problems are not criminals. They are not violent people in the criminal sense of the word; some can be violent at times as part of their illness. They can be paranoid and that can cause them to be violent. They may have anxiety or a chemical imbalance, sparking a violent response. But those are all medical conditions. In many cases when they are in a state of crisis, these people are not able to engage in normal communication. They may not comprehend what is being said; they are often not even able to hear what is being said. They are responding from a different space.

Police are not diagnosticians, nor should they be. They are not knowledgeable in mental health issues. They have the same biases and lack of understanding as ordinary people. They use words like *crazy* to refer to those with mental illnesses. They are trained to take charge, to take control. Their first words tend to be words of control—"Don't do that" or "Don't move" or "Drop the knife"—not words that might defuse a situation or establish a relationship based on communication. They have been trained to treat knives and other edged weapons as they would guns—as just as dangerous and just as lethal.

As Paul Dubé's research showed, between 1995 and 2000, Ontario police officers were assaulted 315 times with edged weapons compared to 51 times with firearms. But they are trained to deal with behaviour rather than the cause of the behaviour, so when a person's response is "No, I won't do that," or the person ignores the command, the confrontation escalates. The police officer may quickly elevate the response to lethal force even though the use-of-force model they are trained on claims to provide for a graduated response and the option to dial down. Too often, an officer will not pull back and realize the person is clearly not engaged.

There are police officers who can communicate well; I have seen this with my own eyes. But here they are using their own judgment, not their police training. There have been efforts to close this gap in ability, but they have not been sufficient. Toronto has created Mobile Crisis Intervention Teams (MCIT), which partner a mental health nurse and a specially trained police officer, but these units are preventative and would not respond to a call concerning a mentally distressed person with a knife. They are what is known as secondary responders; they will respond to calls regarding citizens in mental health crisis as long as the person is not a threat. As well, they only work until 11 p.m. But in British Columbia, in the wake of the RCMP Tasering death of Robert Dziekanski, the province established a Crisis Intervention and De-escalation training standard that requires every front-line police officer, supervisor and recruit to receive de-escalation training. They must redo the course every three years to keep their skills fresh. British Columbia stands alone in this requirement, however.

In the rest of the country, the use of force rules. This is the moral and ethical question that preoccupies me. We are saying it is okay to view the mentally ill person as "the other" who is a threat to society, and to treat that person the same way we treat a violent, criminally motivated individual. Is this an outgrowth of the police culture, of exclusive reliance on the armed, uniformed police officer, or a combination of the police culture and a generational change? There is a saying used by police watchdogs and cited by Dubé: "Culture eats training." It means the reality of policing the street will eventually swallow up anything a recruit was taught.

A popular approach used in policing, usually expressed by a senior officer coaching a probationary constable freshly out of training, goes like this: *Forget what you learned at the police college. Now you're on the street and we'll teach you real policing.* Blair would actually mention this at every graduation of recruits and say, "Do not follow that advice." He would tell them, follow your training, trust your values. He was fighting the cynicism of the veterans. Blair did this three times per year in front of the public at graduation ceremonies. Another thing that isn't being talked about publicly that points to a cultural factor is something I learned from Blair and Mike McCormack, the police association president.

They believed there was a generational factor. The new generation of police officers, the young ones, just don't know when to back off, they said. During a conversation McCormack, Blair and I had in Blair's office some months before he stepped down as chief, McCormack said, "You know, this is a real problem." He went on: "Bill, you and I were street cops and when somebody swore at us or gave us lip, we would back off and say, 'Okay, fine.' But this generation of officers must have the last word." So, if someone swears at them, they get in their face with a "What did you say?" Rather than disengaging and walking away, they tend to escalate confrontation to such an extent that McCormack claimed he was going from division to division to talk to the officers and telling them to lay off.

So here are two pieces of culture—older officers telling younger officers to forget their training and learn from the street, and other police officials saying younger officers are too confrontational. How do these factors play out when armed police officers are the first responders dealing with mental health crises? I have seen good—and bad—policing that involves people showing signs of mental health crisis. Three examples come to mind: one that happened in my own home and two I witnessed on "ride-alongs" (which allow a person to experience a typical police shift first-hand).

During one evening ride-along we came upon a woman sitting out on the street by a subway station. Two police constables were trying to talk to her. Toronto Transit Commission special constables were there as well. They were doing their best, trying to help. She was saying she had ingested a whole bottle of some medication and her body was riddled with pins. She wanted to rip off her clothes. Under the direction of the sergeant I was with, the officers talked to her in the quietest of ways, assured her they wanted to get her help and because she had taken all those pills, she needed to go to the hospital. She did not have a weapon. She had issued no threats to the officers. She was more likely to harm herself. She agreed to go to the hospital in the ambulance that had been standing by. The officers assured her they would stay with her.

We left thinking the matter had been resolved and she would be cared for at a hospital. Two hours later, we got a call from the two constables who had gone to the hospital with her. They wanted the sergeant to come back. "Do you know why they are calling me?" he asked and pointed at his Taser. Constables were not allowed to carry Tasers. Clearly, she was not under control. The hospital had informed the officers that the woman was well known, a "frequent flyer" in their parlance. So they would not take her. They wouldn't even register her. She had locked herself in the public washroom in the front lobby and stripped off her clothes.

Now she was not answering, so the officers thought they would have to break down the door, Taser her and get her under control. But the sergeant did not use his Taser. He talked to her. It was the police officers who got her out of there—who persuaded her to get dressed and who searched again for a way to help her. This was time-consuming, but they were prepared to take the time. This time there was no ambulance. The officers put her in their own car to take her from one end of the city to the other. However, like Sunnybrook Health Sciences Centre, which had turned her away, Mount Sinai would not take her.

It was after nine at night and there was one more place left to try—the Centre for Addiction and Mental Health (CAMH). After directing the two officers to take her there, the sergeant started thinking about a plan in case she was rejected there as well. "She couldn't go back to the shelter [where she was staying] in her present condition. They wouldn't let her in," he said. The only place would be a cell in the police division. At least she would not be on the street and she would be fed, he told me. When he went off-shift, the next sergeant would have to decide what to do with her in the morning.

These actions were a consequence of the failure of our social support systems, but they were also an example of good policing. Police were providing the safety net that others wouldn't. It was hugely time-consuming. Three police officers had spent the entire evening with one person. They were prepared—with the sergeant's support—to do what needed to be done. As my ride-along ended, the officers were taking the woman to the CAMH. This was a case of a sergeant taking an entire shift to deal with a situation because of a shortage of beds. Her repeat visits had become a justification to deny help. It also highlighted the lack of necessary institutional support in the community. The police acted properly, but our social support system failed miserably. In my view it doesn't matter if she had come to the hospital twelve times. Take care of her. That's your job.

The second example involves an incident that happened in our home. A friend who was staying with us hit a crisis point one night. Our guest was bipolar and manic-depressive, and alcohol had acted as a trigger. She collapsed and became unconscious. I was out at the time. My wife was home and had called 911. Paramedics and police responded quickly, not knowing whose house they were attending. They were there when I returned. After some effort on the part of the paramedics, our friend regained consciousness, but the sight of police officers set off a strong physical reaction caused by the fear of being taken away. The paramedics responded very aggressively. "I'm going to charge you with assault if you don't stop," one of them threatened, making the situation worse.

It was the two young police officers—a man and a woman—who gained control of the situation and our friend's trust. "We're not going to lay any charges. We are here to help you and make sure you are okay," they said. They kept talking to her in a calm, friendly voice, calling her by her name and saying, "We will help you, we will stay with you." They got her into the ambulance and on her way to the hospital. One of them stayed with her and kept talking to her, calming her. By morning the crisis had passed. Our friend was fine. Today, she is working and prospering.

I saw the best not necessarily of *policing*, but of *care-giving* by those two officers. This kind of action is highly resource dependent. If police are going to do it, they need to be able to make a significant investment of time and choose the right people. The officers involved in the two incidents did not use threats or intimidation. They took their time and used calm voices and empathy. In both cases, the officers were dealing with women, and both women would have "looked white." I have wondered if that may have ratcheted down the threat level felt by the responding officers.

The third anecdote takes us to the Finch subway station in North Toronto. The sergeant I was riding with that night got a call from some patrol constables. A young man they described as Asian was very upset. He had a speech disorder and his speech difficulties were quite obvious. He was upset because it was very late at night and he was supposed to be taking the bus from the station to his home in Richmond Hill, ending a journey that had begun in downtown Toronto. He said he had been threatened by two knife-wielding older boys who were circling him and touching his body with the knives. The two constables had decided he was making up this story because he was late and was looking for an excuse to escape his mother's wrath.

The sergeant listened to their account and, leaning over to me, said, "Let's go for a walk." Behind the waiting area, there was a newsstand. The sergeant approached the operator, who told him, "Oh yeah, there were two boys. They were bigger than him and they were acting in a threatening way to him." The constables had not bothered to talk to the newsstand operator. The sergeant was furious with them and their inadequate investigation. They had dismissed the young man because he wasn't quite "normal" and didn't speak in a "normal" way. They had prejudged him, and that had coloured their view of the situation. The sergeant chalked this one up as a learning opportunity. They were rookies; they would get better.

So here was an example of a man, visibly of colour, who because of his speech disorder wasn't believed let alone helped by the officers.

They were quick to take on an accusatory, interrogatory tone. The more they did this, the more nervous he became. They acted like criminal investigators, not officers who could help. It was a quantifiably different approach from the one used with the two white-looking women.

Many of the problems that arise when officers deal with those in mental health distress begin at home. How the Toronto police department treats its own is a good indicator of how its members deal with others. The Toronto Police Service, an organization of about 7,300—5,100 uniform and 2,200 civilian employees—has two full-time psychologists on staff. Montreal and Calgary, with smaller workforces, have five psychologists each. (Calgary has a police force of 2,715, 2,200 of them in uniform. Montreal has a force of about 6,000 employees, close to 4,600 in uniform.) One of the Toronto police psychologists, Dr. Carol Vipari, told the police services board in the summer of 2016 that demands on their service continued to increase and they were understaffed. Her lament was familiar: there are only two of us and only so many hours in the day.

Vipari and her colleague, Dr. Catherine Martin-Doto, also reported that more than twice as many officers, 12.7 percent of the force, had sought help compared with two years earlier. Chief Mark Saunders insisted this was because the stigma of seeking help was being overcome and the need to look after one's mental health was becoming embedded in the culture. Yet despite numbers indicating otherwise, Saunders maintained that the Toronto Police Service compared favourably to other law enforcement entities in tending to the mental health needs of its employees. Vipari was able to offer a list of those who would be most in need of mental health help, including officers who deal with child exploitation (who often have to view videos of children being abused); forensic officers; emergency task force officers; those working undercover in drug enforcement; homicide investigators; those who served in Afghanistan, Haiti and Ukraine; and phone dispatchers who deal with people in distress.

The police service was also struggling to implement a program recommended by Iacobucci for officers early in their careers. Under this program, officers in their first year on the force would be seen by a psychologist whenever they first experienced sudden death, homicide or suicide, or were exposed to other traumatic situations they had never had to deal with before. Two years after Iacobucci had recommended that the police service begin such a program, it was under way in only two of seventeen divisions. It initially bumped up against the familiar funding roadblock and another common roadblock—police culture. As Martin-Doto told the board, "We have to change the culture. We need our services to be central, as if you were going to the family doctor. We need to move to a place where it is seen as normal that people look after their emotional health just like their physical health."

Psychological testing for recruits is contracted out and the results are not routinely reviewed by the overworked psychologists on staff. A fairly significant number of police officers have mental health issues. We know this from the number of officers who have committed suicide and the number who have claimed post-traumatic stress disorder (PTSD). But concrete data are hard to come by. At one point I asked the senior brass of the Toronto Police Service how many of our officers had committed suicide over a ten-year period, and they could not tell me conclusively. Apparently, the information was scattered about, not housed in one location.

The Toronto Police Service does not keep track of the incidence of mental health problems, including PTSD. However, according to a recent survey by the federal Department of Public Safety, 7 percent of police officers in Canada suffer from PTSD.[13] By some estimates, the rate for all types of mental illness among police officers could be as high as 30 percent, according to a report from the Mental Health Commission of Canada. Like anyone else, officers have disagreements with spouses or children and are battling pressures outside the job. Then they start their shift and can be confronted by someone with a knife.

When I came in as chair, there was an internal, informal peer-support system in the Toronto force, created jointly by the force, the board and the police union and overseen by the Toronto police chaplain, for people who were feeling emotionally or psychologically unwell: they could talk to a colleague who had been trained in peer counselling. I wasn't satisfied with it. I thought in this day and age, with the complex problems people face, surely we could have an anonymous, professional service of superior quality. So we moved to a more formal family assistance program with services offered by an outside provider that officers or their family members who needed emotional assistance could call anonymously.

The police association was not happy because this move wrested the program from its control. But since the board paid for it and was liable as the employer, we instituted it. I worked very closely with the deputy chief in charge of human resources, Keith Forde, to put in place a modern, professional service. Every supervisor and unit commander was expected to take responsibility if they saw an officer acting erratically or if an employee came to them saying things were not going well. The person was supposed to be encouraged to get help. It did not always happen that way, though.

In one case, Blair felt that an officer who was on probation, Ariyeh Krieger, was not suitable as a police officer because he was too quick to draw his gun or otherwise put people in jeopardy. Before his probation ended, we terminated him. At the board meeting where we considered his firing, Krieger claimed his behaviour was caused by PTSD. In support of this claim, he insisted that he had been seen acting erratically and emotionally, breaking down in tears at the police station, but that no one had helped. We put the superintendent who was his unit commander through the wringer and sure enough, she had been rather blasé about his plight. The police service's procedures required supervisors to be watchful, to be proactive in encouraging anyone who was having trouble to get help, and to provide information about where to get help.

The board felt that the superintendent had been passive in the way she had dealt with Krieger. We still terminated him because of his proclivity for drawing his gun or beating people up. But he went to the Human Rights Tribunal, where his complaint was upheld. The tribunal ruled that we had not been attentive to his needs and had failed to accommodate him. It ordered us not only to reinstate him but to do so at full rank, bypassing the rest of his probationary period. This was a lesson for us: we had to be much more vigilant about our employees' mental health, and in order to be a responsible organization, we had to have a top-notch program to help people.

Krieger claimed he had acquired PTSD through two incidents that happened while he was on probation. At Yorkdale Shopping Centre, Toronto's west end shopping behemoth, he was patrolling with another officer and they saw a young man, a Black man, whom Krieger suspected of having a gun in his pocket. He physically challenged the man and tried to put his hand in his pocket. The young man naturally reached into his pocket to protect what was there—it was a gun—and the officer called on his colleague to shoot. His partner fired one shot that did not hit the suspect. They were standing just outside one of Toronto's busiest shopping malls. This was reckless behaviour. If you suspect someone has a gun, you don't accost him in the midst of mall traffic. (A few years later the man approached by Krieger was killed in another police interaction.)

But now Krieger claimed he was fearful, thinking that had the man's gun even accidentally discharged, Krieger could have been dead. He claimed that this fear had destroyed him and unhinged him.

He told the tribunal that this fear had led to the second incident. He and his partner were working an overnight shift and stopped at a McDonald's in north Toronto. In line in front of him at the restaurant was a man, a big guy, possibly intoxicated. Krieger perceived the man as a threat. He questioned the man, physically grabbed him, put him in a nearby seat and then put the man in a headlock when he resisted, ultimately forcing him out of the restaurant. Krieger was not in control. The chief's reasoning regarding his termination was that if we didn't deal with him immediately we would continue to have a problem on our hands, and the board agreed. Yet we were ordered by the tribunal to take him back into the service. I never heard from him again; perhaps he was put in a job where he posed no threat.

Years before Blair became chief, a unit was created that came to be viewed as the "dumping ground" for people like our young recruit. Known as CARU, the Central Alternative Response Unit, it works out of an offsite location, where it is set up like a virtual police division, with a unit commander and platoons headed by sergeants and staff sergeants. The difference is that just about everyone sent to this unit is on restricted duty due to a physical or mental health issue. At one point we had several hundred uniformed officers on reduced, restricted duty but drawing a full salary. One day, the board asked Blair to account for this financial drain: How many people did we have on permanent reduced, restricted duty who were drawing a full salary?

The number was over four hundred. They were earning an average of $100,000 per year, not including overtime, and a large number of them were never going to be 100 percent. They could be on reduced duty for their entire career. As their employer, we couldn't force them to transition to long-term disability or take early retirement as long as they were able to perform 60 to 70 percent of their duties. We had a duty by law to accommodate them. If they were young enough that long-term disability would not carry them into their pensionable years, we were stuck with them.

What concerned me more than the financial implications was how those who were sent to this unit were perceived by others and treated by superiors. The unit itself, as I have said, was viewed as a "dumping ground." It included people who had been labelled, marginalized, ridiculed and harassed by their colleagues and supervisors for being "less than a man." I heard numerous accounts of the poisonous atmosphere within the unit. Employees who were facing challenges were consigned to this outfit instead of being given the assistance and support they needed. Out of sight, out of mind, as it were.

In the culture that prevails in the world of policing, a police officer admitting to facing mental health–related problems is not looked upon favourably by many. I became involved in the case of an officer who was at one time flying high and receiving praise for the great work he was doing with young street kids—until he had a breakdown. He had been untouchable, an icon of modern-day street policing, but he later confessed to me that he had not been well for some time, had been drinking too much and felt he was having sporadic breakdowns. "I went to my supervisor and I was laughed at. They mocked me," he said. He was ultimately moved from one office to another, including CARU.

Now he was a pariah. He spoke openly about his problems and how the police force dealt with those in similar straits. He took the police service to the Human Rights Tribunal. He was seen as disloyal. Management took disciplinary action against him. When this man was given an office at headquarters for his new assignment, he was greeted by a sign on his door reading Mental Asylum. If this was done to an officer with such a high profile, what happens to those who are unknowns? This was going on as I was leaving my position, but I took a photo of the sign to the chief administrative officer, Tony Veneziano, who oversaw human resources. "Tony, look at this photo. This says something," I told him. "Chair, I assure you we will look into it and deal with it," he assured me.

I don't know if they did but it was a key reason for my recommendation, before I left, that the board set up a standing committee on workplace health and wellness, and adopt the Mental Health Commission of Canada's national standard on mental health and wellness in the workplace. In October 2014, the board agreed to create a standing committee consisting of representatives of the board, the police service, the associations and the families of officers who had suffered from mental health problems. But the police service balked at adopting the national standard, and the standing committee ran into trouble almost from its inception.

Inclusion of family members of officers who had died by suicide became a major source of concern. First, representatives of the service and the association claimed they couldn't identify potential committee members fitting this description. Then, when I invited Heidi Rogers to join the committee, their backs went up. Rogers was the widow of Sergeant Richard "Bucky" Rogers, who had died by suicide in July 2014. In a letter to Heidi and their daughter Lori written shortly before his death, Bucky had said, "I blame the Toronto police for putting me in this state." According to the letter, his repeated pleas for help had gone unheeded. Instead, he had been mocked and isolated. Heidi and Lori had gone public and had begun a determined campaign to hold the organization accountable for their loss.

Senior officials had told me the letter was not accurate; the service had been trying its best to help Bucky and, incredibly, claimed his family members did not know the truth because he had not been close to them. In other words, his last words were not to be believed. The service and the association, therefore, were not pleased to have Rogers at the table. As if to counter her claim that the police service's handling of employees who were having problems was woefully inadequate, Mike Federico, the deputy chief responsible for the mental health portfolio, arranged for Dr. Vipari to deliver an extended presentation demonstrating that the service was already doing everything required under the national standard.

But there is one thing in the national standard that the Toronto Police Service does not do, as I had found: the systematic collection, analysis and publication of data on workplace mental health and wellness. The service came armed with all kinds of reasons why the data could not be collected. It was clear the top brass and the police association had no desire to do this, because that would create an accountability mechanism they did not want. This resistance to accountability is another key part of police culture. One would have expected the police association to enthusiastically support accountability in the interest of its members; instead, it joined forces with the service to resist adoption of the national standard.

I left the board feeling that the standing committee had merely served as window dressing to the work the service was doing: providing inadequate support to members who were experiencing mental health difficulties. Oh, and the need for more psychologists for the police service? A recommendation by Chief Saunders to hire a third psychologist came before the police services board and was deferred—at the same meeting in which the overworked duo providing psychological services patiently explained they could do no more because they were overwhelmed.

Response to mental health crisis constitutes some 30 percent of all police work, not only in Toronto but across Canada. It is safe to safe to say that each day, every single police officer will interact with someone having a mental health–related crisis. It has become widely accepted that police are the first point of contact for people who find themselves in this situation. Often, the only way they can hope to get the help they need is through police. And many officers do respond well to these situations. They do it well because of personal aptitude, empathy, judgment—and training.

However, do all police officers have the proper training? Are the right people being hired? Do they have the right communication skills? Are officers adequately equipped, supervised and monitored? Are those who don't respond properly—or whose response results in serious injury or death—held truly accountable? Are police procedures for responding to mental health–related calls for service themselves adequate?

Look at media reports, coroners' inquests, court decisions and inquiry reports, and you will find these types of questions being asked ad nauseum. Such questions are asked even when people agree that police officers are not experts but have ended up carrying this burden because of inadequacies in the health care system.

I feel grateful for the hard work and commitment of people like the members of the Toronto Police Services Board's mental health subcommittee—Pat Capponi, Jennifer Chambers, Steve Lurie, Dr. Kwame Mckenzie and Judge Ted Ormston. People like the family members of officers who lost their lives to mental illness—the Rogers family, the family of Eddie Adamson. Adamson, a Toronto police staff sergeant, took his own life in 2005, twenty-five years after the death of Constable Michael Sweet, who was brutally tortured and killed inside a Queen Street bar in downtown Toronto. Adamson's Emergency Task Force was ordered to stand down. Hearing Sweet's agonized screams, he finally stormed the bistro but could not save his colleague. He suffered from post-traumatic stress disorder.

His family has been steadfast in its demand that Adamson be commemorated on a Memorial Wall commemorating officers who have fallen in the line of duty. But the big question remains: Why is it that in Canada, the United States and much of Europe, where mental health is a big issue, police are required to deal with this in the first place?

For me, it's not enough to say that this is because of cutbacks to the health care system. There is a far more troubling underlying issue that must be confronted. Canada, the US and many European countries rely on an economic model based on having fewer and fewer social supports in the name of getting the economy right. We are seeing the inevitable results of the embrace of austerity by Margaret Thatcher and Ronald Reagan, and the ascendancy of the neo-liberal economic system. Rather than increasing investments in health care, mental-health care, institutional supports and social care, poverty reduction and affordable housing, as societies we have turned our interactions with people in mental health crisis into a matter of law and order. Social responsibility has taken a back seat.

The ultimate result of this is that we are saying, "Okay, police officer, you can kill some of these people." The police culture tells them that such deaths are unfortunate but unavoidable. And because they are unavoidable, the officer who kills or does serious injury to someone in crisis—whose behaviour is caused by an illness and who is not a criminal in the common meaning of that term—shall not be considered guilty of a criminal act. A person suffering from mental illness is society's "other"—not normal—and history is full of examples where those in power have responded to "the other" with similar acts of control. People called "mad" were incarcerated; people considered unfit to bear children were forcibly sterilized; people considered "retarded" were lobotomized.

Have societies in the age of neo-liberal economic policies pushed these boundaries and accepted that it is all right to kill this new "other"? This, to me, is the defining moral, ethical and political question that we who call ourselves civilized must face. If not, people will continue to die, and those who kill them because they feel an "imminent threat" to their safety will continue to go free, perhaps with a slap on the wrist. What else can society expect when it turns a matter of social responsibility into a matter of "law and order" and "public safety"?

6

Stirring the Gravy

I WORKED WITH three mayors while I was chair. David Miller was the first, and he was an example of how a mayor ought to participate in the governance of policing while respecting the political independence of the police services board. There were, of course, certain additional factors that contributed to this period of productive collaboration. In the first place, Miller and the police board had a common agenda: making the police service truly reflective of the community it served, developing a strong model of community-based policing, addressing the problem of racial bias in policing, reducing gun violence and bringing down rising costs—and through this fostering greater public trust.

Further, the Miller era was marked by a period of rapid growth in the city, and that contributed to the spirit of co-operation. As Toronto grew, so did the police service. New facilities were built. Budget was a concern and board members were uneasy about the ballooning police costs, but in those years of growth, the city was not demanding budget reductions. Instead, it asked for smaller annual rates of increase, which we complied with. In my first budget presentation to the city as board chair, I explained our approach: we would continue to bring down the annual rate of increase until it plateaued in four to five years, at which point we would look for ways to bend the curve downward.

My first five years on the board were also helped by a favourable response from the community. At his inauguration as the new chief of police, Bill Blair had spoken frankly about racism and his commitment to dealing with it. With a focus on hiring and promoting people of colour, diversity training, and engaging with the community, there was hope that the relationship between police and the public would improve. Blair was widely viewed as someone who would bring about big changes. Believing that change required a period of stability and continuity, the board agreed in 2009, Blair's fourth year, to give him another full five-year term. However, dark clouds were gathering.

Reports in the *Toronto Star* showed that police interactions with racialized people—particularly Black youth—were as problematic as before, and might even have become worse. And Blair's performance leading up to and during the G20 summit in 2010, including his failure to be transparent with the board, left board members feeling betrayed. He was losing significant support from the public as well. By then, the board was focusing its attention on other difficult issues, such as police response to people in mental health crisis and Blair's handling of police discipline.

Personally, I had begun to pay more serious attention to cost and models of policing. In a speech at the 2009 conference of the Canadian Association of Police Governance, I talked about the need for renewal in our model of policing. I suggested there was a serious mismatch between what police services did and the resources they used, dispatching uniformed police officers for every function. Around the same time, in a presentation to the Federation of Canadian Municipalities, I addressed the issue of policing costs and called for a new system of funding. After four years on the board, my thinking on these questions was evolving.

Within a year, a seismic change would occur in Toronto's political landscape. Miller decided not to run for re-election. Rob Ford, a brash right-wing figure from an influential conservative family, became the mayor. His brother Doug took Rob's seat as councillor. The Fords had run on the slogan, "Stop the gravy train." A neo-conservative populist, he strongly believed that elimination of waste and corruption was the answer to rising municipal costs, not the imposition of more taxes. This view and his populist persona gained him a huge following, somewhat anticipating the rise of Donald Trump.

The Fords came from a political family with ties to Ontario's Progressive Conservative Party. Their father, Doug Ford Sr., had been an influential provincial politician in the 1990s as a member of the provincial legislature and a close friend of Premier Mike Harris and federal finance minister Jim Flaherty. My only contact with Rob Ford before he became mayor had been on those few occasions when he had asked a question about some aspect of the police budget on the council floor that I had to answer. There had been one instance of informal contact when intruders had broken into the Fords' parental home, shot at sister Kathy and made off in their father's car.

Pam McConnell, the board chair at the time, had phoned me while I was on my way to an evening meeting at the Toronto Police College. We agreed that we should go see Councillor Ford and offer some support as a courtesy. I asked the driver to turn around, pick up McConnell and take us to the police station in Etobicoke where Ford was. We met him, extended our sympathies and asked if we could be of any help. A gruff man accustomed to projecting the image of a tough guy, he said he was fine and didn't need anything. However, some days after the event, he sent me a very warm and friendly note conveying his appreciation for us reaching out to him. That had been the full extent of our acquaintance when he became mayor. Otherwise I did not know the man who would become globally infamous due to the extensive press reports of his use of crack cocaine, his "drunken stupors," his lies, his lewd and racist remarks and his unhinged attacks on the media.

As I have mentioned earlier, I was seen by the right wing as "Miller's man." So there was a lot of speculation as to whether I would survive as chair under Ford. But my membership on the board was secure. As I was getting to the end of my term as city council's appointee on the board, one of the provincial spots became vacant. When I told the minister of community safety, Rick Bartolucci, about my status, he recommended to the premier that I fill the provincial vacancy.

It came as a pleasant surprise that Ford wanted me to continue as chair, and not only did I remain chair for his entire term, I developed a good working relationship with his team and his brother Doug, who was his key adviser and vice-chair of the council's budget committee. I believe the basis of our relationship was that we agreed on the need to reduce the cost of policing in Toronto. To this end, Mayor Ford and I had a brief conversation at the Mayor's New Year's Levee. It was widely thought that Councillor Michael Thompson, a Ford ally and the only Black city councillor, wanted to be the new chair of the board. Ford appointed Thompson to take Miller's vacant spot on the board and replaced councillors Pam McConnell and Adam Vaughan with Frances Nunziata, a close Ford ally who had served on the board once before, and Chin Lee, a quiet, middle-of-the-road politician. Lee would be replaced two years later by Mike Del Grande.

For the seat to be filled by city council with a public appointment, Ford opted for Andy Pringle, a wealthy businessman and successful fundraiser with strong ties to the Conservative Party. Pringle had been John Tory's chief of staff when Tory was leader of the Ontario Progressive Conservative Party. He was a key fundraiser for a pair of Conservative federal finance ministers, Jim Flaherty and Joe Oliver. He later became a major fundraiser for the Conservative leadership campaign of Kellie Leitch, a controversial and ultimately unsuccessful candidate who proposed that new arrivals to this country would have to pass a test for "Canadian values." When his association with Leitch became controversial, Pringle stepped away from the campaign.

Pringle was expected to play an important role in budget matters. Soon to go, one by one, were the citizen appointees: Judge Hugh Locke, Hamlin Grange and Judi Cohen. All brought strengths to the table—Locke was the senior member and dispensed timely and judicious advice, Grange was a champion of human rights, and Cohen had spoken out on ethical issues. Locke's term had ended earlier, with the province appointing me in his place. The province replaced Grange and Cohen with Dhun Noria, a senior medical doctor at Scarborough Hospital with Liberal ties, and Marie Moliner, an executive with the federal government known for her community ties.

Thompson became vice-chair. Although he and Nunziata were initially distant and suspicious, considering me to be a Blair ally, by the time the issue of racial profiling broke, we had forged a strong alliance. This was helped by another development. Soon after the appointment of the new board members, Keith Forde, now retired as deputy chief, organized a get-together of Toronto's Black police officers. Thompson was invited, along with Grange and me. The turnout at his home was impressive. Following dinner and informal conversation, Forde spoke with great passion about the treatment of Black officers in the police service. He acknowledged the work that people like him, me, and Grange had been doing together to change it, with the support of Deputy Chief Sloly, Superintendent McLeod, Sergeant Stacy Clarke and many others.

Forde's message to Thompson was clear: Black and other minority members of the Toronto Police Service were counting on him. Then the three board members—Grange, Thompson and I—were asked to speak. Grange and I reinforced what Forde had said, outlining our own efforts at the board table and airing our frustrations. When his turn came, Thompson spoke from the heart about growing up in Jamaica and the choices he had made to get ahead in the largely white political world of Toronto. None of us had heard him speak so openly. What he said was very different from a public position he had taken previously that police should stop and document every Black youth. He had evidently played the white man's game to build credibility with voters.

Thompson's words brought to mind my encounter with a previous chair, Phil Givens. In the mid-1980s, the primary target of racially motivated violence in Toronto was the South Asian community. As an activist involved with Indian Immigrant Aid Services, I was part of a delegation that sought a meeting with Givens and the police chief to request greater police attention to this problem. When we entered the chair's office, no courtesies were extended. Givens and Chief Jack Ackroyd sat behind a huge desk and did not bother to stand up, greet us or even offer us chairs. As we stood across the desk, Givens barked, "What do you want?" We stated our case. Completely misrepresenting our submission, Givens turned to the chief and asked, "Chief, do we have racists in the force?" The chief answered, "No, sir," and we were dismissed.

Later that evening, my home phone rang. It was Givens. He wanted to assure me he was not a racist, because he himself came from a minority background. Givens was Jewish. I was bowled over. What he was saying to me was that he had to make choices to be accepted as a member of the establishment and to get ahead. I was a non-entity and he was a powerful member of the Toronto elite, yet he still felt the need to make this call and plead for understanding. The incident has always stayed with me. Twenty years later, the event at Forde's house appeared to have allowed Thompson to show his true self. A relationship between us was born that night; we were to be good partners during the rest of our tenures.

Nunziata had initially been unsure about her position on the carding issue, seeing some merit in the practice, but she had come around. Thus Thompson, Nunziata, Del Grande and I were often able to work as a majority on the seven-member board. This did not sit well with some of the other board members. In particular, Pringle and Noria were friendly with Blair. They disapproved of my ties to Thompson, Nunziata and Del Grande. Pringle, with his business background, was uncomfortable with the confrontational approach favoured by the politicians and preferred to resolve issues behind the scenes.

A new tone was set virtually from the first meeting of the new board: the era of confrontation was here. It began soon after the new board took office, when the police service requested funding to replace its main IT system. Thompson was deeply skeptical that this was necessary, arguing that the existing system could be modernized. It was a big-ticket item, and the new members from city council were determined to question all large expenses. The police brass believed they had already done due diligence, that the problem warranted the expenditure and that we were losing valuable time. It took almost seven months before the project was approved, and the delay rankled the police service. It was also miffed by the aggressive questioning it had faced.

Another aspect of police culture had been challenged: that the chief must be given great deference. There was consternation about the combative way he had been grilled and the openly skeptical way in which his responses had been received. A new tone had been set: we were trying to show the board was in charge. This tone, the aggressive style and the refusal to show deference to the chief were upsetting to some of the board members, who would personally call me to ask that I do something about it.

The main focus of the Ford administration was the cost of doing business. The mandate of the councillors who had been sent to the police board was to bring that focus to the cost of policing. It did not help that there was not a great personal warmth for Blair in Ford's circle. I agreed with the councillors' view that we needed to act now to bend the curve of policing costs downward and that the political conditions were right to work on this objective. In my view, the Ford administration's support for the next set of changes that needed to be made was very important. With majority support on the board, I could push for significant changes, even though I chaired a divided board and it was a poisoned environment in which to provide governance. The collegiality of 2005 had been replaced by distrust and cliques that would persist throughout the next five years.

When Rob Ford became mayor, he called for a 10 percent reduction in the city's budget. He declared that "heads will roll" if any agencies, boards, commissions or departments failed to meet the target. The police board had accepted the 10 percent reduction target, and the city agreed with our plan to do it over two years. As the 2011 budget had already been set, our first year to target for a reduction was 2012, which we set at 4.6 percent. But we were met with immediate resistance from the police service. In discussions with city manager Pennachetti, deputy city manager and chief financial manager Cam Weldon, and the mayor's chief of staff, Amir Remtulla, Thompson and I were encouraged to stay the course and not back down.

Pringle, who found out that Chief Blair lived four houses down from him, decided to try the personal touch—he invited Blair over for a beer in his backyard and even to his fishing cottage in New Brunswick to attempt to get him onside. To no avail: led by Blair, the police service's budget and finance officials made it clear there was no way the 4.6 percent target could be met. Frustrated by this inflexibility, Thompson expressed his anger in public, echoing Mayor Ford's "heads will roll" comment.

On October 2, 2011, I received an email from Blair:

Good morning Alok,

I have read the various media reports and comments by a Board member, threatening my tenure as Chief for doing my job. I will retain counsel and seek advice from the Ministry.

Bill

I replied:

Good morning Bill,

I expect you will do what is necessary and in your interest. Thank you for advising me.

Alok

Around the same time, I wrote to Thompson:

Michael,

I have seen your comment in the *Star*. There will likely be some legal developments on the basis that the Chief is being threatened with dismissal for doing his job. I will watch for any developments. We will discuss a process when we meet tomorrow afternoon. In the meantime, it would be best to not say any more and to keep the Mayor and the City out of it. As far as they are concerned, this is a matter for the Board. Let us act with the least legal ramifications.

Regards,

Alok

While we were engaged in this sparring, Blair and I had gone to England as part of a team of Canadian police officials to observe and learn about how police forces there had met very draconian reduction targets laid down by then–home secretary Theresa May. Chatting during the lunch break one day, Blair shared his difficulties with reducing his budget by 4.6 percent. He said the types of cuts we were suggesting would only yield a million here and a couple of million there, not the $40.6 million the board was asking him to find. I replied that those millions here and there would add up to what we were looking for. I added that he was the expert, he knew his operation better than anyone else, and we needed him to scrutinize his budget to find the savings. It was my view that this would be a better and less radical approach than a massive cut to one area.

Working with Thompson and the city manager, I had begun to consider options. I concluded that something drastic would have to be devised in case the service failed or refused to come through. At the board meeting on October 5, 2011, I proposed that we consider offering an exit package to up to four hundred people. With salaries of approximately $100,000 per person, that would reduce the budget by $40 million. I had spoken to the city manager about the city providing the money to pay for this approach, and had talked to McCormack and Blair as well.

Neither was pleased, but McCormack had understood our predicament and said that if he had a fight, it would be with the city, not the board. Blair, who had presided over a major expansion of the police service, was not as agreeable. However, he had opened the door by offering a similar package to eighteen senior officers—twelve police officers and six civilian managers—to save a little over $2 million. The relationship between Blair and me was entering a new confrontational phase. The spirit of collaboration that had characterized our relationship since 2005, when we both assumed our positions, was over.

Blair's response to the situation was twofold. First, he attempted intimidation with his email threat of legal action against a board member. It did not work. Instead, it made us even more determined to assert the authority of the board. Blair then played the political card: he circumvented the board and went directly to the mayor. The night before the October 2011 board meeting where his budget was to be considered and approved by the board, he met with Ford, city manager Pennachetti and chief of staff Remtulla.

Remtulla called me as the meeting was getting under way and said I should join. I refused, saying it was improper if not illegal for the mayor to involve himself in board matters. The law gives no such authority to the mayor. Eventually, they were able to persuade Thompson to join. At the meeting, Blair presented Ford with an alternative plan for achieving the reduction target. It was a patchwork of small cuts, unspecified savings and deferred costs. The oddest part of his proposal was that the city would put up $5 million to $6 million for the police service's annual contribution to its reserve funds maintained by the city. Ford bought this plan and promptly met the press that night with Blair at his side to announce how for the first time the police service had reduced its budget, thanks to the chief's leadership.

It was an illusion, but Blair had won the day, undermining the authority of civilian governance of the police service. The board had no choice but to approve the budget that had been accepted by the mayor already, and put the best spin on it. In fact, the reductions turned out to be illusory and the budget ballooned by at least $14 million. The point had been made: the police service would not hesitate to play politics to have its way with the board.

Del Grande experienced this personally when he tried to raise a question about police ethics at a public board meeting. As a city councillor, he claimed to have been told by organizers of a major cultural event in his neighbourhood that some police officers expected free food and drinks when they attended. The organizers felt pressured. Del Grande apparently raised the matter with Blair in private but got nowhere. One day at a public board meeting, he stood up and repeated his claim in a very dramatic manner while making a point about the importance of holding police officers to a high ethical standard. An enraged Blair promptly, menacingly announced that he would be conducting an investigation immediately.

Two days later, I got a phone call from a shaken Del Grande. He had been contacted by Toronto police detectives demanding to speak to him about his allegation. He felt threatened by their manner, as if he were the accused. He requested legal representation, which I arranged for him. The investigation, which was completed with surprising speed, did not support Del Grande's allegations. Intimidation can take many forms.

The Earl Witty saga proved that to me. After someone in the service had leaked the information to reporters, I confirmed to the media that Witty, a police superintendent, had arrived at work drunk on the morning of February 10, 2012. Blair informed me that I might be guilty of violating my oath of confidentiality and could be the subject of a complaint of misconduct by Witty or the senior officers' organization that represented him. The day after Blair spoke to me, I received a letter from the organization's lawyer, Joseph Markson, objecting to my "decision to publicly confirm and comment upon the internal Toronto Police Service investigation presently being conducted into the circumstances of Superintendent Earl Witty's fitness for duty on February 10, 2012." Markson was not making a formal complaint; he was essentially urging me to cease and desist. The letter was copied to Blair.

I found it a curious power play to cover up the fact that it was Blair's service that had leaked like a sieve on this matter. It was also an example of the double standard that prevailed in the police service. On the same day the Witty incident had occurred, Blair's communications director, Mark Pugash, confirmed details of another professional standards investigation, this one into the conduct of officers accused of fraud. I was puzzled. Why was Pugash's action acceptable but not mine? The answer came a few days later on February 20. That morning, Blair's executive officer, Stu Eley, issued the following order on behalf of the chief to all senior managers:

> As you are no doubt aware, there recently was an issue about the release of confidential information by a Board member to the media. As a result, the Chief has ordered:
>
> - that ALL interaction with the Board will be through the Office of the Chief.
> - that no member of the Service will provide information to the Board office except in the form of a Board report, submitted through the usual chain of command through the Office of the Chief.
> - that if requested by the Board to provide information, members will provide the requested information to the Office of the Chief and this office will be responsible for providing it to the Board.
> - that any clarification or direction required by a member on the content or submission of Board reports, provision of Board Minutes will be directed to the Office of the Chief.

With this order, Blair was choking off my and the board's ability to receive information readily and directly from members of the service, and making his office the gatekeeper. The board was not notified of this huge shift in the culture of open communication that we had worked together since 2005 to create and nurture. He had taken advantage of one incident to make this move—an incident in which one of his people had leaked information in the first place. Ironically, Eley's confidential memo was provided to me and Thompson anonymously in brown envelopes by someone who had received it. Clearly, not everyone thought this was a good order.

It evidently did not matter to him that this would inconvenience his own people. Everything had to go to Eley, who was already overworked; stuff would sit on his desk and requests would go unanswered for days and weeks. And we were back to the old days when no one from the police service was allowed to communicate with the board—even physically come to the board office—without approval from the Office of the Chief. As one senior officer who worked closely with the chief told me, "I feel as if I can't breathe." A chill had set in.

Blair and I had entered the picture at a time when relations between the board and the chief were poisoned and the board was viewed as dysfunctional. Chiefs before him had used the vague separation in the *Police Services Act* between policy and operations like a firewall to exercise total control over everything the police service did, including non-policing administrative, labour and fiscal matters. But Blair would drop by my office quite regularly to talk about all sorts of subjects. On many occasions late in the day, he would show up coffee in hand to engage in thoughtful conversation about the direction of policing, discuss what was happening in the community or throw out some new ideas. There was a free flow of information. Eley's predecessor, Superintendent Bob Clarke, would keep me informed about serious incidents occurring in the city and make sure important events were on my calendar. We did away with a liaison officer who for years had served as the go-between, and we agreed that board staff and service staff would deal with each other directly. Whereas before, interaction among people working for the board and the police service had been strictly controlled,

Blair showed a willingness to loosen this control—except on matters of police operations—and work in concert with the board.

For my part, I had given considerable thought to the experiences of past board chairs and concluded that our ability to do our job successfully required that we develop a relationship marked by openness, dialogue, information sharing and trust. And during the early years of my tenure as chair we worked to do that. We had board members who—though independent minded, tough and committed to making change—understood and practised a collaborative model of governance. They were not hesitant to challenge the chief, ask difficult questions or strongly express disapproval when they were troubled by an action or issue.

Board members participated in a tough budget process. They grilled the chief and his team intensely and year after year forced him to reduce his request. Similarly, they were not sparing in their criticism of the way in which the police service dealt with officer misconduct or conducted reviews of incidents that had been investigated by the province's Special Investigations Unit. In the early years of my tenure, although board members reflected a pretty broad political spectrum, they showed a remarkable ability to work together, listen to each other and engage seriously with issues.

Blair's actions during 2011–12—circumventing the board and going to Mayor Ford to get his way with his 2011 budget, and moving to shut the board down by clamping down on information sharing—were primarily in reaction to our conviction that the policing model needed comprehensive organizational transformation. I had set down such proposals in a discussion paper, "Avoiding Crisis, an Opportunity: Transforming the Toronto Police Service," in June 2011. I shared this paper with Blair and a few other close confidants who were experts in policing and organizational change. Others supported the paper enthusiastically; from Blair there was silence.

The discussion paper reflected the culmination of my thinking since 2005 about the costs of policing. I had concluded that a two-pronged approach was needed. On one side, efforts had to be made to reform the collective bargaining process, which had served the police associations very well but not the boards and the public. To the extent that wages and benefits constituted 80 percent or more of the police budget, they had to be tackled. But this was not easy, as board after board had found out. The agreements in Toronto had been very much in line with what had happened elsewhere. However, given the size of the organization, the impact in actual dollars was huge.

On the other side, we had to tackle the way the police service as an organization did business, managed itself, used people and technology, and delivered services. The theory was that if the service adopted a new model that used people more efficiently, becoming less hierarchical and deploying innovative practices and strategies, it would become more cost effective. My proposals in the discussion paper of 2011 were based on this theory. The paper sought to shift our focus away from temporary fixes to long-term, systemic answers.

When I became police board chair in 2005 there was little talk of busting the police budget piñata. In fact, there had been nothing but growth in police spending across the country between 1990 and 2005, with spending going from $5.25 billion to $9.3 billion. Of course, the annual rate of increase in Toronto had slowed compared to previous years and had continued to decline each year, from 5.7 percent in 2005 to under 4 percent in 2009. This was due mainly to the approach that Mayor Miller and his administration had taken to combine moderate growth in the cost of services with using the city's newly acquired powers under the *City of Toronto Act* to look for additional revenue sources.

But that approach changed dramatically when Ford came to power, with his single-minded commitment to balancing the city's budget by reducing the cost of government and not raising taxes. The city had commissioned reviews by consultants from KPMG to identify opportunities for sharing services among its departments and agencies, and had undertaken an examination by Ernst & Young of different operations, including the police, to find efficiencies that could yield cost savings. Even though we were poles apart politically, Ford and I were allied on the question of police costs. Like a lot of other people, I saw Ford's obvious flaws, but when it came to police budgets, I believed that his position and election mandate had created an unprecedented opportunity.

Our efforts to control police costs had in fact begun five years earlier, during the 2005 contract negotiations, when we tried to tackle the question of shift schedules. The subject had been studied regularly over the years, but through the combined efforts of chiefs of police and the police association, these studies had been just as regularly shelved. A study we commissioned in 2006 identified savings of several million dollars by changing the system that had been in place for decades. The study had come about as part of the 2005 collective agreement negotiations between the board and the police association. But the police service and the police association could not reach agreement beyond a minor fix that was quite inconsequential. Twelve years later this system remains unchanged. It was flagged yet again as part of the 2017 report of the Transformational Task Force jointly chaired by the board chair and the police chief. And once again, the police association agreed to a joint committee to study it.

Let's also take a look at the gold standard of perks, paid duty. Anyone who has spent any time in Toronto has seen them: uniformed officers standing in the street watching the manholes; standing beside the pylons to separate cars from movie equipment during film shoots; standing beside other pylons for a lane blocked by a private condominium under construction; providing security at sports arenas, nightclubs, bars, street festivals and fundraising events; or directing traffic at shopping malls or door-buster Boxing Day sales at electronics stores. The employer does not set the hourly rate for paid duty in Toronto. The union sets it. A constable earns $65 per hour, and even if it's a five-minute shift, they are paid for a three-hour minimum. If the duty requires three officers, there would need to be a sergeant on site making $85 per hour. And for more officers you need a staff sergeant, who would get paid even more.

In 2010, Toronto Auditor General Jeffrey Griffiths put a $29 million annual price tag on paid duty, a sum including officers' pay, administrative fees and equipment rental fees. The auditor general found that in 2009, 3,695 Toronto officers worked 40,919 paid-duty assignments totalling 370,562 hours of service, earning $24 million in wages. He found that 40 percent of the $29 million price tag, $11.6 million, came from public functions administered by the province and the city—in other words, taxpayers.[1] By 2015, there were still 39,716 paid-duty assignments for 3,132 officers over 381,584 hours. The pay rate had gone up to $68 per hour for constables, and officers received $25.5 million in pay. The total price tag had risen to $30.5 million.

We pushed Blair and his inner circle on how much of this work was optional and how much was legally required. We didn't get an answer. However, Chief Administrative Officer Tony Veneziano finally conceded that the majority of paid duty was optional. It has long been my position that a large portion of this type of work can be outsourced to private security companies, leaving Toronto police more time to do real police work and saving Toronto taxpayers millions of dollars.

The *Police Services Act* allows paid duty, so we could not ban it. The Ontario government, in a major overhaul of police oversight it tabled in November 2017, promised to look at the "core duties" of officers with an eye to hiring others to provide security for the likes of construction sites.

In the autumn of 2014 we considered recommending that paid duty be limited to three hours per week for any officer, so that there would be no negative impact on their fitness to perform regular duty. We also wanted to recommend that paid duty be eliminated at events that are not covered by bylaws, such as bar security or outside sports arenas. Our lawyers told us we couldn't be specific about cutting back hours—the old bugaboo of the board treading on police operational matters—but we were able to ask the chief for alternative methods of providing security instead of officers on paid duty. But this got lost in a mist of other political turmoil.

We expect police to be professionals. In my mind, it is demeaning for them to be doing such low-level jobs, standing around when somebody is changing traffic light bulbs or becoming a uniformed flag person on a construction site. How is this core police work? The *Police Services Act* defines core policing services as crime prevention, law enforcement, providing assistance to victims of crime, public order maintenance and emergency response, in that order. Nowhere does it mention standing beneath a traffic light while a bulb is being replaced. It is akin to a doctor standing guard outside the operating room in his off-hours to ensure no one walks into the operating room—and getting paid for it by the patient!

There should be a limit to how many hours of paid duty officers can do in a week. They are working a full shift, quite often doing overtime, and then taking on paid duty. After working all those hours, how rested and physically fit is an officer to come and perform regular duty the next day? There are officers who put in paid duty at a construction site before their shift begins, then work an eight-hour shift, then go to a nightclub to provide security through paid duty. When do you sleep if you are so busy filling your bank account? One constable drew praise from police brass as a "high flyer." "We don't know when he sleeps," Deputy Chief Kim Derry once told me in wonder. "Doesn't that worry you?" I replied.

Blair had instituted a system that made the opportunity to do paid duty more equitable, not just the domain of those working in downtown divisions. But he didn't cut it back. The chief once said in a conversation where I was present that he liked to put an extra $10,000 or so in the pockets of his men and women each year. I was stunned. So much of the paid-duty gig seems like a monopoly fleecing the public for its self-interest. Here was a chief who not only had your back, he was also watching your bank account. The upshot is that you have constables making $160,000 to $200,000, by taking on overtime and paid duty—in many cases, doubling their salaries. It all adds up.

Most residents probably don't know Toronto police run a lifeguard program, despite it overlapping with the city-run system that is visible at beaches and pools.

Then there is the question of crossing guards. The Toronto Police Service runs the network of school crossing guards across the city, budgeting $6.8 million for the program. In each division, a police constable or sergeant co-ordinates the guards, keeping tabs on who is working, who is sick and who needs to be fired in their division. Nobody really counts the cost of using up to twenty officers to manage a duty that is not a core function of policing. It may be popular with parents, it may be necessary, but it is not a core police service. Crossing guards are generally paid $12 to $15 per hour, but when they are ill or otherwise absent from work, Toronto police officers fill in at full salary.

In 2015, Toronto police officers were making sure children got across the street safely for 3,138 hours, taking the officers away from core police duties. Blair delighted in telling everyone that his first job, as a rookie constable, was crossing-guard duty. I once proposed outsourcing the crossing-guard duty and I have the scars to prove it. I wanted to maintain the function but get it out of policing, but my move was misinterpreted by parents and the blowback was enormous. Apparently they thought I was recommending their kids dodge traffic on their own. I was simply questioning whether this was a core police function and a good use of highly paid police resources.

It was against this frustrating backdrop of history and culture that the board accepted Ford's target of a 10 percent budget cut. As I have described, Blair met the first year's 4.6 percent target by selling a patchwork of cuts to Ford directly. By the next year distrust between board and chief had escalated. The feeling among board members was that the chief was not serious about finding savings, and there was no point wasting time if he was not going to move. Whenever the board asked a question, the answer from the police service was, "No, you can't do that. No, that's not possible." There was no longer any dialogue or consideration.

After approving the 2012 budget with a 4.6 percent cut to police spending, we needed further cuts in 2013 of 5.4 percent. But when the new police contract was figured in, the 2012 budget actually came in at $936 million, $6 million higher than the 2011 one. We had always understood that Blair's backroom deal with Mayor Ford would only delay real action—ward off the day of reckoning. And so, when approving the budget in October 2011, the board had directed Blair to engage outside expertise to conduct a comprehensive organizational review to identify options for meeting the next year's 5.4 percent target. The board had also asked that the proposals in my discussion paper be considered as part of this review, along with recommendations from the city's shared services and efficiency studies.

Blair had told the board there was $250,000 left in the coffers that could be used to pay for this review. But before the board dealt with the matter, Blair asked me that we let him oversee the review. My reaction was, "Chief, you are the expert. You should oversee the external review." All I asked was that he get the board's support and buy-in for the work by involving it in developing the review's terms of reference and the process for the selection of a consultant. And this is what the board had approved. But Blair did not follow through on either of these things. When some months had passed and there had been no contact with the board about the review terms of reference and the hiring of a consultant, I sent him a memo requesting an update. There was no response.

Then one day one of his deputies, Mike Federico, requested to meet with me over lunch about the matter. Federico told me they were proceeding with the review and would bring in a consultant. However, to save costs, the preliminary information gathering was being done internally under his direction. I had some misgivings about this approach because I thought information on how the force operates day to day and who does what would be better collected independently. However, I understood the logic behind this approach and was reassured that a consultant would be brought in. I assumed that, as per the motion approved by the board, we would be consulted as well.

That did not happen. Blair did not initiate a consultation or give us updates. Instead, he launched his own review, grandly called the "Chief's Internal Organizational Review" or CIOR, complete with a fancy website and all the bells and whistles imaginable. An army of police officers and civilians from all ranks was deployed; Federico was named the project sponsor, and a project charter, mission and anything else you could possibly want were created. This was not an external review and the board had remained excluded. It came to a head one day some months later. By then, the CIOR was well under way. I requested that Blair join me, Thompson and Pringle in a meeting in the seventh-floor boardroom at police headquarters. The purpose was to discuss the agreed-upon review and how exactly it would help us reach the 5.4 percent reduction in the next budget.

Blair talked about his CIOR and how comprehensive it was. It was as if there had been no conversation about a review by an external expert or the board's involvement in developing the terms of reference and the hiring of a consultant. So I brought out the minutes of the relevant board meeting. Blair said he couldn't remember. Then he said that, in any case, he didn't have any money. He was reminded about the discussion in which he had said he had $250,000 to pay for it. He got sarcastic and retorted that this was a $1 million project, what was he going to do with $250,000?

I had no option but to simply lay the information before the board and leave it up to the members to decide what should be done. It didn't surprise me when the board, upon receiving my report, chose to do nothing. It failed to hold Blair accountable and meekly went along with a review that was different from what it had approved and would not be completed in time to be of any help in preparing next year's budget. Before the review could be completed, the time to prepare next year's budget was upon us. Not only did we not have any recommendations from an outside expert, we had also been informed by Blair that he could not give us a budget that was in line with the target—his budget would be off by more than $19 million.

The board's budget subcommittee found itself at sea and all but stopped functioning. Thompson and I realized that to achieve the 5.4 percent, we would have to act unilaterally. I made a list of options and we sat down to come up with a strategy. The night before the board meeting to finalize the police budget, scheduled for December 10, 2012, I got city manager Pennachetti and budget director Josie La Vita on the phone and described to them a plan that combined a hiring freeze, personnel cuts and the deferral of certain expenses among a set of measures aimed at achieving the target. The bottom line? A 5.4 percent budget cut.

We discussed the pros and cons of the options on the list and La Vita crunched the numbers. We had a plan, which I wrote up as recommendations for the board. The next morning, before the confidential meeting of the board at 9 a.m., I shared the plan with Thompson, who backed me. We decided against sharing the recommendations with anyone until the board's public meeting later that afternoon. We did not want to risk a leak, which would allow Blair time to mount a counterattack. Our strategy worked. The police service budget came up for the board's consideration at the public meeting. We first heard public deputations and then I opened the item up for questions and comments by board members.

Finally, the item was ready for consideration by the board. Only board members can participate in discussion at this point in the meeting, unless there is a question. This is when I announced that I had some recommendations on the budget and gave copies of my proposal to the board members. This was not unusual; as chair, I regularly made recommendations on reports that were before the board. It was only when my colleagues saw the recommendations that they realized the significance of what was being proposed. The board was being asked to set aside the budget being put forward by the chief and substitute its own. Under the board's meeting procedures, Blair would have no chance to respond. The motion passed unanimously and we had a budget that met the reduction target.

Blair sat at the table and watched as the budget cuts passed. He and Chief Administrative Officer Veneziano, sitting next to him, looked at each other as if to say, "What just happened here?" He had been silenced and sidelined. Pringle described the recommended solution as "elegant." We had met our target, but it was a pyrrhic victory.

Thompson and I had concluded some months ago, following the meeting with Blair about the CIOR, that the transformation work that was needed would not happen under Blair's leadership. It was our assessment that in his second term, Blair was more interested in defending and preserving his legacy. And that was probably as far as he would go in terms of creating significant change. The direction we wanted to go—a new model of policing and a different way of doing business—was one he would not support. We had nothing against Blair as a person. We just didn't think he could go any further in terms of being a change-maker.

If anything, Blair's actions—circumventing the board about the previous year's budget, the threat of legal action, Eley's memo cutting off the supply of information to me and the board, the refusal to respond to inquiries about several policy issues including the strip-searching of people detained by officers and ignoring board direction on the organizational review—showed a deliberate intent to chart his own course. In any other organization, be it in the public sector or the private sector, if the CEO acted in this way the directors would not accept it. In policing, the *Police Services Act* and the chief's contract make it virtually impossible to let the chief go. Some of the matters that caused us concern may have looked like insubordination but as our legal counsel advised us, the definition of insubordination by a chief in the *Act* made it an extremely hard case to argue.

Thompson and I had concluded that our only recourse was to buy out the remainder of Blair's contract. I sought the advice of the board's legal counsel about the process that would be involved and explored with city officials their willingness to provide the needed funds. But before going to the board, Thompson felt that we should get the mayor onside, so he spoke to Ford. We were in for a surprise: Ford wanted to get us all in one room with Blair to try and resolve the issues we were concerned about. We had no choice but to agree. So Ford convened a meeting where he would be the mediator.

One day in March 2012, Thompson, Nunziata and I sat on one side of Ford's conference table. Blair sat facing us and Ford chaired. He opened the meeting and asked me to share our concerns. I had prepared a briefing note for the mayor listing five concerns and went through them. Ford then turned to Blair and asked him to respond. Blair went on for a while without acknowledging any of our issues. Ford then looked at his watch and said he had another engagement. He concluded the meeting saying that we clearly had major differences and he would like us to work them out. End of mediation. We all left—in a worse situation than when we had come in.

A few days later, the mayor's brother Doug called me. He said, "Doc, you know that Rob has his own issues, and the chief is popular. If you let him go, there will be a reaction and the heat will be on Rob. He doesn't need another controversy. Please manage." So the confrontation phase continued. Blair knew where the chair and the vice-chair stood. Some board members who were close to him had also come to know about what Thompson and I wanted. Now I had a board that was even more divided. Blair began to come to meetings accompanied by his lawyer. He would bring a big notebook and make a show of writing down his conversations with members. His supporters suddenly started finding more faults with how the board functioned. We were back, once again, in the viper's nest—the description Heisey had used when he resigned in frustration.

The board was fractured, marked by suspicion and distrust, and relations with the chief had hit rock bottom. But of course the work on CIOR chugged along, with little information given to the board and little involvement by it in the process. Finally, Blair produced a report that essentially recommended a shifting of chairs, some new titles, some housekeeping and little else. He advised the board that he had already started implementing the recommendations that were strictly operational and did not require board involvement. The report was presented in public with great fanfare, as if it were a blueprint for transforming policing in Toronto.

And keep in mind that Blair brought out his shiny CIOR well after the budget had been approved. The report was supposed to have been completed a year earlier, as it was originally intended to help with budget preparation in 2012. And the savings? Blair trumpeted a cost-cutting amount of $1.8 million. This did nothing to achieve the reduction target of 5.4 percent. Not only that—as an assessment by consultants from KPMG would point out—it had cost more than that to do the work on CIOR. The KPMG consultants pegged the price tag at $2 million, not including all the time put in by salaried staff assigned to the project. The cost was double what Blair himself had claimed it would take to do an external review.

Although Blair had not followed up on his original recommendation for an external review, he did bring in an external expert—a team from Ernst & Young headed by a former assistant commissioner of police from England. They had done two studies: one in response to my proposal to reduce the layers of hierarchy, and the other answering the question posed by the city's budget chief and, subsequently, a board member, Mike Del Grande: What is the "right number" of police officers the service needs to provide "adequate and effective services" as required by law?

My discussion paper had suggested that we do away with two ranks: staff inspector and staff superintendent. Ernst & Young recommended that only the rank of staff inspector be eliminated. Regarding Del Grande's question about numbers, lo and behold, they had come up with the same number of officers Blair had advocated. It was the number we already had. In effect, what the Ernst & Young recommendation did was say that Blair had it right all along.

When Blair shared the results of his CIOR study with the board, not one member reacted. There was no discussion. The board received his report politely without giving any recommendations or direction. How else could it have reacted? This glitzy report from a project that had taken two years was not what we had asked for, and its results were no help in re-engineering the organization or reducing the cost of policing. A few months after the CIOR report was presented, the board approved my recommendation to contract an external expert to assess the results of this project and provide the board with a road map for change. With funding from the city, we selected KPMG for this task. It was clear from KPMG's assessment that many of the projects done under CIOR had not been done properly and were of little value. KPMG also showed us what could be done today, in a year and in three years. It gave us an accounting of what it would cost to implement its recommendations for a major trans-formation of Toronto police.

As these developments were happening, Mayor Ford's personal life began to come under scrutiny. A slow trickle of rumours got big-ger over time—rumours about his drinking, his family life, his drug addiction, as well as rumours about police shielding him. Several people—journalists and city councillors—told me they found it odd that Ford was never caught or charged with drunk driving. He always insisted on driving himself and adamantly turned down offers to have someone from the police service drive him around. Only much later in his term was he prevailed upon to get a driver. Rumours that he was drinking in his office were later confirmed by his chief of staff of the day, Mark Towhey. Rumour even had it that, on occasion, police had escorted him home when he was found to be driving impaired.

I was informed that certain reporters were probing the matter and that a story was imminent. I shared this with Blair and asked for assurance that there was no truth to the stories about police that were making the rounds. He insisted they were totally false and said he had made it clear to the force that the mayor was to be treated no differently than anyone else.

One incident that raised journalistic eyebrows was a contro-versial 911 call that Ford made in the early hours of one morning following a domestic dispute with his wife, Renata. Apparently, the Fords got into an extreme argument and the mayor called 911 for assistance. It was alleged that during the call he was being a bully, using foul language, identifying himself as the mayor in a threatening way, and addressing the female dispatcher using vulgar, sexist language. Somehow, the incident became public and the details were reported in the press. First thing that morning, Blair retrieved the audio recording of the exchange and placed it under lock and key in his possession. As a result, the content of the conversation could not be ascertained.

But within a day Blair publicly claimed that, on the request of Doug Ford, he had personally reviewed the recording and determined that while the mayor had used strong language, he had not said anything vulgar or sexist. This stunned seasoned reporters; they could not recall anything like this taking place before. Blair went one step further and turned the recording over to the commissioner of the OPP for his personal review. The commissioner then made a public statement that backed up Blair's.

This was one instance of the way in which Ford's personal life drew media attention. There was much talk of loud, late-night arguments between the inebriated couple and how their two children were not receiving proper care. Some reporters even attempted to camp out outside the Ford residence. The media attention had become so intrusive that there was a full-time police presence outside the home's front entrance to keep people at bay.

People told me they saw these things as proof that Ford was receiving preferential treatment from the Toronto police. According to them, although there was no evidence that Ford had ever raised a hand against Renata, he was committing verbal assaults that were severe enough to merit investigation as domestic violence. Further, they argued that this home environment was causing neglect of the children that was sufficiently serious that the police should have called in Children's Aid. It puzzled them that the police had taken no such action despite being present at the home, as surely they would have if these things were happening in another home. The only answer, they were convinced, was that the police were protecting Ford.

Therefore, it came as a big surprise when the Toronto police began investigating allegations about Ford's drug use and his connections to gang members. The American online publication *Gawker* had broken a story, verified by the *Toronto Star*, about the existence of a video showing Ford smoking crack cocaine with some unsavoury companions and making off-colour comments, including what sounded like a homophobic slur against Liberal leader Justin Trudeau. As the story mushroomed, so did the police investigation. I was questioned about the propriety of Toronto police investigating the city's mayor—whom many members of the media and the public inaccurately considered to have ultimate authority over policing.

I answered that the mayor exercises no authority over the police except when participating as a member of the police board, and further, it was a test of the independence guaranteed to the police service by law that it could carry out a proper and honest investigation of the city's highest official. However, not all of my fellow board members took this view—especially a couple of the city councillors. In an informal conversation with Blair in my office, they told him that while they realized the board had no jurisdiction over an operational matter like a criminal investigation, they felt strongly that having Toronto police investigate the mayor was inappropriate. The Fords did, however, make an attempt to involve the board.

After the video evidence had been acquired and reviewed by investigators, Blair, while speaking to journalists, commented that as a resident of this city, he was "disappointed" by the mayor's conduct. A war of words had been going on between him and Doug Ford. Doug Ford reacted angrily to Blair's remark, claiming that it had damaged the mayor's chances of getting a fair trial should he be charged. He asserted that Blair had engaged in political partisanship. One morning while being interviewed by CBC Radio's *Metro Morning* show, Doug Ford announced that he would be writing to me demanding an investigation of Blair's conduct. He followed this up with a phone call to me in which he said he would be sending a formal written complaint. He did so several days later.

I explained to Doug Ford that under the law, the board could not direct the chief in operational matters and did not have the authority to undertake a conduct investigation. I further advised him that the right course for the Fords would be to lodge a public complaint with the OIPRD about the chief's conduct. If the OIPRD accepted the complaint, it would direct the board on a proper process to follow. He said he would take my advice but eventually dropped the matter. The net effect of these dramatic developments was that we could not count on the mayor and his ever-evolving team to continue their strong political support for our reform efforts.

By the time the KPMG report was completed, the board had decided against extending Blair's term and John Tory had been elected the new mayor. When the report was presented to the board, there was an enthusiastic response. Mayor Tory said that the changes outlined in the report were exactly what we needed to do. And Pringle, who was helping to organize a board retreat for strategic planning, had decided to structure it around the KPMG report. It appeared that we were finally moving in the right direction, despite all the difficulties that had come our way. And there had been many. Despite all that, the board's work had carried on.

7

New Mayor, New Chief

ON APRIL 25, 2015, Bill Blair would complete ten years at the helm of the Toronto Police Service. His employment agreement required him to inform his employer, the police services board, nine months before the end of his term whether he wished to continue. The board would then have three months to make its decision. Blair had written to the board requesting another extension to his tenure. On July 30, 2014, all seven members of the board met to consider his request. I opened the discussion by reminding the board we were not undertaking a performance appraisal of Blair, but determining the future leadership of the organization in light of our major strategic priorities.

There was a clear consensus that Blair had provided good leadership since assuming office in 2005 and had brought about significant changes to the police service. At the same time, there was virtually unanimous agreement that the challenges we now faced in transforming the organization would require new leadership. Indeed, the board members were so focused on the issue of transformation that they felt strongly that we should look beyond the Toronto Police Service—even internationally—for Blair's successor. On this basis, the board decided by a majority of 6–1 to deny his request for an extension. I called Blair at his cottage after the board meeting and conveyed the decision. The board had decided that a public announcement would be made immediately after I had spoken to Blair. During our phone conversation, I read him the text of the announcement.

There was intense public speculation about his successor, with a significant section of the community backing Peter Sloly. However, this was not to be. Yet another episode in this long-running drama began with the entry of a new actor, John Tory, who was elected to replace Rob Ford as mayor in October 2014. A week before taking office, on November 27, the mayor-elect proclaimed that he was "not at all satisfied" with the relationship between the board and the police service, and declared that he planned on taking "a strong leadership role" in addressing this issue: "I understand the fact and accept that there will always be some healthy tension in these relationships. However, without any attempt to assess blame, I believe those relationships have become increasingly polarized on all sides and this has led to a lack of progress on achieving our goal of safe, effective policing and of maintaining the confidence of the entire community in our police services."[1]

This was widely interpreted as a rebuke of the board. I responded that I entirely agreed with what he had said, including his recognition that there should be a "healthy tension" between the board and the police service. And then I added, "However, that tension appears to be heightened currently because both the Board and the Service are involved in dealing with particularly complex and tough issues related to the long-term sustainability of the policing services and the relationship between the police and the community in our city. These are difficult issues that both of us are committed to resolving. And we are committed to resolving them together in the best interest of the community."[2]

The extended and painful dance around the policy on racial profiling and carding was clearly one of these complex issues. We did not know where Tory stood on the issue. During the election campaign he had avoided the subject. He had, however, been asked by a reporter whether he believed in the existence of "white privilege."

"White privilege?" Tory had replied. "No, I don't know that it does [exist]. I think there are people left behind, and what I think they need is a hand up from people of all skin colours and religions and backgrounds."[3] This statement had drawn considerable criticism.

It was well known that Tory was a friend and strong supporter of Blair. At times when Blair had been the subject of severe public condemnation—for his role in the G20 debacle, for example—Tory had defended the chief vociferously on the talk show he hosted on Toronto's CFRB 1010 radio. Most recently, when the board had decided not to extend Blair's contract, Tory had publicly criticized us.

When Tory ran unsuccessfully for mayor in 2004, he received a public endorsement from the Toronto Police Association. He had accepted the endorsement, raising questions about his judgment. Only much later, after losing that election, did he acknowledge his mistake. This action subsequently led to the board implementing a policy prohibiting the involvement of police officers and by extension their association from engaging in political activity during municipal elections. They were not to endorse or campaign for any candidate.

The impression that Tory had close ties with the police association and its president, Mike McCormack, persisted. After Tory became mayor, there was intense speculation as to whether he would take the seat reserved for the mayor on the police board. As the speculation continued he played coy but continued to comment on policing matters. Given his evident interest in them, it was surprising to us that he had not asked for a briefing from the board. It was rumoured, however, that he had come to police headquarters several times to meet with Blair.

He did finally request a meeting with me and I agreed to meet with him for an hour that same day. All board members except for Thompson and Nunziata attended (Del Grande had decided not to run for re-election in 2014). It was a cordial meeting in which I gave Tory an overview of the key issues the board was dealing with and explained how this was a historic moment for policing. If the board succeeded, its legacy would be a transformed system of policing.

Tory listened and engaged in the conversation. I hoped that the briefing would give him a first-hand appreciation of what we were grappling with. As he was leaving, he said he would come back for more discussion. He never did.

Tory was to become a major actor in this long-running battle over racial profiling and carding. We were soon to find out how he intended to demonstrate his promised "strong leadership role." He announced his decision to join the police board, and he also radically changed the equation within the board by dropping Thompson and Nunziata and appointing Shelley Carroll and Chin Lee. It was clear from his other actions and pronouncements that he meant to be actively involved in the police board—not as one of seven members but as the leader.

Lee had been a member before. He was well liked and was seen as a reasonable, level-headed politician with a low-key style. I knew Carroll from her days as the city's budget chief during the David Miller era. We had worked well together and shared concerns about the cost of policing. Although I was not disturbed by the appointment of Lee and Carroll, I had lost three valuable and strong allies: Thompson, Nunziata and Del Grande. They had stood by me and had not been intimidated by the tactics meant to undermine the board's efforts to enact change.

The public gaze was on Tory. People even speculated that he would rescind the board's decision on Blair's contract and keep him on. Amid all this speculation, a young Black journalist named Desmond Cole had published an article in the April 2015 issue of *Toronto Life* describing in very powerful language his encounters with Toronto police. He claimed that he had been stopped and documented more than fifty times simply for being Black and being in the wrong place. The article changed the debate, and suddenly the fight against profiling and carding was no longer limited to community activists, lawyers and a handful of reporters.

A new group was born, Concerned Citizens Against Carding, with membership drawn from the city's elite. It was the initiative of

Gordon Cressy and his partner, Joanne Campbell, a dynamic duo and veterans of city politics. Both had been city councillors. Cressy had gone on to other important positions, including president and CEO of the United Way of Greater Toronto. Campbell had served as the president of Toronto's housing authority, the largest public landlord in the country. Cressy had also been born and raised on the same street as Tory; they had attended the same schools.

Cressy and Campbell were deeply affected by Cole's *Toronto Life* piece and concluded that they needed to join the battle. They came out of retirement and convinced an impressive list of powerful voices to take a strong public position on this issue—stop carding. At a press conference hosted by Thompson in the lobby of City Hall, a who's-who lineup delivered that message to Tory. Apparently some of them, like former Ontario cabinet minister Mary Anne Chambers, who had endorsed Tory during the election campaign, had attempted to contact him on their own and Tory would not return their calls. But now, after Concerned Citizens Against Carding made its demand in public, Tory wanted to meet with them.

I was asked to join Tory in a meeting with Cressy, Chambers and Dr. Anne Golden. Chambers was not just a former provincial cabinet minister; she had been a senior bank executive and a highly respected leader in the Black community. And Golden had been president of the Conference Board of Canada and, like Cressy, head of the United Way. Tory began by expressing his disappointment that they had gone public and not tried to contact him directly. Cressy bluntly told him to get over it because it was more important to address the issue. And Chambers pointed out that his claim was untrue as far as she was concerned—he had not returned her calls.

Chambers had come armed with information about what had been going on, and concrete proposals about what should be done. She had stayed in close contact with many of us throughout the imbroglio with Blair over carding, and speaking and providing advice to people like me and Audrey Campbell, who was a steady hand as the community co-chair of the PACER advisory committee and former president of the Jamaican Canadian Association. At a time when the level of trust between the police service and the community—especially the Black community—had cratered, Chambers had performed her difficult role honourably, professionally and with great clarity about the objective she was pursuing.

So when Tory spoke about his support for the policy the board had been struggling to implement under Blair and referred to conversations that had taken place between him and people like Campbell, Chambers pulled out printouts of emails she had received that provided a very different account of what had transpired. Tory brought me into the conversation and asked that I tell the delegation about the hard work we were doing. I kept things objective, avoided criticism of anyone like Blair, and gave an overview of our goals and the concerns we had heard. In the end, Cressy, Chambers and Golden spoke individually and said bluntly that carding had to stop.

In the meantime, in late December, word got out that Blair had done just that: in a quiet move, he had issued a confidential order to his officers that they were no longer required to fill out so-called contact cards. In response, even astute people like Howard Morton, a prominent lawyer and former head of the Special Investigations Unit, had reacted favourably. However, when I read the fine print of Blair's order, I realized he had not actually ended carding. He had driven it underground and made it harder to monitor.

Individual officers did not have to submit contact cards for every interaction. They were to retain the details in their memo books. At the end of an officer's shift, his or her supervisor was to review the memo book entries in accordance with two other service procedures and decide what information was to be retained in the police database. Members of the public would no longer be able to ask police about contact card information about them, since there would be no such thing. Information would now reside in officers' memo books, which were not shown to the public, and no one would know what information was in the police database. As people began to realize the implications of Blair's actions, the initial sense of relief vanished.

So public pressure continued when Tory attended his first police board meeting on December 15, 2014. The room was packed and there was a long line of deputations. People who had spoken to the board many times before came again, except this time they were there to speak to Tory. The night before the meeting, he called me to discuss how I intended to handle this item. He was worried about the meeting getting out of hand and people becoming uncivil. I assured him that we had done this many times before and that the people who had asked to address the board knew the rules. However, I did offer to draft some possible motions as the deputants spoke, based on what they had to say. I don't know if he was reassured, nor what worried him. That he would be attacked by a phalanx of Black community activists?

As the meeting convened, it was clear that all eyes were on Tory. There were deputations by several individuals and organizations and included people like Barbara Hall, chief commissioner of the Ontario Human Rights Commission, Noa Mendelsohn Aviv of the Canadian Civil Liberties Association, Anthony Morgan of the African Canadian Legal Clinic and Valerie Steele of the Black Action Defence Committee. They made impassioned pleas. Tory sat next to me, listening, as I drafted possible motions. The deputations lasted two hours. Once they were finished, I asked if any of the board members wished to speak. Silence. Tory asked to make some comments. He had been writing as people were speaking and he made a masterful speech, incorporating and acknowledging many of the submissions. He didn't mince words, called racial profiling "corrosive" and unambiguously called on the police service to move forward with the implementation of the board's policy on community contacts or carding. Then some of the board members spoke up in support of what Tory had said. A pattern had been established, it would seem. From then on, board members would take their cues from him.

On my suggestion, Tory moved the motions that I had drafted. The board voted unanimously to "reaffirm its commitment" to the April 2014 policy directing Blair to go back to the table with Frank Addario and the board subcommittee to finalize the missing parts of the policy, and Blair and I were to report back the following February with a completed policy and an implementation plan. Blair sat in grim silence. But Tory later told me that he believed Blair wanted to do the right thing and very much wanted to bring the matter to a close before he stepped down. I replied that this would be in keeping with what I had come to know about him and his values from a decade of working with him. I expected that Tory would use his relationship with Blair to break the logjam.

By February of 2015, however, there had been no progress. I was out of the country when a special meeting of the board was convened at Tory's suggestion in which he proposed that we seek mediation by a well-respected senior judge. I joined the meeting by phone from Barcelona. This was an unprecedented approach; I was not aware of any instance in Canada where a police board had sought to resolve a policy dispute with its chief—an employee—in this way. Board members, apparently grasping at the straws, eagerly agreed with Tory's idea. So did Blair. But, I wonder if this was a charade.

We set to work finding a mediator when I returned. Former chief justice of Ontario Warren Winkler agreed and could meet with us on very short notice. Both the board and Blair were happy with the choice of Winkler. We met for two and a half days in March. Blair came with his executive officer, Inspector Stu Eley, and I was accompanied by Andy Pringle, Marie Moliner and Addario. I felt confident that Winkler had briefed himself well through separate preparatory meetings. And Addario had put together an excellent written submission setting out the issues. Blair provided no such material; he was jovial and even nonchalant. At the end of the process, a new document emerged that purported to incorporate most of what had been in the policy that the board had approved and had fought for all along. It was presented to the board on April 2, 2015, for approval, almost a year to the date after it had approved the original policy. The new policy recognized a police officer's "discretion in the performance of his or her duties" but specified that this discretion must be exercised in a "principled manner, reflecting the values of fairness, respect, individual dignity and equality." It also proposed that the name of the policy be changed from "community contacts" to "community engagements" and it set out several principles. These principles were by and large a reiteration of the elements of the April 2014 board policy.

The name change was not just cosmetic. The title of the previous policy placed the focus on the issue that bothered the community—police officers stopping and making contact with people, especially Black and other racialized people, who were not under criminal investigation for the purpose of questioning and gathering information in the name of public safety. The new title sounded more benevolent by suggesting that the policy provided guidance to police officers on how they should engage with members of different communities. In so doing, it recast contact between police and community as merely a component of positive interaction integral to community-based policing. It thus took the focus away from the issue that was agitating the public mind. As well, of course, the name change appeared to align the board policy with the police service's initiatives, namely PACER.

Though the proposed policy claimed to incorporate most of what was contained in its predecessor, gone was the requirement for police officers to advise people of their right not to remain when stopped during an informal interaction and their right to not answer questions. Officers would do so only if asked by an individual. At the same time, officers would not use these informal occasions to engage in "psychological detention." And while they would no longer have to automatically offer a receipt with all the details of the interaction, they would provide a business card with their name, badge number and contact number. There would be a review of the implementation in a few months' time, at which point the board would have an opportunity to make any necessary improvements.

Blair promised to move forward promptly with this new accord. He felt it was balanced. I believed we had gone as far as we could under the circumstances and once a new chief was in place, the pieces that had been eliminated or watered down could be restored.

On the night of the second day of the mediation, Pringle called me at home to confess he was not comfortable with the outcome. "Andy, there will be a firestorm of controversy, and all of us will have to work very, very hard to win public support. But what choice do we have?" I told him.

So on the third day all of us signed off. After Blair and Eley had left, Winkler wanted to talk to Pringle, Moliner and me. He made a very strong case for the board appointing an independent monitor who would have the freedom to go anywhere to observe all functions of the police service and thus tell the board if the policy was in fact being followed.

We didn't get that far. Around 11:30 p.m. on March 17, Tory emailed me a long message outlining his vision for rolling out the results of the mediation and new policy publicly. Tory's two key backroom boys, Chris Eby and Vic Gupta, also called me. They pushed me to work the phones to get people from the Black community, especially the "reasonable" ones, behind the new direction. When I did call my key contacts, I got a guarded reaction. They were suspicious and wanted to know what the deal—which they believed had been engineered by Tory—had cost in terms of watering down the original policy approved by the board.

While these conversations were going on, a meeting of the police service's PACER advisory committee was scheduled for just a few days after the mediated resolution was reached. Blair suggested we divulge the deal to the group, even though the board had not yet made it public. He and I shared with committee members the broad strokes of the deal. There was skepticism in the room, but no move to reject the deal. Blair's supposed abolition of carding elicited many questions. Finally, a joint press conference was held at police headquarters on March 27, 2015, in which Blair, Tory and I announced the result of the mediation. Winkler was present but did not comment.

I went first, saying that the new policy "strikes the right balance" and reassuring the community that "nobody expects this policy and the service's procedure to be a final, perfect solution to community engagements." I said that as we received feedback and analyzed data, modifications might be required. My comments were intended to signal to the community that the mediated policy was only an interim measure. Blair followed, resolving to fully implement the revised policy now that his operational concerns had been addressed. Lastly, Tory, speaking as mayor, hailed the resolution and congratulated the board and the chief.

A volley of questions followed. They were directed primarily at me and Blair. But slowly, Blair took over and spoke in his usual voluble way. From the questions, it was clear that there was a lot of suspicion—what exactly had the board given up to gain Blair's support? The worst was yet to come, and it came very soon. When the board held a special meeting on April 2 to approve the new policy, it faced a roomful of angry community advocates and ordinary members amid mounting criticism. Casting about for a way out, the board deferred consideration to yet another meeting on April 16 with the following caveats:

1. there will be a public report from the chief of police that describes the details of the data collection, retention and disclosure of personal information that will occur in accordance with...the Community Engagements policy,
2. board members will consult with the PACER advisory committee, and
3. there will be a public report from the Community Engagements Sub-Committee (Andy Pringle, Marie Moliner and Alok Mukherjee) that outlines the criteria the board will apply to a future review of the policy.

Tory's backroom boys called me again. Eby was upset and tried to pin the blame on me, saying I hadn't done enough to line up support in the Black community. "Chris, are you now blaming me for this fiasco?" I asked. I pointed out that I had made calls, but Blair had upstaged us by disclosing the deal at the PACER advisory committee meeting before we had the opportunity to implement a proper communications plan. And furthermore, I pointed out, I did not work for the mayor and it was not my job to protect his ass. Eby backed off, saying it was his job to protect the mayor's interests. I responded that he should do his work and not dictate to me. As board chair, I worked in the board's interest, not the mayor's.

While all of this was unfolding, I met with Addario and his team to decide what more we could do to build public support. Former *Globe and Mail* journalist Kirk Makin was brought in to provide communications strategy. With Makin's assistance, we decided to publish an op-ed in the *Toronto Star* jointly authored by Blair, Tory and me. Tory's people agreed. Addario contacted the newspaper's op-ed page editor, who held space for us in the next day's paper. Makin helped us prepare a draft, which we shared with Tory's staff. They suggested some modifications, which we incorporated. The revised version was then sent to Blair. It was late in the afternoon, and the *Star* could not keep the space open any later than 5 p.m.

Eley finally called to say the chief would not sign on to the piece. He had a few objections, but in particular he was not prepared to give the *Star* any credit. The article acknowledged the role the newspaper had played in bringing the issue forward, alongside many other interested people from the community. Eley told us Blair would be calling Tory directly to convey his objections. We weren't surprised when Eby advised Addario that Tory would not be signing on if Blair wouldn't. I told Addario that I would not agree to an op-ed with my name only. So at the eleventh hour, we informed the *Star* that the op-ed would not be submitted.

Clearly we were no further ahead, and the deal agreed to with Winkler's guidance was gaining no traction. The board met on April 16 to consider the policy along with the reports it had asked for at the previous meeting. Blair's report committed the police service to clear criteria for the collection and retention of personal information and more importantly to a time limit of one year, after which records not required for "any historic investigations or judicial proceedings" would be purged. This was a huge gain—until now the chief had not been willing to accept such a short period for storing these data. My report recommended very specific and detailed criteria for a review of the implementation of the new policy. The board strengthened this further by adding that the review would take place in six months and that "the policy will continue to be reviewed every six months."

We hoped that these modifications and commitments would satisfy people, but the community would not budge. In deputations and in the media, there was an avalanche of criticism. When the board met on April 16, people lined up to castigate it for caving in and selling out. Thus, Blair's term ended with the issue unresolved, even though the policy was approved that day. The board had lost public credibility. Its contortions had made it a laughingstock.

On April 25, 2015, Blair served his last day in office. There was a warm ceremony in the lobby of police headquarters. Employees turned out in large numbers to greet him, bid him farewell and take photos with him. I went down too. We embraced and had a last picture taken as chief and chair. Along with hundreds of people, I applauded as the Chief's Ceremonial Unit marched him out of the building. He was a proud man to the end. Despite our disagreements and conflict, I respected his intelligence, his love for the city, his socially progressive values. He had served the city well. I felt emotional as he left.

We had brought in an excellent facilitator, Maureen Brown, to solicit public input in the hiring of a new chief. She organized community consultations right across the city involving the general public, young people, police community liaison committees, businesses and all three levels of elected politicians. We also re-engaged Paul Stanley and Tanya Todorovic from the executive search firm Odgers Berndtson to plan and execute a global search. They had helped the board in 2005 with the selection of Blair and his deputies.

Late one evening the previous December, Gupta from Tory's staff had asked to meet me for coffee. We met at the Starbucks directly behind City Hall. Gupta said the mayor would like to work closely with me on selecting the new chief. I answered that this would be very helpful and that it made absolute sense because the chief would have to have a good relationship with both the board chair and the mayor. Then Gupta posed a question that made me sit up. He asked if I could think of any internal candidate for the job other than Peter Sloly.

Sloly was the senior-most deputy chief and one of a handful of Black senior police officers in Toronto. He was young, had risen through the ranks rapidly and had been assigned to a variety of roles in the service, so he knew the organization well. He had an MBA and enjoyed an international reputation as an innovative thinker and reformer. He was leading PACER, the police service's critical project on the controversial issue of police interactions with members of racialized communities. He was community oriented and had a strong public presence and credibility. Within the organization, he was known for his commitment to inclusive, non-discriminatory and anti-racist practices. Along with a handful of other Black officers including Keith Forde and David McLeod, Sloly had risked his future by challenging former chief Fantino and speaking up about racism within the force.

From the day that Sloly became a deputy chief, there had been speculation that he was headed for the chief's chair. This attention did not sit well with Blair. He had joked about it, but I had learned that behind the scenes it made relations tense. Sloly had detractors in the police association. He was not "one of the boys." Several complaints were made by the association about Sloly's management style and even his character. The association didn't like Forde or McLeod either. A curious thing—these were all Black officers. Blair himself rarely had a good word to say about Sloly. On the contrary, on several occasions he had spoken disparagingly about "Young Peter." All of which is to say that Sloly had been a marked man ever since he had stepped into the limelight.

So here we were—Gupta and I—talking about an alternative to Sloly for the chief's job. In answer to his question, I made the following points. First, if the mayor was looking for another internal candidate because Sloly was not ready, then I had to say that others were even less ready. I gave all the reasons why in my view, Sloly was the most ready to take on the chief's job. Second, I reminded Gupta that when the board had decided not to extend Blair's term, it had made it clear that we would conduct a global search for someone who could lead the kind of transformational change that we wanted.

And finally, I suggested that if the mayor was concerned about Sloly's readiness, the board could look for a tough outsider for a fixed term of three to five years, someone who could withstand the pressures of implementing major change with no internal allegiances or loyalties except to the board. One of the responsibilities of this chief would be to mentor Sloly as his senior deputy. Once the foundation for the new model had been laid, Sloly would take over the task of rebuilding. Gupta agreed that this suggestion had merit, and we left it at that. I still believed the board was serious about a global search.

Our Odgers Berndtson consultants undertook an international search and we received several applications from interested candidates within Canada and abroad. The three deputy chiefs—Sloly, Mike Federico and Mark Saunders, the latest addition to this rank—were among the internal applicants. The board decided to interview all three deputies in addition to several external candidates from both Canada and overseas. After that we were left with three internal and three external candidates. Among the externals, there were two Canadian candidates with reputations for being tough, community-oriented, progressive and open to innovation. One was former Ottawa police chief Vern White, now a senator, the other a deputy minister of community safety in another province. The third was a solid, down-to-earth police chief from England. These six were a very good group from which to pick the right person for the job we needed done. It also put our internal candidates up against some of the best.

As we were going through the process, supporters of Sloly launched a campaign to promote his candidacy. They sent letters and made phone calls to board members. They initiated media stories. While all of this was going on, Tory came to speak to me. He said he had heard rumours about Sloly and wanted to check them with me. One of them went back to the time when Sloly was a young inspector assigned to communications. The chief of the day had dealt with a complaint about Sloly's management style, though clearly since this time he had learned and matured.

The other rumours had little substance. Despite a dubious source, one had been thoroughly investigated by the service's professional standards unit and Sloly had been cleared. I confirmed to Tory that at the time of shortlisting, I had asked Blair to review the conduct files of all three deputies and advise the board if there were any concerns. Blair did so and all of them were in the clear. Tory thanked me and said he had wanted to check only because he had heard the rumours.

In the final round of interviews, we were left with two internal candidates, deputies Sloly and Saunders. The one remaining external candidate, Dale McFee, was deputy minister of community safety in Saskatchewan and former police chief of the city of Prince Albert. He had a solid reputation as an innovative police leader with a strong social justice outlook, as well as being a tough manager with an entrepreneurial background. He was also Métis.

For the pre-final round, we had prepared questions, and candidates were provided with the topics our questions would cover. In addition, each had to make a presentation on transformation and change. For the final round, board members were free to ask questions on any subject; therefore, there could be no prepared answers. After we had completed the interviews and scored the candidates, I asked each board member for their ranking of the three.

Everyone was highly impressed by the external candidate. He had the most experience, strategic thinking and leadership capability. Properly, McFee should have gotten the nod. He was a deputy minister overseeing policing throughout the province, one of his initiatives had become a national model, and he had considerable management experience; however, he did not pass muster–Tory convinced several board members that he would not be acceptable to Toronto residents because he hadn't led a big city police force.

So we were left with Saunders and Sloly, both Black candidates. Sloly had excelled in the final round of interviewing. And outside of the interview process, their track records, achievements and experience were not comparable. Again a discussion started around the table. Some of my colleagues did not approve of the "lobbying" for Sloly, which they believed had been instigated by him. I found this strange because there had been lobbying for the position in the past without criticism. They were also dissatisfied with his failure to co-operate with the board in developing the policy on carding, quite ignoring the fact that he was carrying the can for Blair. They thought his interview performance had been *too* slick, even though in the final round, which had precluded preparation, he had answered all questions superbly.

I pointed out the reputation and respect he enjoyed within the community. I also drew attention to the fact that Sloly had a broader breadth of experience in the organization, having worked in many different roles, while Saunders had a very narrow breadth, exclusively within uniform policing and most of it in homicide. His experience with community-based policing was limited to his brief tenure as head of a police division. My points were heard, but minds were made up. Tory claimed that he liked and respected Sloly, but that his choice here was based strictly on the selection process.

I felt that since there was consensus among the six other board members, there was no point in continuing the discussion. Their choice was clear: Saunders was chosen. Tory countered that he would prefer a unanimous decision. I said fine, go ahead. It made no difference anyway. I was extremely disappointed in the board members who, going in, I thought would prefer Sloly. Given that the board had made the ability to bring about transformational change a key expectation, based on the information it had about the three finalists' backgrounds and track records, the psychological assessment, and above all performance in the interviews, one of the other two candidates should have been the choice.

After much thought, I am left with two disturbing conclusions. One, that the fix was in. It seems work had begun on grooming an alternative to Sloly soon after he was made a deputy chief by the board against Blair's wishes. Saunders's rise through the senior ranks—a meteoric rise—began almost immediately after Sloly's appointment and the public speculation about Sloly being the next chief. Unlike Sloly, Forde, McLeod and other Black officers, Saunders had kept his head down, had never spoken about or involved himself in issues of discrimination, had made the right friends and had not rubbed the chief or the police association the wrong way. He was an ideal alternative, part of the establishment, someone who wouldn't rock the boat—and he had the right skin colour.

Second, this was an example of the insidious ways in which racism manifests itself. There had been a general sense that Toronto was ready for a chief who was from a racialized background, preferably Black. It would have been extremely problematic, in light of the deep concerns about the relationship between the police service and the Black community, if the board had not selected a Black chief. But this had to be balanced against the interests and comfort level of those who exercise social, economic and political power. A Black chief who was seen as too invested in the Black community, too radical, too independent of the establishment—not "one of the boys"—would not have been acceptable. But a chief who was Black and yet "one of us" would fit the bill.

Underlying this type of thinking is the notion that all the Black community cares about is the colour of the chief's skin, not what they stand for or represent. To me, this sort of thinking is racist. And I cannot shake the conclusion that the grooming and selection of this chief is an example of that. I have called it insidious because the outcome did not serve anyone's interest—not the community's and certainly not the board's. And that, too, is part of life in "the viper's nest."

Blair used to say to me, "Alok, my job is easy. I am the chief and when I give an order, all my men and women will follow it. Your job is the more difficult one, even though it involves only the seven of you. Your members are not required to follow you." It is not only about the role of the chair. Civilian governance of policing is complex. It is immensely political, not guided by clear rules, and performed by a small group of people who are thrown together by a chaotic appointment process. It is supposed to protect and defend the independence of professional policing. And yet it cannot function without having working relationships with city government, especially the mayor. And as I have shown, even though the mayor has only one vote on the board, how he or she chooses to interact with the board can and does have a huge impact on the board's ability to provide independent oversight of the police service.

Union Coup

BY ITS VERY nature, a coup relies on speed and surprise for its success. It must catch its target in an unguarded moment. In December 2014, when my efforts to transform policing in Toronto had become too much for the Toronto Police Association and its president, Mike McCormack, the union reached back for tactics that had served it so reliably over the years, resorting to intimidation to remove an impediment to the status quo. I was the target of a direct, personal and unexpected attack that aimed to get me out of the way.

The intervention of the city's new mayor at the time, John Tory, made the situation worse. The mayor's role in the attempted insurrection created more than just a headache for me as I sought to fight back. His behaviour brought into sharp focus the consequences of the role of politicians and others—including the police board—in legitimizing destructive political activity by organized and powerful police unions.

December 5, 2014, began early and well for me. I was invited to the opening session of an annual conference of the Elementary Teachers' Federation of Ontario at the Toronto Congress Centre near Pearson airport. The event would cap a week of engagements and activities that were all related to transformation, a topic that consumes the Toronto Police Service to this day. I arrived at the

conference on the Friday morning in a good mood and found myself seated beside Bill Blair in the front row. We listened intently,
sharing notes and conferring cordially. The speakers reinforced
my view that we should be investing more in education, rather
than policing.

The keynote speaker, Wab Kinew, told the audience we should
not allow police to destroy or damage the life chances of young
people with the ruinous practice of racial profiling. We should be
more innovative so that the police service is genuinely community-
based, is accountable to the public it serves, and functions as a true
partner in building safe and caring communities. Only then can
policing be a true partner in the democratic project. Kinew was elec-
trifying, enlightening and encyclopedic with his moving account of
the resilience of residential school survivors and the need for true
reconciliation in this country. And then my phone started buzzing.
And buzzing. In fact, it was suddenly manic with phone calls and
emails coming in.

I checked a couple of the messages and realized that for some
reason, McCormack had called for my resignation. Reporters were
trying to reach me from just about every Toronto newspaper, television network and radio station. Evidently the police association's
call was related to a meme from Occupy Wall Street that I had shared
on my Facebook page the night before, which had nothing to do with
the conduct of Toronto's or Canada's police officers. It was about
the current police situation in the us. How could this be grounds
for my resignation?

A message from *Toronto Sun* columnist Joe Warmington alerted
me:

> Ok. They are really going after you doc. Hopefully you can
> explain to me what was with the poster. Hang in there. The
> smear campaign seems to be in full stride.

By noon, I had received the association's statement:

ALOK MUKHERJEE MUST RESIGN

The Association is calling for Chair Alok Mukherjee to immediately resign from the Toronto Police Services Board (TPSB).

Mukherjee has crossed the line. His lack of objectivity indicates he is no longer fit to sit on a police oversight body.

Yesterday he shared activist group Occupy Wall St.'s poster on his Facebook page which not only compares police officers to terrorists but implies they are in fact far more dangerous.

His sharing of this poster is clearly unprofessional, clearly unethical and clearly seeks to undermine the very people he is paid to oversee.

We find it absolutely ironic that the chair of a civilian oversight board, set up to ensure the integrity and ethical behaviour of a police organization, would engage in this type of behaviour.

Mukherjee's obvious disdain for police, apparent lack of judgment and his personal agenda discredits and compromises the integrity not only of the Board he chairs, but the Toronto Police Service itself.

The Association will also be filing a letter of complaint with Premier Kathleen Wynne, the Solicitor General, Mayor John Tory, the Toronto Police Services Board and the Ontario Civilian Police Commission.

The communiqué went to all media and was simultaneously circulated as a poster on the association's letterhead to all units of the police service. Recipients were asked to "PLEASE POST AND READ TO ALL RELIEFS [officers coming on shift]." It had been issued in the name of the association's board of directors. This was unprecedented. Never in the history of Toronto police had the association done anything like this or engaged in this type of political activity. My immediate reaction was that I was the target of a coup attempt being staged by McCormack and possibly his vice-president, Dan Ross, claiming to be speaking for all members of the police service.

Until this point, my relationship with McCormack had been occasionally combative but generally good. His predecessor, Dave Wilson, had had a very adversarial relationship with Blair. McCormack took over as president after Wilson stepped down, emphasizing negotiation and collaboration. McCormack was the son of a former Toronto police chief, had siblings working for the service, and was thus well connected within the ranks. With him at the helm, the relationship between the union, the board and the police service started out well, with grievances dropping considerably—something he needed to do to save the association from facing a huge financial crisis. Arbitrations did not drag on—he would often call me directly even as one was in progress and I would then work with our labour relations staff on a fair and balanced settlement. Not only did it save on legal bills, it served every party's interest.

We would meet periodically, along with his vice-president, Ross, over coffee to catch up, exchange information and share ideas. McCormack and Ross knew well how my thinking about policing was evolving. We did not always agree, and we knew that our interests were not always identical. Tensions had begun to surface, especially after I took a hard public position on carding and racial profiling, and after the board accepted Mayor Ford's recommendation to reduce the police budget by 10 percent. It had not helped that I had forged a close alliance with board vice-chair Michael Thompson and the two other councillors appointed by Ford. Thompson spoke bluntly, questioned the police service's sincerity about cost reduction and was prepared to challenge the chief publicly in a not-so-subtle manner.

McCormack and Blair had a close relationship, and that had become a complicating factor. By this time, the relationship between Blair and the board—and me personally—had deteriorated to the point where he had his executive officer circulate the memo limiting communication between the police service and the board to formal requests made through the chief's office. But Blair and I were still talking to each other, even if we sometimes argued and disagreed.

In an attempt to keep the lines of communication open and preserve our relationship, when we were all in Ottawa in 2012 for our annual joint meetings, Tom Stamatakis, a Vancouver cop who was president of the Canadian Police Association, had organized a late-night meeting for McCormack, Ross, himself and me. He thought we had worked well together and had dealt with issues before. "So, sit down and fight if you need to, but work it out," he told us.

Stamatakis invited us to the bar in the Lac-Leamy Casino, across the river in Gatineau, Quebec, ordered a bottle of superlative single malt Scotch and some excellent cigars and urged us to get to it. We talked, shouted at each other and disagreed vehemently, but we were frank and open and did not lose our good humour. This lasted late into the night. We came to an understanding, although, in terms of my ideas about changes in the model and cost of policing, we didn't find common ground. Had this been a sign that our relationship was in decline? Should I have been more vigilant? I don't know, but I was determined to forge ahead with my call for big changes to policing in Toronto.

Just a few months earlier, in September 2014, the association's magazine had published a provocative cover with the headline, "All Those in Favour of Disarming Cops... Raise Your Hands." It showed the back of a man in prison garb raising both hands. Atop the headline was a quote attributed to me: "and that could even include taking away guns from some (or many) police officers." The cover was a reaction to my comments in the media on a new model of policing. I had drawn a comparison with policing elsewhere and said there was no reason why every cop in the city should be armed and why neighbourhood policing could not include special constables who were not armed and whose job it was to work with local communities on safety, as opposed to criminal issues.

When the cover caught the attention of the Toronto media, McCormack initially tried to laugh it off, saying it was meant as a joke. This portrayal of me would continue until I left the board, a decision celebrated on the association's magazine cover with a cartoon of me peeing on a police car and walking away. I was drawn as an ugly, doddering old fogey. But the association's public attacks on me began over something I had posted on my personal Facebook account the night before the teachers' conference.

I remember checking the day's fare, especially the many items of topical interest shared by my friends, colleagues and family. One item that caught my attention was a meme related to the ongoing controversy in the US about police use of deadly force and the deaths of ordinary people, mostly African-Americans, during encounters with police. This meme had been produced by an activist group that had attracted widespread attention, Occupy Wall Street. It was in the form of a poster comparing the number of Americans killed by Ebola, ISIS terrorists and the police. The numbers were three, two and five hundred plus. The poster was signed "Occupy Wall St. with Samantha Hippysam Artifoni," and at the bottom was the following message in small type:

> Just a reminder of who the enemy is in this world. #ShutitDown #BlackLivesMatter #YaMeCanse #WeAreTired

Quite frankly, due to the late hour when I came across the poster, I had not paid attention to the small print at the bottom. What had caught my eye was the attention-grabbing strategy that had been used to highlight an issue that was agitating people in the US and many other parts of the world, including Canada. The three numbers pertained to three "top of mind" concerns for Americans at that time. It seemed to me that by juxtaposing them, the meme was raising the issue of deaths caused by police in the US in a dramatic and intriguing way.

At approximately 11:15 p.m. on December 4, I shared the meme on my timeline, with the following caption in quotation marks: "I can't breathe." These were the dying words of Eric Garner, who died in a police chokehold in New York on July 17, 2014. The forty-three-year-old father of six died after police confronted him about selling loose cigarettes. Like the Sammy Yatim incident, Garner's death was captured on video. As he struggled for air, Garner told police who had him in a chokehold that he could not breathe. He told them eleven times. The words I had quoted had become the slogan for massive protests and demonstrations across the US. By placing the phrase in quotation marks, I thought I was making it clear that I was reproducing someone else's well-known and extensively quoted words.

My Facebook timeline was accessible only to those who had been accepted as a "friend." Over the years that I have used Facebook, I had posted numerous items on a wide range of subjects drawn from countless sources—from mainstream media to academic journals and alternative media. I had been as likely to share good-news stories about the contributions, good works, achievements and successes of members of Toronto police as I was to post thought-provoking news items about controversial issues near and far. My purpose had always been to share useful or interesting information and to encourage thoughtful conversation.

I had enjoyed the fact that so many people from the Toronto police force had asked to be "friends" on Facebook and as a policy, I had accepted every request once I was satisfied that the person was friends with other members of the police service whom I knew. Their presence validated Facebook as a democratic space. In the hierarchical culture of policing, only those in the highest ranks had access to the board chair. Unless I met them at a meeting or an event, people in the lower ranks generally could not contact me. But here, people of all ranks were sharing information, sending messages and commenting on articles, events and issues.

However, between the night of December 4 and the early morning of December 5, this open space was to cause me great trouble. When I checked my Facebook account in the morning, I found three responses to the Occupy Wall Street meme, from India, England and Canada. But as I was making my way to the teachers' conference, a comment appeared from a member of the Toronto Police Service, Michael Minogue, who had been a regular on my timeline for quite a while. Minogue reacted negatively to the meme, referring to the hard work done by Toronto police officers to "serve and protect" the community. At 9:24 a.m. while being driven to the conference, I responded on Facebook as follows:

> Michael, thank you so much for sharing your reaction to the post. I think it is important for us to know what is happening in other countries without taking that information as a reflection on ourselves. We do things very differently; it is useful though to know that in 2013 for example, there were 0 deaths from police interactions in the UK and 3 in Germany. These are not judgments but reasons for asking how this happened. We learn to continuously make ourselves even better. In the US there is an unhappy situation and history. The public reaction from the President to the Mayor of NYC to folks on the street is very disturbing. On November 19, I participated in a Town Hall in Baltimore with police leaders, elected leaders, academics, public and young people. There was a very intense emotion shared by them all, and they were amazed to hear about our systems and processes. You know how our Chief responded to one tragic event in the recent past; he brought in a top former Supreme Court Judge to do a review and tell us what we should do differently. Deputy Federico and I and our College folk work closely with members of the community to improve the way we train. And several times a week at every opportunity I celebrate exactly the reasons why we are so proud of how we do things. That does not stop us from asking questions of ourselves and looking for ways to do even better. We should never be defensive or close-minded.

A few minutes after I posted my response, Minogue's comment disappeared from my timeline. Comments by others from the

Toronto Police Service criticizing me for the post would appear much later, after the association's campaign was well under way.

I have no way of knowing how the association caught wind of the post, but clearly it launched an extremely well-organized campaign early in the day based on a Facebook post from late the night before. It was a coup, and the association was attacking on all fronts. On my way back to the office, I realized I would need professional support. I could not involve the board's staff or counsel, as they would have to advise the rest of the board on the police association's complaint of misconduct against me. I would need to find my own supports. After a quick mental review of my choices, I contacted Sarbjit Kaur, who had done strategic communications work for me when I was president of the provincial association of police services boards.

Kaur grasped the urgency of the situation and came on board immediately, without hesitation. She agreed to start working on a strategy and a statement right away, and to meet me in my office as soon as she could. Minutes after making these arrangements with Kaur, my phone rang again. It was Michael Thompson. Without any small talk he said, "Alok, I'm with the mayor. He wants to talk to you." Tory came on the line and after some quick formalities, I asked point blank, "Mr. Mayor, are you calling for my resignation?"

McCormack had done a round of media interviews and had been saying that Tory should demand my resignation. Reporters were seeking an answer from the mayor. Tory replied, "No, I am not going to call for your resignation, but I want you to get in front of this issue. You need to make a public statement immediately about this posting. You have to make it clear that you were not making any comment on Toronto police officers and express regret for any misunderstanding that the posting may have caused. But you have to do this right away." I told him that this was exactly my intent and I had already started drafting a statement, which I would share with him for his feedback. We ended our conversation on that note.

Ironically, Thompson had been ousted from the police board by Tory despite strong and widespread public support for his work on the board. I remain convinced that had it not been for Thompson's intervention, Tory would have called for my resignation right away. I made some revisions to the draft statement that Kaur had emailed me, and around 1:35 p.m. I sent it to the mayor's office for Tory's perusal. The mayor's office did not yet know that I was receiving professional assistance and had assumed that it would be telling me what my statement would say. While we waited to hear back from the mayor's people, Kaur held the media off. We had decided on our initial strategy: there would be a statement but no interviews. We would see how this played out over the weekend and then take further steps. We decided we could not wait for the mayor's response, so we called his senior staff, Chris Eby and Vic Gupta, who conveyed the mayor's feedback.

They told me that the mayor wanted me to apologize for the posting, but this was unacceptable to me: I regretted the reaction it had caused, but not my attempt to contribute to an important conversation that was playing out across the continent. So we considered the mayor's suggestions, accepted improvements to the language of the draft, and finalized the statement. It was sent to the mayor's office with the message that I would be releasing it shortly; if the mayor had any concerns, we needed to hear from him promptly. We waited for a bit but there was no further word. At about 3 p.m., this statement was released:

Statement by Dr. Alok Mukherjee, Chair, Toronto Police Services Board

December 5, 2014

This morning the Toronto Police Association has called for my resignation as Chair of the Toronto Police Services Board, claiming a Facebook posting I shared on my personal page in regard to the Eric Garner death shows lack of objectivity on my part.

Let me say that I very much regret the reaction caused by the posting.

I would like to make it very clear that the item was shared as a topic of interest, intended to encourage conversation and reflection. The share was not meant as an endorsement of any views contained. It was not intended to be a negative commentary in any way on members of our police service or on our practices. I am very proud of our approach to policing, our practice of continuously learning from our experience, our systems of accountability and the efforts we make to maintain positive relations with our community.

I take every opportunity to celebrate the work our police officers do to keep our communities safe and to build good relations in our neighbourhoods.

I have the utmost respect for members of the Toronto Police Service and I strive at all times to serve as Chair in a fair and professional manner.

We decided to make no other moves over the weekend, with one exception. The *Toronto Sun*'s Warmington, who had kept in touch throughout the day, was keen to talk to me. At 4:52 p.m. he emailed: "Hey Doc. You callin? Day's getting old. You okay?" I thanked him for his concern and suggested we connect over the weekend.

Overall, the press coverage my statement received during the next two days was balanced and fair. The statement appeared to have cleared the air for most media people. Other members of the community, having read or heard about the imbroglio, had also begun to respond. From a strategic point of view, it made sense to stand back and let those voices be heard. Audrey Campbell, in her capacity as the immediate past president of the Jamaican Canadian Association, had written to Tory stating that "No rational person sees this poster as an indictment of our police service." Messages like this had begun to come in from other people too, those who knew me and those who did not. They were sent to me directly, or to the premier or the mayor with a copy to me.

On Sunday I met Warmington for a lengthy interview on what I believed was the real issue driving McCormack's campaign against me—my push for a complete transformation of our model of policing, far-reaching changes to how the Toronto Police Service delivered its services and managed its business practices, and province-wide reform of collective bargaining in the police sector. This would be the response I would give in countless media interviews on Monday and Tuesday: I regretted that my post had been misinterpreted, reiterated my intention in posting it, insisted that the post was not meant to cast aspersions on Toronto police, and said I believed that McCormack was using it to sabotage the big changes the board was seeking under my leadership.

McCormack vociferously rejected my assertion and, in a burst of literary flourish, said that "the veil had been lifted on my true feelings about the police." And he had found a new line of attack: he said the statement I had made on Friday was not acceptable because I had not said explicitly that I was sorry. Sorry for what? That he would not say. But in heading down this path, he had found an ally—Tory—who had suggested an apology when given a preview of my statement but did not disapprove of the final wording. Now he was saying I should have said sorry to the members of the police service for my post.

Tory added, in the *Toronto Sun*, "I feel quite strongly that all people in public positions of responsibility like this, especially sensitive public positions, have to be extra careful about what they put on their Facebook page or put out on Twitter—they just do."[1] Tory's intervention added fuel to a fire that had appeared to be dying down. However, I was not prepared to do what Tory and McCormack wanted—for the simple reason that while I regretted the reaction and misinterpretation, I did not agree that I should be sorry for posting the meme. Kaur and my legal counsel, Howard Morton, shared my view.

The more thoughtful reporters had begun to see through the posturing and agreed with my position that this was motivated by resistance to change and concern about the collective bargaining that was set to begin soon. It appeared that by the late afternoon of Tuesday, December 9, McCormack's campaign was fizzling, especially after I went on Jim Richards's radio program on Newstalk 1010 and said I was sorry that I had offended some people with the Occupy Wall Street post. Richards clearly understood that the campaign was subterfuge—a move in anticipation of the coming contract negotiations, intended to weaken my position as management. Tory heard the interview, and seemingly deciding it amounted to the apology he sought, had his staff call Kaur to convey his approval.

But some ex-cops were not content. The Toronto Police Pensioners Association had initiated its own campaign against me to support what McCormack was doing, mobilizing its membership. A handful of retired members of the Toronto Police Service posted critical comments on my Facebook page. I also received sixty email messages beginning on the morning of Monday, December 8. At 11:51 a.m., Andrew Davie emailed: "Shame... how unprofessional." A minute later, David Watt wrote: "RESIGN!!!" Four minutes later, Peter Phoenix added, "You should quit now." At 1:13 p.m., Wilf Townley emailed, "Get out of Office and join the rabble you seem to identify with." And at 1:17, John Nosredna said, "do the right thing...pack your bags... we never wanted an immigrant in that seat to begin with!!!!" Gary Thompson's message, received at 4:24, appeared to me to sum up what these writers were saying: "I'm entitled to express my views to [sic]. YOUR [sic] A POLICE HATER."

A majority of the writers had retired after thirty to thirty-five years of working for the Toronto Police Service; a few had retired as far back as the 1980s. What they were objecting to when they accused me of being a "police hater" or a "thorn in the side of the Toronto Police Service" was my advocacy for a new, accountable, transparent and truly community-based model of policing under strong civilian governance. To me, their criticism was proof of the true mission of the police association in coming after me—to sabotage any agenda of change.

I was not the only one in a public position to face this wrath. While McCormack was going after me, his counterparts in New York had started a similar campaign against the new mayor of that city, Bill de Blasio. De Blasio's crime was that he had reacted strongly and emotionally to Garner's death, as the father of a mixed-race son, and he had put a stop to the odious New York police practice of "stop-and-frisk" after complaints that it disproportionately targeted Blacks and Latinos. Since he was an elected public official, the New York police union could not demand his ouster, but it was showing its disapproval in other, equally intimidating ways.[2] Even President Barack Obama had not escaped the opprobrium of the US police unions for saying that if he had a son, he would be afraid for his son's safety. It was as if police unions across the US and Canada were drawing from the same tactical playbook.

But by the afternoon of Tuesday, December 9, it was clear that McCormack's coup attempt was not working. He had not succeeded in turning the media against me; the community had responded strongly in my favour. There had been a stream of letters sent and phone calls made in support of me to the powers that be. In addition, as early as Saturday, December 6, some people had started a petition on Change.org addressed to Premier Wynne and Mayor Tory, telling them I should not be asked to resign. The petition was to garner hundreds of signatures very quickly.[3]

But it turned out those who wished me harm were not done yet. At 1:04 p.m. on December 9, I received an email from Natalie Alcoba of the *National Post* asking if I could call her. It turned out she wanted to talk to me about a second meme from my Facebook account that had been provided to her by someone in the police association. Grabbed from my Facebook timeline and posted some time ago, it compared marriage to "a deck of cards. In the beginning all you need are two hearts and a diamond. By the end, you wish you had a club and a spade." I had posted it not because I thought it was funny, but because to me it raised troubling questions about why some marriages don't end well. Alcoba, though, wrote that it trivialized domestic violence.[4]

I found it hard to believe that the timing of the leak was coincidental, or that the way the meme was publicized was happenstance—

sharing it with someone in the media who was most likely to react negatively to it and who worked for a newspaper that is generally sympathetic to the police.

Once again, Tory jumped with alacrity and criticized the post. He expressed no curiosity as to why the police association would go to the trouble of going through my personal Facebook account and digging out that old post from among thousands of entries. With Thompson, Nunziata and Del Grande gone, I no longer had majority support on the board. The direction the board would take would depend very much on what Tory wanted. He had already pointed the way with his criticism of the second post.

I did not think I could survive a second onslaught. I felt despondent and told Kaur and Morton that this was likely the end of the road. I would resign from the board. They were disappointed, as we had prevailed so far. Morton counselled me against making up my mind so quickly. "Are you sure," he asked, "that this is the end of the road? Think about it." I agreed to do so. Kaur remembered having seen the post. She said she had found it clever, but definitely not offensive to her as a feminist. (As I was to learn, the meme had in fact been created by a feminist.) So we agreed to consider the options. In the meantime, on my advice, Kaur contacted the mayor's office to tell them what I was contemplating.

I called my wife, Arun, to prepare her for the worst. She said she would accept whatever decision I made because she did not think the job was worth the stress, the insults and the chicanery I had endured. At the same time, as a senior university professor of literature, a feminist and an anti-racist, she was aghast. She could not comprehend how Tory could be so obtuse, and she could not see how the post trivialized domestic violence. "Quite the opposite," she said. My next conversation was with three close friends who, like Arun, would not hesitate to tell me if I was off-base. They were indignant that I was thinking of quitting.

So I returned to the office with my little "market survey." It had lifted my spirits. While I was engaged in these conversations, Morton and Kaur had been busy as well. Morton had contacted some of the city's leading feminists and sought their response to the post. Independently of each other, they had all been incredulous that Tory would read it in the way he had. They had no difficulty distinguishing a metaphor that raised serious issues from a factual statement advocating violence. None of them had accepted that even metaphorically the meme promoted domestic violence.

Instead of feeling like throwing in the towel, I was energized to stand up once more to the bullies. Morton, Kaur and Arun were delighted. But I would not legitimize the story by engaging with it or debating it with reporters. Instead, we would issue a very brief statement that put this attack strategy in the context in which we saw it—that of the board chair being prevented from doing the work that was necessary. The statement we prepared simply said this:

> I do not recall this post as it seems to be from almost two years ago. This is nothing more than another desperate attempt to drive me from my position on the Board and distract from the serious work we have to do. It's time for us to focus on moving forward and stop this campaign of harassment.

Before I issued the statement on December 9, Tory's office was informed that I would not resign and would be responding. This was not well received.

We took one more action: to prevent any further muckraking of my Facebook account, we shut it down. We made sure that reporters knew this. On the advice of Morton and Kaur, I declined to engage in any further conversation about the issue and gave no interviews. My statement was to speak for itself. By the afternoon of Wednesday, December 10, media coverage of this second move by McCormack and his cohorts had stopped.

What had this coup attempt achieved? A handful of ex-cops from another era of policing had lambasted me, prompted by the association. Other serving members of the police service had communicated their support for me. From members of the public I had received overwhelming support, with many of them writing to me, the premier and the mayor. The media had treated me fairly. Besides McCormack and his association, the only other person who had been on the receiving end of harsh public criticism was the mayor, Tory. Belatedly, in an op-ed in the *Toronto Sun* on Monday, December 22, McCormack tried to seek public sympathy for his actions. They had been motivated, he claimed, by a concern for the safety of police officers. He wrote the piece after a police officer was shot and killed in New York. He claimed that "irresponsible anti-police rhetoric" by politicians, groups and individuals was partly responsible for jeopardizing officer safety.[5] Few people were persuaded by this new posturing.

Now the ball would be in the police board's court, as it would have to decide how to deal with McCormack's formal complaint against my conduct. It would be a challenge for a new police board, heavily influenced by Mayor Tory, who was committed to harmonious relations with the police association and had already publicly criticized me and my leadership more than once. As I looked to the upcoming meeting where my fate on the board would be decided, I couldn't help but reflect on other board members who had been caught in the crosshairs. Several people who had attempted to bring about reforms in policing had paid dearly for their efforts: Susan Eng, chair of the police board in the 1990s; Alan Heisey and John Filion in the early 2000s; my colleagues Michael Thompson and Mike Del Grande more recently.

I had been identified as one of the enemy, joining the ranks of former board members like Roy Williams, Arnold Minors and Olivia Chow. They were all hounded, formally or informally. They were all tarnished with allegations of being anti-police. Williams, the first Black member of the police board, had defended the right of Dudley Laws, founder of Black Action Defence Committee, to publicly express his condemnation of police behaviour toward members of the Black community. He was castigated for defending a "radical."

Minors, a member of the Eng-led police board in the 1990s and widely perceived to be on track to be the first Black chair of the board, saw his entire career go down the drain. His crime? When asked by reporters why people from the Black community were not co-operating with a police investigation of a shooting in a nightclub frequented by young people from the Black community, he had said this was precisely why community-based policing was needed and unless that happened, certain communities could see the police as an "occupying force." All hell broke loose because it was wrongly reported that he had called Toronto police an "occupying army." Minors was cleared after an independent investigation but his future was sealed. He did not make chair. The delicate sensitivities of the police mattered more to the powers that be.

Chow, a board member at the time, had been riding her bike when she observed police behaviour that she felt was worsening the situation at a downtown community protest. She stopped and suggested officers might try a less confrontational approach. She later had to step down as a board member because, supposedly, she had intervened in an operational matter. The possibility that she might have had a suggestion that would have helped police resolve the situation peacefully did not matter. Williams, Minors and Chow were all racialized people. In their own way, each had attempted to bridge the gap between police and members of marginalized groups—people whom the police considered radical and therefore suspect.

Now I had joined their group by appearing to endorse another radical group, Occupy Wall Street. Except that when I noted the racial connection to previously ostracized board members, McCormack got indignant and commented in the media that I was playing the "race card," which is the cheapest response a white man in power can give to people of colour when he doesn't want to deal with the facts. The facts were that all of us were from racialized backgrounds; all of us had been activists in the community; all of us had joined the police board precisely because we wanted some significant change from the perspective of the community; and all of us wanted to help build a police service that truly and equally served and protected everyone who lived in this city.

But this is perhaps too complicated for a culture and ideology that divide society between "us" and "the radicals." And by appearing to be siding with the radicals, we—Williams, Eng, Chow, Minors and I—were being anti-police and showing our true agenda. Well, yes, I guess we had shown our true agenda. And no, we did not belong to the club in which you scratch each other's back and get along. Accountability, social justice and the public interest were for us concepts with meaning, not empty platitudes or insincere slogans. But by following these concepts and pushing for changes that the establishment could not accept, I had proven that I did not belong.

It was up to the board now to determine what to do with the complaint—and me. The board had its regularly scheduled meeting on December 15. On December 8, board member Dr. Dhun Noria, as the acting vice-chair, had forwarded McCormack's complaint to the other members. Noria had also written to me asking for a response to assist the board in its review. The board would consider the complaint and my response confidentially and could choose to hear from me or question me in person before making its decision. The board would then announce its decision at the public meeting that afternoon.

I turned my attention to preparing the response with advice from Morton and Kaur. We decided that rather than being combative, my response would be somewhat contrite, reiterating the regret I had already expressed publicly, acknowledging that I could have been more careful, and giving the board a way to put the matter behind it. Rather than going down swinging, I knew it was important to those who supported me that I stay and continue to push for the changes they and I had advocated. This was my response:

I must state categorically that I had absolutely no intention of disparaging, accusing or calling into disrepute policing in Toronto. In fact, among the posts on my Timeline there is a very large number of posts that pay compliment to the work and contribution of our police officers.

At no time have I impaired or attempted to impair "public confidence in the abilities and integrity of the board" nor have I "discredited or compromised" or "attempted to discredit or compromise the integrity of the board or the police service."

I reminded them that I had responded to McCormack as quickly as I could, clarifying my intent and purpose in sharing the meme and expressing regret that it had sparked such a reaction. Noticeably absent from my response was any mention of Mayor Tory's interventions. He would now be sitting in judgment of me. We did not gloat about the fact that there had been tremendous public support for me, question the association's motives or make any suggestion that Tory should recuse himself because there could be the perception of a conflict of interest given his public comments. I assured them that I would stay inactive on Facebook as long as I was a member of the board.

It soon became apparent that we had given the board a way out. At the meeting on December 15, we were asked to remain in the room as the board deliberated. Tory led the way. After some comments about how those of us in public positions need to exercise better judgment in using social media, he recommended that considering my explanations and assurances, it was time to put the matter to bed. Other members quickly agreed. At the end of the meeting, the board decided that no further action was needed, and acting vice-chair Noria made a public statement announcing this at the board's public meeting that afternoon. So, the ten-day ordeal ended, and the board had skirted a minefield.

But many disturbing questions were left unanswered about the way the matter was handled. The Law Union of Ontario and the Toronto Police Accountability Coalition had raised these questions publicly, and the board was aware of them. Paul Copeland, a lawyer, Law Society Bencher and recipient of the Order of Canada, quoted in the law union statement made on December 9, raised an important legal issue: "Lobbying the mayor and the premier to replace a civilian overseer of the police force is a political activity and it is illegal." He also raised an issue that related directly to the board and its code of conduct: "Unfortunately, by aligning himself with the Toronto Police Association's attack on the chair of the Toronto Police Services Board, Mayor Tory risks undermining the progress that the Board has been making to build public confidence in the police."

In a letter to members of the police board on behalf of the Toronto Police Accountability Coalition, John Sewell, a former mayor of Toronto, also asserted that the police association and McCormack had contravened the *Police Services Act* and the board's policy against involvement in political activity. Further, the letter had emphasized my right under the Canadian Charter of Rights and Freedoms to speak my mind on critical issues. In part the letter read:

> It is improper for the police association to intervene in political matters. Asking for resignation of the chair of the body to which your members report is a political act. The Police Board policy which implements this regulation states that members of the Police Association are subject to the Police Services Board and its regulations, and that the chief will discipline anyone who contravenes the policy.
>
> The chair of the TPSB [Toronto Police Services Board] has the right to speak his mind. We live in a society governed by the rule of law and a Charter that guarantees freedom of speech and expression. Subject to the regulation noted above, the Police Association has every right to challenge the Chair's opinion, which it did not do. Instead, it attacked the person who was speaking out. We wish the Police Association would speak out about people dying at the hands of the police, and also state that it is concerned for its members. Sadly, this has not happened, and there was silence from the TPA [Toronto Police Association] when Sammy Yatim was killed eighteen

months ago as well as in the far too many shooting deaths by Toronto police in the past.

We are glad that the chair of the TPSB is speaking out against police killings. We think most people are appalled when such events happen, whether in Toronto or New York or Ferguson. Toronto would be a better place if the representatives of Toronto police officers, the Police Association, expressed that sentiment too, and worked to ensure that deadly force is minimized as much as possible.

Sewell went on to acknowledge the association's concerns about the upcoming budget and our push on carding. But he concluded by saying the association should be disciplined for attacking me and engaging in unauthorized political activity.

This intervention was particularly gratifying to me. Sewell had not always backed me. He had castigated me and the board countless times for what he had viewed as our failures and in my case what he viewed as an unacceptable proximity to the police chief. Indeed, after the G20 fiasco, he had called for me to step down as chair because he believed that I had been too close to the police.

But the board had a different reaction. Not a single board member referred to the important legal and policy questions that these responsible and thoughtful people had asked. I might have been spared, but the board missed an opportunity to delve into questions of far-reaching significance directly affecting its ability and that of its members to discharge their responsibilities without fear or favour. Questions like these are fundamental to effective and meaningful community-based civilian control of policing in a democratic society.

The policy that Sewell referred to about political activity by police officers was passed by the Toronto Police Services Board in 2005. We recognized their Charter rights but said they should refrain from engaging in municipal politics where they serve. This also covered the police association as an entity. Before every election, the chief is required to send out a directive to this effect. Each time I had to

remind Blair to do it, and the association would say we had no jurisdiction to issue that order. The Facebook snafu was also political activity, bringing a campaign against the head of the police oversight
authority. It works both ways: police unions have the power to do
favours for politicians but also the power to punish or try to punish.
And they have the power to influence public opinion.

In Toronto and elsewhere, there has been a history of attempting
to undermine critics by both the union and police leaders, using intimidation and bullying. Susan Eng, police board chair in the 1990s,
found out that her phone had been tapped. She had angered police
brass by exercising the authority of the civilian board on the police
force. Alan Heisey, board chair in 2003, found his name besmirched
in the press and was falsely branded as soft on pedophiles after a
conversation he had with Detective Sergeant Paul Gillespie and an
email from then–chief Julian Fantino's inbox on the matter were
leaked to the media. Around the same time, Fantino had found the
terms offered for renewal of his contract to be unacceptable. City
councillor John Filion, board member in the 2000s, believes his
marital difficulties were revealed to the press and his home placed
under surveillance. He was considered to be part of the left-wing
faction on the board, which was staunchly opposed to extending the
police chief's contract.

Underlying the experiences of all these board members are
certain common factors related to the culture and environment of
policing. It is a highly politicized institution, accustomed to using
its muscle to get its way. It understands well the power that comes
from withholding information and using it strategically. And it is
not shy about deploying political connections and information to
force "uppity" board members into line. The police chief is hugely
connected, politically. He controls information and uses it to his
advantage. These, too, are aspects of police culture.

Welcome to the Security State

WITHIN A FEW months of becoming mayor and joining the police board, John Tory had strong-armed the board on two extremely significant matters with huge future implications: carding and selection of a new chief. It was clear to me the majority of board members were content to let him have his way. I concluded that I was chair in name only, and only as long as I carried out Tory's wishes. So at the board meeting of June 18, 2015, I announced that I would step down as chair and leave the board altogether at the end of July. I departed three months after Blair. Pringle, who had been my vice-chair, took over as interim chair.

Also at the June 18 board meeting, Tory made a last-ditch effort to salvage the doomed carding policy that had been watered down through mediation to appease Blair but had proven to be wildly unpopular with the public. Tory moved to rescind the April 16, 2015, policy and reiterate the original policy, which had been approved a year earlier in April 2014. The board was back to square one, but with far less public credibility. The impasse continued. While the issue remained unresolved in Toronto, reports had started coming in about the existence of identical practices in other jurisdictions across Ontario—and even across the country.

Carding and police bias against Indigenous people and people of colour were being reported in other regions. The CBC, using access-to-information requests, found in 2016 that the police force in Edmonton was ten times more likely to stop Indigenous women than white women for non-criminal checks. More generally, Indigenous people were six times more likely to be stopped by Edmonton police than white people, and Black people were almost five times more likely than white people to be stopped on the street by Edmonton police.[1] In Lethbridge, Alberta, a prominent defence lawyer used access-to-information laws to show that in this city of about 100,000 people, Blacks were nine times more likely than whites to be stopped by police, and Indigenous citizens five times more likely than whites to be carded.

In the northern Ontario city of Thunder Bay, relations between police and Indigenous people are at a breaking point. The Office of the Independent Police Review Director announced in November 2016 that it was probing the police force for "systemic racism." The police are under fire for what Indigenous leaders believe are inadequate investigations of the deaths of young Indigenous students—seven between 2000 and 2001. Five bodies were found in the city's rivers; two died in their boarding rooms. There have been more deaths since.

Two recent deaths, in May 2017, of seventeen-year-old Tammy Keeash and fourteen-year-old Josiah Begg, are now being probed by York Regional Police from the Toronto area.[2] And in late September 2017, the body of twenty-one-year-old Dylan Moonias was pulled from the Neebing-McIntyre Floodway. The Thunder Bay Police Board, which has consistently backed the police force, is also under investigation by the Ontario Civilian Police Commission. A 2016 inquest into the deaths of seven Indigenous teens, including two who did not die in the rivers, ripped the bandage off the racism many Indigenous citizens said they encountered, much of it from police.

In the introduction, I referred to the York University study of 81,902 traffic stops in Ottawa over two years from 2013 to 2015, which found that people whose background was perceived to be

Black, Middle Eastern, East Asian/Southeast Asian, South Asian or Indigenous were stopped at rates that were vastly disproportionate to their presence in the city's population. The study stemmed from an Ontario Human Rights Tribunal settlement in the case of an eighteen-year-old Black man, Chad Aiken, who was pulled over by Ottawa police in May 2005 while driving his mother's Mercedes-Benz. Aiken said an officer taunted him, then punched him in the chest in a case of racial profiling. He shot video of the incident.[3]

And in Toronto in July 2017, the *Star*'s Jim Rankin struck again, this time with colleague Sandro Contenta and data analyst Andrew Bailey, analyzing ten years of marijuana possession busts by Toronto police from 2003 to 2013. They found Blacks three times more likely to be arrested for marijuana possession than their population would warrant. During the period studied, Toronto police arrested 11,299 people (whose skin colour was noted) for possession, with 25.2 percent of them being Black. The 2006 census data said Toronto's population was 8.4 percent Black. White possession arrests almost perfectly mirrored the population. The census pegged the white population in Toronto at 53.1 percent and they represented 52.8 percent of the marijuana possession charges.[4]

The *Star* found other important discrepancies. Blacks were far more likely to be held for bail hearings after a pot possession charge (15.2 percent of the time compared to 6.4 percent for whites) and Rankin and Contenta also found the greatest number of simple possession charges were made in neighbourhoods where Toronto police most aggressively carded. The carding and marijuana charges were more prevalent in poorer, racialized neighbourhoods and less prevalent in more affluent, whiter neighbourhoods.

Two days before I announced my departure, Ontario's then minister of community safety, Yasir Naqvi, announced that the practice of carding was unacceptable and that by fall, the province would develop a regulation forcing police services to deal with it appropriately. Naqvi said, "We have all heard the personal stories about the negative experiences associated with street checks...experiences of members of racialized communities going about their business, having done nothing wrong, and stopped for no reason. And because they are facing a police officer, they feel compelled to identify themselves, answer the officer's questions and then have that information recorded in a police database. It is clear that the status quo in these cases is not acceptable."

As the province got in on the act, Toronto's police services board suspended its efforts. It was believed by many that Premier Kathleen Wynne, a John Tory ally, had stepped in to save the mayor from his own fumbling with the issue. Naqvi set a very aggressive timetable for developing the regulation and began province-wide public consultations to seek advice. While the public was telling the minister to ban carding, police representatives were insisting it was an important policing tool.

By this time, I had accepted an invitation from the president of Toronto's Ryerson University, Sheldon Levy, to join the university as a distinguished visiting professor cross-appointed to the Office of Equity, Diversity and Inclusion (since renamed the Office of Equity and Community Inclusion) and the Department of Criminology. I took up my position on September 1, 2015. Soon after, I invited a large group of community activists, lawyers, representatives of the human rights commission and Ryerson professors to discuss the carding question. I had two questions: First, can we define from a community perspective what exactly we want banned? And second, can we develop a joint position on the problem, including a set of principles or benchmarks by which we can measure whether the new regulation meets community expectations effectively? There was a large turnout, and I quickly learned these people had never gathered at the same table to work together. We had an excellent discussion and to follow up, the group struck a small writing team to develop a joint position. The writing team worked very hard to develop a thoughtful submission to the province.

In the meantime, I was invited by Naqvi to meet with him and his deputy minister, Matt Torigian, over breakfast to lay out my thoughts. We had a very good conversation. Of all the things we discussed, two points I made have stayed with me. My first was that this was a historic opportunity because the ministry did not have a history of writing regulations dealing with social justice, human rights or Charter issues. So it was important to get it right. My second point was in response to Naqvi's comment that he would be consulting with all stakeholders to ensure he got it right. I stated that it was the government's job to make policy on behalf of the public. Police personnel, whether chiefs or police associations, were professionals whose job it was to give advice on how a policy decision could be implemented; it was not their job to determine or influence policy. And in that sense, they were not stakeholders in the same way that municipalities, police services boards and the community at large were.

I felt it necessary to make this point because we have politicized the policing profession by treating the chiefs and associations as equal stakeholders and deferring to them on policy matters. I hold the view that it is for society, represented by elected officials, to decide how it will be policed; the job of police professionals is to make it happen. In Ontario's ministry of community safety there was a culture of decision by consensus, and if the police chiefs and associations disagreed, that killed consensus and policy matters died. I have lived through this many, many times.

I do not know if my meeting had any effect. However, when the joint submission by the Ryerson group was ready, Naqvi and Torigian gave its representatives a good hearing for a couple of hours. When Naqvi was informed that we would be going public the next day with our proposals, he encouraged us to do so. He felt the conversation so far had been dominated by the police, and by going public we would be changing the channel. The day after it met with Naqvi and Torigian, this ad hoc group released its recommendations at a press conference.

On October 28, 2015, Naqvi announced the regulation. Every police services board in Ontario was now required to establish a policy consistent with the regulation. It provided mandatory direction on what information would be collected by police officers and retained by police services. The minister established an advisory committee that included eminent community representatives such as Barbara Hall and Mary Anne Chambers to work with the province's police college to revamp police training. As well, an independent review of the implementation of the regulation would be completed by January 1, 2019, to identify further changes or improvements.[5]

All of this looked positive; however, as many of us pointed out, the regulation had two major flaws. It did not deal with the police stop, that first interaction where problems began, but with the aftermath of the stop. And it created a broad set of exemptions to which the regulation would not apply. In many ways, these exemptions were not much different from the porous definition of public safety that Toronto police brass had proposed and we had rejected.

It appeared that yet again the voice of the police had prevailed over that of the community. And once more, the community was asked to live with half measures. Was the political default of deferring to the police, as if their concerns were on par with those of the entire community, too entrenched to be overcome? Had the organized voice of policing proven more powerful than the persistent but less organized voices of the community? Or, was it that the arbitrary stopping and carding of people who were not the subject of a criminal investigation was seen as indispensable in the context of the securitization of the state?

Many caring people, in a powerful demonstration of good citizenship, worked with great passion, solidarity, integrity and perseverance to force change.[6] They forced the government to sit up, take note and implement rules. This was unprecedented because governments have no track record of regulating policing in relation to racial or other forms of bias and discrimination. The broad principle in the *Police Services Act* that policing should be respectful of the public's human rights and Charter rights is supposed to suffice. So perhaps carding (in whatever name) will no longer be practised formally. But will that put an end to anti-Black, anti-Indigenous, anti-homeless and other forms of discriminatory profiling?

I ask this because of the dogmatic insistence of police chiefs and police associations that stopping people at random and gathering information about them and their friends is an important and valuable policing tool. They strenuously deny that the use of this tool is motivated or influenced by bias or discrimination. They argue that if some neighbourhoods—and some communities—experience greater contact with police, it is a result of efforts to deal with differing incidences of crime, violence and social disorder in different parts of the city. Despite their failure to produce one iota of evidence that this indiscriminate and massive collection of information about innocent people makes the city safer, police professionals have not changed their minds.

In the Greater Toronto Area region of Peel, for example, chief Jennifer Evans disregarded her masters, the police board, when the board requested that she at least suspend this practice until the new provincial regulation had been announced. Another *Star* investigation, in 2015, found that Blacks in Brampton and Mississauga (both part of that region) were three times more likely to be stopped for "street checks" than whites. Evans refused to suspend the practice and was eventually given a two-year contract extension by the police board she had been feuding with; she will remain at the helm until at least October 2019.

By the time Naqvi and the provincial government implemented the racial profiling regulation, Blair's successor had been in the top job for several months. Curiously, Chief Mark Saunders declared that he would have to find an "Option B." Saunders was a relative unknown with no public position on carding, but one reason he was apparently favoured within the police service was that he was known as a "cop's cop." It had been expected that as Tory's chosen chief, Saunders would be amenable to implementing the board's original policy, which had been reiterated in Tory's motion. One of the knocks against Sloly's candidacy for chief had been the claim by certain board members that he had not been helpful in developing the policy when Blair delegated him to assist the board and Frank Addario in this work. I harboured the suspicion, however, that he was constrained by Blair's instructions.

After the "cop's cop" took office on April 26, 2015, he turned out not to be so malleable after all when it came to implementing the board's policy. He claimed carding was a valuable investigative tool important for public safety, criminal investigations and national security. That last item was a new justification, though it went virtually unnoticed. The policy was no closer to being implemented; we were having the same discussion all over again. In his early months as chief, I had numerous one-on-one conversations with Saunders. But as I told board staff, these were not really conversations. Saunders would hear me out, call my point "interesting," ignore it and tell me what he was thinking. It was like listening to a broken record. He would repeat this over and over.

Exasperated, I finally sent him an email on racial profiling in which I said that if collecting and retaining information about innocent people—people not involved in or suspected of any crime—was a valuable policing tool, then it might as well include personal information about all 2.4 million residents of the city. Who knows who might be a useful source of information during a police investigation? Saunders appeared to be incapable of making a distinction between gathering information related to a police investigation and storing information about innocent people—predominantly Blacks and other minorities. In private conversations and public comments, he repeatedly justified carding by talking about criminal investigations despite repeated reminders that the debate was about the innocent, not the criminal. In an op-ed in the June 5, 2015, issue of the *Toronto Star* I expressed concern about surveillance in today's security state.[7]

It is axiomatic that policing depends on good-quality information. However, I worry about the magnitude of the information that is now being collected based on a supposed risk profile, and the methods by which this is being done. It seems it is a direct consequence of the type of society we have become because of state policies related to neoliberal ideology and the post–9/11 securitization of the state. The pursuit of neoliberal ideology in Canada, the US and much of the Western world has created greater economic and social disparity at the same time that withdrawal, reduction and outsourcing of support systems in the name of cost saving and deficit cutting have made life harder at the bottom. Society has become less caring, less just and less fair.

Less social justice equals less social order. It seems inevitable that governments choosing this course will be fearful of its consequences and increasingly rely on policing to maintain order. We can now add to this mix the post–9/11 fixation on national security and the global war on terrorism. In Canada and around the Western world we have seen an ever-increasing reliance on systems of policing and security, and the criminal justice system more broadly, to deal with these two matters. When this is combined with the state's need to control the potential consequences of neoliberal policies, there is bound to be an impact on the nature and methods of policing.

It is expected by those in power that police forces will not only react effectively to social disorder but also act proactively to prevent its recurrence. Stringent laws have been enacted, reliance on punishment has increased and police powers have been enhanced. The protection and promotion of people's rights and liberties has diminished. We see the consequences of these political developments. One of them is the phenomenon of the militarization of policing. There is a growing public perception that police reliance on weapons, including lethal weapons, has increased. At the same time, police uniforms, vehicles and tactics convey the message of a coercive system of command and control.

The issue of the militarization of American police forces came on the radar in North America after the killing of Michael Brown in Ferguson, but alarms were being set off before that 2014 shooting.

In a June 2014 report entitled "War Comes Home," the American Civil Liberties Union (ACLU) examined more than eight hundred SWAT deployments conducted by twenty US law enforcement agencies during the years 2011 to 2013.[8] These were almost invariably drug raids in which heavily armoured officers carrying assault rifles used battering rams to break down doors, used stun grenades to disorient residents, and used unnecessarily violent and intimidating equipment such as armoured personnel carriers to carry out their operations. If there were children in the home, so be it. This was war.

The ACLU reported that "the militarization of American policing is evident in the training that police officers receive, which encourages them to adopt a 'warrior' mentality and think of the people they are supposed to serve as enemies." The ACLU reported that a total of 15,054 battle uniforms or personal protective equipment were received by sixty-three police agencies during the study period. It estimated that five hundred law enforcement agencies received Mine-Resistant Ambush-Protected (MRAP) vehicles built to withstand armour-piercing roadside bombs. When paramilitary tactics were used in drug searches, the primary targets were people of colour, especially African-Americans, but when paramilitary tactics were used in hostage or barricade scenarios, the primary targets were white. Overall, 42 percent of people targeted by a SWAT deployment to execute a search warrant were Black and 12 percent were Latino. Overwhelmingly (68 percent of the time), police were looking for drugs in these deployments that targeted minorities.

The militarization of American police began with the 1990s-era Department of Defense 1033 program, born at the height of the War on Drugs, which transfers military equipment to local police forces for free (the municipality pays the transportation costs). It requires local forces to use the war equipment within a year of receipt. Between 1996 and 2014 the US government transferred $4.3 billion worth of military equipment to local forces. Among the five hundred police forces with an MRAP was the Ohio State University campus police, apparently needed to keep everyone in line on football-game days.

Some American police forces also have a Ballistic Engineered Armored Response Counter Attack Truck (BearCat), a particular favourite, along with the armoured personnel carriers. Keene, New Hampshire, has been widely mocked for accepting a $286,000 Department of Homeland Security grant to purchase a BearCat. The town of 23,000, which had only two murders from 1999 until this desperately needed BearCat arrived in 2012, had told DHS it was concerned about unforeseen terror attacks at its annual pumpkin festival.[9] The trend is not as pronounced in Canada, but some of the police forces that have acquired armoured vehicles in recent years include those in Winnipeg, Windsor, Hamilton and Saskatoon. A $300,000 light-armoured Cougar was donated to Windsor by the Department of National Defence. Winnipeg police spent $343,000 on a Gurkha Armoured Rescue Vehicle (ARV1).[10] And Ottawa city police patrolling the airport have been issued military-style carbine rifles.

Even as he was upgrading to more firepower by providing his front-line officers with carbine rifles, RCMP commissioner Bob Paulson lamented the militarization of Canadian police. The RCMP is a force that also has armoured vehicles, drones and machine guns, but Paulson expressed concern about an "us versus them" mentality during a February 2017 appearance before a Senate committee.[11] Paulson rightly believes this armed-to-the-teeth approach moves Canada away from the community-based, preventative, problem-solving policing model.

Toronto has its own militarized equipment. A prime example, buried in the budget in the hope that no one will find it, is a fixed-wing surveillance aircraft equipped with a high-resolution camera, supposedly for finding marijuana grow-ops. It costs $1 million per year to operate—a hell of a lot of money to spend ostensibly looking for pot. Toronto leases the plane, but with maintenance and crew costs, you get to the $1 million price tag pretty quickly. As well, Toronto police have armoured vehicles and Chief Saunders has put shotguns in every police division.

In addition to militarization, the other result of the onset of the security state has been the ever-increasing police need for information for both proactive and reactive purposes. We well know the relentless pressure placed on governments by police leaders—like the Canadian Association of Chiefs of Police and its US counterpart—to give police the legislated ability to intrude upon the public's right to privacy in order to gather information. The response has been a sympathetic hearing from their governments and a public that has been made fearful by the spectre of terrorism. I believe that the insistence of police chiefs that police must randomly stop people who fit a supposed "risk profile" and coerce them into giving up personal information must be examined in this broader context. It is not a coincidence that Saunders referred to national security every time he defended carding. The role and culpability of governments in this must be questioned.

That Black people, Indigenous people, other racialized people and poor people are the primary targets of the practice of making random stops and collecting information is not an accident or a coincidence. In our diverse societies marked by racial, economic, political and social disparities they are "the other" considered most likely to create social disorder and threaten security. When police deny that they are deliberately racist, they are probably right—for the most part. However, they are engaged in massive surveillance on behalf of the state. And who but the dominant society's "other" will be the target? Is it surprising, then, that all the Ontario government could offer to those demanding an end to biased and discriminatory policing as epitomized by carding was a half measure?

We are left with a conundrum. The same government that requires all local police services boards and police services to put in place confidential plans to deal with national security and terrorism threats also promotes, through the *Police Services Act*, community-based models of policing. While protection of national security and prevention of terrorism are federal matters, the federal security agencies are inadequately resourced for the job. Local police forces are better able to gather intelligence about the communities they police. Canada is not alone in this regard; this is the arrangement in the US and the UK as well. But it inflicts a seriously negative impact on the relationship and trust that should exist between these police services and the communities that are seen as "the other." One cannot expect an agency to provide community-based policing to the same community it puts under surveillance.

The Elaborate Illusion of
Police Accountability

IT WAS HAPPENING again. Sleep would not come to Andrew Loku. That was all he wanted on this midsummer night in 2015, nothing more. Sleep. But the incessant noise and loud music coming from Apartment 302 was keeping him up again, as it had so many other nights. It had become a problem so chronic he sometimes went to a basement laundry room in search of an elusive night of peace.[1]

But on this night there would be no laundry room. This night was different. Here was a man suffering from PTSD and possibly depression. The father of five was lost at times, enduring a prolonged separation from his family a continent away, a man who had existed largely on his own since arriving as a refugee in 2004. His mind would often flash back to the torture and the beatings that had rained down on him from the hands of rebels who kidnapped and held him for two months during the civil war in his native land, now known as South Sudan. But this was also the man who sang Christmas carols over the phone to a sister in Saskatoon, a man described by residents of his building as a gentle, hulking giant of a man. This was a man who had led a life alien to anyone born in this country.

On this night, July 4, he had been drinking. In fact earlier that evening, police had picked him up on Toronto's busy Don Valley Parkway as Loku puttered down the expressway on an electric bike.

He had more than three times the legal limit of alcohol in his system. On this night, Loku had apparently hit a breaking point. He decided to confront the noise problem—with a hammer in his hand. When the call went out to police, this troubled refugee, who had recently graduated from the George Brown College Craft Construction Program, was described as "large, violent and armed," someone threatening to kill a neighbour with a hammer.

Loku's apartment building had several units designated for people with mental health issues; these were rented to clients of the Canadian Mental Health Association. The fact that a number of tenants in the building were dealing with mental health issues had apparently not been relayed to police so as not to "stigmatize" others in the low-rise. By the time two constables—thirteen-year veteran Andrew Doyle and the rookie he was coaching, Haim "Jimmy" Queroub, a mere eleven weeks in uniform—arrived and found the man with the hammer in the narrow hallway of the Gilbert Avenue building, a witness said Loku had been calmed down. Yet twenty-one seconds after the officers' arrival, he was dead, shot by Doyle. His rookie partner said he had cocked his own gun and would have pulled the trigger if the senior officer had not fired first.

Loku's death unleashed a toxic stew that cut to the heart of police accountability in Canada: secrecy and lack of transparency by Ontario's Special Investigations Unit (SIU), the way officers deal with SIU investigators and yet again how police deal with people who have mental health problems, particularly people of colour. Doyle was exonerated by the SIU, but it took two years and considerable community pressure to find out why and a coroner's inquest to learn his identity. And for almost two years we didn't know why there was a gap in the CCTV video recorded inside the building at the moment of the shooting—and only on the floor where the shooting had occurred—and we didn't know why another officer had inserted himself into the investigation by downloading the surveillance video, something that had angered the SIU director Tony Loparco.

We had to wait almost two years to learn that it was Toronto police inspector Peter Moreira, a man with twenty-six years' experience, who arrived to secure the scene of the shooting before the SIU arrived. He took it upon himself to try to collect video evidence. This was after consulting with an SIU liaison officer, he said. Witnesses were called to maintain that there had been no tampering with the video. But actual video of the shooting never surfaced.

After the decision not to lay charges against the officer was announced, members of Black Lives Matter Toronto camped out in front of police headquarters for two weeks demanding more answers on Loku's death, including the identity of the officer who had pulled the trigger. They protested at Queen's Park, and Premier Kathleen Wynne eventually met with them. When Chief Saunders was pushed to meet with them, he said, "I'm not going to go there and be yelled at by a bunch of kids." Neither police board chair Andy Pringle nor Mayor Tory would meet with them, despite their stated commitment to dealing seriously with issues of mental health and policing as well as the killing of Black people by police.

The *Toronto Star* launched a campaign pushing for SIU transparency, and in the newspaper's path stood Ontario Attorney General Madeleine Meilleur. A month after the SIU cleared the officer and with protests swirling, the *Star*'s veteran Queen's Park bureau chief, Robert Benzie, revealed Meilleur had not even read the report explaining the decision.[2] Shortly after, she resigned and left politics altogether, resurfacing briefly when opposition parties in Ottawa forced Justin Trudeau's Liberals to withdraw her nomination for the position of Official Languages Commissioner, a move that smacked of a patronage appointment to an independent agency.

The Loku fallout also led to a wide-ranging review of police oversight in this province led by Ontario Court of Appeal Justice Michael Tulloch, the first Black person appointed to the province's top court. Beyond the SIU, Tulloch also reviewed the two other agencies that comprise the troika of police oversight in the province: the Office of the Independent Police Review Director (OIPRD), established in

2009 as a successor to the Ontario Police Complaints Commission dismantled by the Progressive Conservative government of Mike Harris; and the Ontario Civilian Police Commission (OCPC), which sits for police discipline appeals as part of a broad set of responsibilities. It is the only body with authority over police boards, chiefs and even members of city council, including the mayor. It is also the entity responsible for ensuring there is an adequate and effective policing service in every community in the province.

In reality, only the SIU and the OIPRD are real players in police oversight. The OCPC, on which I served as a member in the mid-1990s, has slid into irrelevancy for reasons I will deal with later. As far as police chiefs and police unions are concerned, the two main independent entities do an effective job of holding police officers accountable. They are independent, they have vast powers and they are objective—or so goes the narrative from the police perspective. The fact that they absolve the vast majority of police officers they investigate is proof that officers act lawfully and legally and do not misuse their authority—again, from the police perspective. These two institutions create the illusion of independent oversight and accountability. They also do not disrupt the status quo. But it is merely that: an illusion. Politicians, chiefs and police associations all go around saying how they are held accountable, but when you look at the consequences of that accountability you are looking at a very slim volume with dubious outcomes.

From the public's perspective, the fact that the vast majority of police officers who are investigated are absolved should be a huge problem. The Special Investigations Unit, I should note, is supposedly an independent agency created under Ontario's *Police Services Act* to investigate every police interaction in which there has been a serious injury or death, the discharge of a firearm by a police officer, or an allegation of sexual assault by a police officer. It is responsible for determining whether the action of the officers involved is in breach of the Criminal Code. The job of the SIU director is not to decide the innocence or guilt of an officer. Instead, the director is limited to considering whether there is enough evidence to justify laying a charge. If a charge is laid, the courts determine guilt or innocence.

Clearly, the SIU has a very narrow mandate. If an officer's conduct does not meet the high standard of violating the Criminal Code, resulting in the laying of a charge, the SIU has no further role. The SIU was established by the Ontario government in 1990 in response to the killing of Lester Donaldson on August 9, 1988, by Toronto police and the December 8, 1988, killing of seventeen-year-old Wade Lawson by Peel Regional Police. The Lawson killing in particular sparked outrage. Police said Lawson had steered the stolen car he was driving in the direction of police, endangering the constables, but a subsequent autopsy showed one of the bullets that killed the teen entered the back of his head. The creation of the SIU was heralded as a much-needed move to bring police accountability into the twentieth century.

The entity has fallen far short of that goal. When SIU directors lay charges, it is often when they have before them video that forces their hand, or when pressure from the media and the community cannot be ignored. Choose any time frame you like, but the numbers are not flattering to SIU investigators. In figures provided to Justice Tulloch for his report, the SIU said it had been involved in 3,932 incidents and laid charges in 129 cases.[3] In the 2016 calendar year, 327 cases were opened by the SIU, the second-highest number in its history. It closed 296 cases during that year, resulting in twenty officers being criminally charged in seventeen cases, meaning charges were laid in 5.7 percent of cases closed.[4] Analyzing data in the first twenty years of the SIU, the *Toronto Star* found that of 3,400 investigations, ninety-five criminal charges were laid, but only 16 resulted in convictions and only three officers were jailed.[5]

These statistics raise a number of questions. The SIU might be doing a good job and police officers might be operating lawfully. But we have no way of knowing, because the SIU does not tell the public after each investigation how it came to the conclusion that an officer's use of force was reasonable or that taking someone's life was justified under the circumstances. The SIU is simply not transparent. Even if it acted thoroughly and impartially, there is no way of knowing because of the way police respond to investigations. Too much is stacked in favour of police and there is understandable suspicion of how officers come up with their versions of events with police association lawyers before the SIU is able to do its work. Secrecy and collusion are the order of the day.

And so on an early April day in 2017, Tulloch strode to the podium in a packed hotel ballroom in downtown Toronto to release his report. He had spent seven months looking into the problems with police oversight in Ontario, meeting with more than fifteen hundred individuals during seventeen public meetings and more than 130 private meetings.[6] He did not shy away from discussing the distrust of police and their oversight bodies by Indigenous people and Blacks in Ontario. This distrust is rooted in history, Tulloch said. The Indigenous-police distrust stems from colonialism "beginning with North-West Mounted Police and continuing through to modern police services," he wrote.[7]

Early police interaction with Indigenous peoples involved the enforcement of discriminatory laws or the removal of children from their parents, he recounted. Blacks were considered property in Canada well into the 1800s, and a US slave patrol law allowed Blacks to be pursued and monitored to the Canadian border during that time. "Within Black communities," Tulloch wrote, "there is a prevailing perception that they have always been over-policed and targeted as criminals. This, some say, reinforces insidious stereotypes associating Blacks with criminality."[8]

Tulloch pushed the envelope in his probe, but he drew the line at naming officers under investigation by the SIU, recommending only that they be named following an investigation that resulted in charges being laid. Instead, he recommended more transparency in SIU investigations, including the release of all reports to the public dating back to its inception in 1990. The Ontario government

immediately committed to doing this, promising to release reports
dating from 2005 to the present by the end of 2017 and reports from
1990 to 2004 by the summer of 2018.

Tulloch also called for the collection of demographic data, so
that there are firm numbers on interactions with police oversight
bodies based on race, religion, age, mental health status, disabil-
ity and Indigenous status. Another key recommendation was the
creation of a College of Policing, which would, among other things,
develop common and clear entry-level academic requirements for
police officers and develop a curriculum that touches on areas of "social and cultural competency, mental health, domestic abuse, serving vulnerable communities and anti-racism and equity studies."[9]

As well, he found during his consultations that many were surprised to learn that complaints to the OIPRD were often referred back
to the officer's force for investigation, creating a "blue on blue" investigative process. He called for the under-resourced OIPRD to receive
better funding so it could independently investigate all public conduct complaints—recommending that within five years it become the
sole body to investigate public conduct complaints. He also called
for it to change its name to something more easily understandable,
reach out to a public that is largely unaware of its existence, and
streamline its complaints process to make it more accessible.

Tulloch also recognized the bitterness many Indigenous people
feel toward police and the futility they feel about engaging with
oversight bodies. He called for mandatory Indigenous cultural
competency training for all oversight staff and ongoing recruitment
of Indigenous people for senior positions in oversight bodies. And
the province accepted his recommendation that the government
provide funding for legal assistance at inquests to family members
of people killed by police. The province moved just in time for the
inquest into the death of Michael MacIsaac, who was killed in 2013
by Durham police constable Brian Taylor.

And then, less than six months later, the dam broke. On November 2, 2017, the Ontario government, building on Tulloch's

work, introduced the most ambitious overhaul of police oversight in twenty-five years. In addition to the existing power to lay criminal charges, the proposed legislation would give the SIU director the authority to lay penalties—a fine of $50,000, a year in jail or both—on officers who refused to co-operate with investigations. It built on Tulloch's call for transparency. Even when no charges are laid, the SIU would have to explain the decision, provide details of the case and release any video, photos or audio available (although the name of the officer would not be released).

The SIU would be able to investigate not just officers on duty, but former officers, off-duty officers, members of First Nations police services and police constables working for private enterprises. Police oversight agencies would have to provide diversity training to their employees, including training on the rights and cultures of First Nations, Inuit and Métis people. A cap could be put on the number of former cops who could investigate current cops at any given time on behalf of the SIU or the OIPRD, which is to be renamed the Ontario Policing Complaints Agency (OPCA). And the OIPRD would no longer refer a complaint back to the police service where the incident had originated—no more blue-on-blue probes. Instead the OPCA would investigate on its own.

It was a good day for those who, like me, had fought for years for changes to police oversight.

But. There is always a *but*. These agencies will now have to be properly funded, given their new mandates.

The real battle for the SIU continues to be dealing with police culture. Let's look at the battles fought by former SIU director Ian Scott—skirmishes that culminated in a historic Supreme Court of Canada decision. I worked with three SIU directors before I left the police board in 2015—James Cornish (2004 to 2008), Scott (2008 to 2013) and Loparco, who replaced Scott in 2013. Since the SIU's inception in 1990, there have been two directors—Howard Morton (1992 to 1995) and Scott—who were fiercely independent and truly believed in accountability. Morton felt there was no reason to keep everything confidential. He told me that when he was director a great deal more information was released to the public.

For all his battles over collusion and police access to lawyers, Scott did not share Morton's zeal for openness. He believed personnel matters and even names should be kept confidential. Scott became SIU director in October 2008 and began making waves almost immediately. Writing in the 2014 anthology *Issues in Civilian Oversight of Policing in Canada*, Scott said he had been in office barely a month when he learned of a police practice, mainly in Toronto, in which a police association lawyer would arrive at an SIU incident scene before the SIU was even notified and would advise and confer with all the officers on the scene before they wrote up their notes.

Scott was not the first to address this issue. In André Marin's 2011 report *Oversight Undermined*, the former SIU director turned provincial ombudsman quoted a lawyer representing Hamilton police: "I was tempted to have a pencil manufactured with the slogan "Shut the F up" embossed on it so that when police officers began to write their notes, they would pause and first give me or their association a call...The first few hours of an SIU investigation are the most important. They decide the future of your career. They may even decide your liberty."[10]

Scott said a review of all SIU files involving Toronto police from January 2006 to December 2008 showed that in forty-six out of 175 SIU investigations, multiple officers involved in probes conferred first with association lawyers.[11] He cited another case in which a union lawyer showed up at a jail ten minutes after a woman was found dead in a cell; the SIU was notified eight hours later.[12] In another case, Scott only learned of a March 2009 incident in which a man was Tasered four times by Toronto police, suffering a complex fracture to his face, when he read about it in his morning newspaper.[13] None of this was news to Scott, who even four years before taking over the SIU had written that police accused of using excessive force stood less than a one in five chance of being dealt with as sternly as civilians.

"It is an ineffective use of state resources to investigate, charge and prosecute cases in which the high probability is...acquittal," Scott wrote in 2004.[14] Time after time, he complained loudly and publicly about suspected collusion among officers as they prepared their notes on an event, their refusal to answer questions during an investigation, and the potential problems with the fact that several officers were often represented by one legal counsel. He also raised concerns about the number of times the siu was not contacted immediately after a serious incident had occurred, as required by law.

Scott had appeared before the Toronto Police Services Board to share his concerns about the quality of the co-operation he was receiving from the service as well as the integrity of officers' notes. I told him at the meeting and also in subsequent conversations that the board could take action only if he provided concrete proof. Scott and I spoke regularly about—and often clashed over—the issues of cooked notes and officers' access to lawyers. The *Police Services Act* requires the police board to indemnify officers, so the board pays for these lawyers. For cost reasons, the board does not provide a separate lawyer for each officer on the scene, only the "subject officer" who pulls the gun, fires the gun, causes the death, causes serious injuries or is accused of sexual assault.

The math was daunting. If there were twelve officers on the scene, the board would be looking at a prohibitive legal bill for providing twelve lawyers. In fact, we wouldn't be able to round up twelve criminal lawyers on such short notice even if we wanted to. So in our contract with the police association, we had agreed that the board would pay one lawyer per six witness officers, while each subject officer would have separate legal representation. For us, this was a reasonable solution. Scott had a huge problem with this because under Law Society of Upper Canada rules, a lawyer representing more than one client on the same issue can't withhold information from the other clients. To him, this was a recipe for collusion.

I had suggested to Scott that perhaps he and I should approach the Law Society together and recommend that in these instances there should be an exemption for lawyers representing police offi-cers, so a lawyer would not risk professional misconduct if he or she did not share information. Influenced by Scott and Law Society com-mittee member Julian Falconer, the Law Society instead entertained a change requiring each officer involved in an SIU investigation to have separate counsel, but the board pushed back. The Law Society ultimately backed off and clarified that lawyers in these cases would not be in breach of their oath if they withheld information from other clients they were representing on the same case.

But did it make any difference? Only the subject officer was compelled under the *Act* to answer questions from SIU investiga-tors. Witness officers did not have the same obligation. So when that question was posed, the witness officer would look to the lawyer and the lawyer would tell the officer he or she did not have to answer that question. Then came the answer, by rote: "On the advice of my counsel, I will not answer that question." Scott's investigators used an array of questions to try to establish factually that there had been prior consultation and that their identical stories had been cooked, but the answer from every officer remained, "I would rather not an-swer that question" or "On the advice of my lawyer, I will not answer that question." They claimed they were co-operating, but they were providing non-answers.

Blair had maintained that officers were put in separate rooms with clear procedures that directed them to write their notes in-dependently. The notes had to be contemporaneous, they had to be accurate and they had to be comprehensive, he said. Officers were obligated to follow this procedure. Blair insisted to me that if officers were not following the procedure, he would charge them under the *Act*. So the board was caught between Scott and his frustration over the perceived cooking of notes and Blair's insistence that officers were obliged to follow a clear procedure. I would have liked to have received something more substantive from Scott, because in my heart I suspected he was right.

As this drama was playing out in Toronto, Levi Schaeffer, a thirty-year-old man diagnosed with schizophrenia, panic and other personality disorders, hopped on his bike at his Peterborough, Ontario, home and headed north—way north—with a plan to buy some land. On June 24, 2009, he was camping on Osnaburgh Lake near the community of Pickle Lake, Ontario, some nineteen hundred kilometres north of Toronto. Two OPP officers, Constable Kris Wood and Acting Sergeant Mark Pullbrook, were dispatched to investigate reports of a stolen boat. Their search took them to the campsite of Schaeffer, where the officers claimed he came after them armed with a knife and bear spray. Schaeffer was alone and frying up some lunch, but the threat was sufficiently alarming for the duo that Wood shot him dead.

The Schaeffer shooting came a mere forty-eight hours after an OPP officer in Elmvale, Ontario, fatally shot fifty-nine-year-old Douglas Minty, who had threatened a pushy door-to-door salesman whom he felt was being too aggressive with his eighty-six-year-old mother. Like Schaeffer, Minty had mental health challenges. As with Schaeffer, the officer who shot Minty, Constable Graham Seguin, felt threatened by a man coming at him with a knife—although there was disagreement about whether the blade of the folding knife was actually out. Seguin shot Minty five times as his distraught mother watched.

Based on the investigation by the SIU, Scott exonerated the officers in both cases, but there were troubling parallels in both shootings that played precisely to Scott's beliefs on police collusion. Wood and Pullbrook contacted their superiors at the Pickle Lake detachment and were specifically ordered not to write up their notes until they had talked to a union lawyer. That lawyer advised them not to write up notes, but instead to prepare a set of confidential draft notes for the lawyer's eyes only. When the lawyer arrived in Pickle Lake a couple of days later, he perused the confidential notes he had requested, met with the two officers, and told them to go ahead and write their official notes. He refused to provide the SIU with a copy of the original notes he had requested.

Seguin received the exact same advice and acted in the same way as the officers in the Schaeffer shooting—he did not compile his notes until he had consulted with a police association lawyer. When Scott exonerated Wood, he pointed out that he had been denied the opportunity to compare the first draft of the officer's notes with the final version and could only make his decision based on union lawyer–approved notes. "Because I cannot conclude what probably happened," Scott wrote, "I cannot form reasonable grounds that the subject officer committed a criminal offence in the firearms death of Mr. Schaeffer." OPP commissioner Julian Fantino fired back at Scott, "If your intent was to inflame an already-volatile situation for all concerned, I can now inform you that you have succeeded."[15]

Falconer, a dogged advocate with a brilliant legal mind, took up the case for the Schaeffer and Minty families. It took four years but ultimately the Supreme Court of Canada ruled in favour of the families and Scott in December 2013. In the majority 6–3 decision, the court reasoned, "Permitting police officers to consult with counsel before their notes are prepared is...anathema to the very transparency that the legislative scheme aims to promote. When the community's trust in the police is at stake, it is imperative that the investigatory process be—and appear to be—transparent."[16] It said allowing officers to fully consult with counsel at the note-making stage created the impression of collusion, the very problem the SIU had been created to overcome.

But the lack of transparency at the SIU remained unchanged. Its default to maintaining privacy and bare-bones detail is not a legal question. Nowhere in the statutes does it say, "Thou shalt not make information public." The only thing enshrined in law is that at the end of an investigation, the director provides the full report, in confidence, to the Attorney General only—not even to the police board or police chief. The police chief receives a letter with a very high-level summary of the matter and the director's conclusion. In Toronto, there is a practice that when the chief provides his administrative review of the matter to the board, he attaches the director's letter. Following the board's directions, the chief answers or clarifies any concerns the director may have raised in the letter. Confidentiality applies to those two documents, but the rules under which the chief provides his administrative review stipulate that the board may make that report public.

The chief would routinely recommend that the board not make his report public. This was a cause of great unease for successive boards. After years of back and forth, there has been a resolution that every time there is an administrative review of an SIU report, the board will make the results of that review public. But names are not released. Details are kept to a minimum. Usually the board says it had an SIU report and a chief's review and that the officers acted lawfully—as the numbers show, the result is almost always "acted lawfully."

The new Ontario legislation aims to end this level of secrecy.

When we look at a rare decision of the SIU to charge, such as with Constable James Forcillo in the shooting death of Sammy Yatim, it is usually due to significant public exposure and pressure. In that case, the pressure came as a result of a widely viewed video of the killing. This clearly established pattern raises serious, critical questions about the real intent behind the establishment of oversight agencies like the SIU and the influence of police organizations on the oversight process. In effect, the creation of these agencies is tantamount to hoodwinking the public into thinking that it exercises control over those who have the power to deprive us of our liberty and our life. An SIU investigation is not the only investigation, of course. In law, there is a rather elaborate system of accountability for police actions.

Whenever there is an investigation by the SIU, the law also requires the police chief to initiate an administrative review. This should include a review of policies, procedures, training, equipment and conduct involved in the incident. It must be completed within thirty days of the SIU investigation and its results are to be reported by the chief to the police board. The law does not make the intent and purpose of the review clear, but in Toronto we took the view that it should not only look at whether the officer's conduct was in compliance with policies, procedures and training, but also whether these things were satisfactory and if any changes or improvements were needed.

So in theory, even if the SIU has "cleared" a police officer, he or she could still be found guilty of misconduct in a chief's administrative review, be charged under the provincial *Police Services Act* and sent to a disciplinary hearing. Depending on the severity of the charges, the disciplinary hearing could result in the demotion or even termination of the individual. However in reality, these reviews follow the letter rather than the spirit of the law. They are largely paper exercises involving the checking off of a bunch of boxes in a report to the board to say that the officer complied with policies, procedures and training; that the equipment used was also in compliance; and that there were no conduct issues. When the SIU says it had no reason or lacked sufficient grounds to lay charges, the chief's review invariably repeats that conclusion. To me, the review is a classic example of how the systems of accountability put in place by law are manipulated to protect police interest.

Given this record of manipulation, the administrative review of police officers' actions or inactions in the killing of Yatim presented a huge challenge to the police service. Risk avoidance is a primary motivating factor in how the police institutionally deal with or manage difficult public relations issues. And when things go awry, they are very good at damage control. With the video circulating and the media demanding answers, the Yatim shooting was a disaster from the word go. Damage control began shortly after Blair and I spent a few quiet moments in my office discussing the video, and it played a key role in shaping the chief's administrative review.

The OIPRD and its director, Gerry McNeilly, warrant less attention in any analysis of police oversight. The biggest problem with the OIPRD, as Tulloch reported, is that the vast majority of complaints it receives are referred right back to the police service to be investigated and approximately 90 percent are dismissed. The OIPRD was created by Dalton McGuinty's Liberal government in 2009 with a mandate of accepting public complaints about the conduct of a police officer or the policies and services of an entire police department. Ontario previously had a robust independent public complaints commission, which the Harris government shut down. The function was transferred to what was then known as the Ontario Civilian Commission on Police Service (OCCPS, now called Ontario Civilian Police Commission).

When McGuinty became premier, he appointed a respected jurist, Justice Patrick LeSage, to recommend ways to revamp the public complaints system. After extensive consultations, Justice LeSage recommended a fairly tough system; what the McGuinty government put in place was a pale version of it. Police chiefs and unions wouldn't have accepted anything more vigorous. The OIPRD says it begins an oversight role from the moment it receives a complaint until the end of an investigation, but police chiefs or the OPP commissioner are responsible for any disciplinary hearings. It can also hold systemic reviews—as it did when it announced, in November 2016, that it would probe the Thunder Bay police service for "systemic racism" for its handling of investigations of Indigenous persons who have gone missing or died. It also has a mandate to educate the public about the complaints system. The truth is the OIPRD is largely toothless and its educational component is a sham.

McNeilly is prepared to take on a more muscular role under the new Ontario legislation by 2022—if he receives the requisite funding.

I gained first-hand knowledge of the citizen complaint process when I filed a complaint against Chief Saunders in 2015. I had written an article pointing out that the key components of the 2014 Iacobucci report on police encounters with citizens with mental health problems had not been implemented. In an interview with the *Toronto Star*, Saunders was asked about my comments and the chief said as a practice he does not respond to statements that are inaccurate. I wrote to Saunders's employer, the police board, asking for its help in getting an answer from the chief as to what was inaccurate in my article. The board under new chair Andy Pringle did not respond. Then I got a letter from the vice-chair of the board, Chin Lee, saying my recommendation would be taken into consideration when the board did the chief's performance review.

I wrote back saying I hadn't made a recommendation, but that I wanted their help because Saunders was casting aspersions on the accuracy of what I had written. The board ignored the second letter and I filed a complaint with the OIPRD against Saunders and with the OCPC against the board, which I believed was shirking its responsibility to oversee the chief's performance. The OCPC ignored me, but the OIPRD accepted my complaint. I advised the OIPRD that I had also drawn the attention of the OCPC to the board's conduct. Even armed with that information, the OIPRD referred my complaint right back to the police board for it to handle. I have no idea why it would do that.

A lack of manpower and funding is only part of the problem. McNeilly, a man with solid credentials, spent a great deal of time setting up the commission. There was a big push during its design for it to be closely connected to the public and for there to be mechanisms for regular consultations with the community. As he designed the organization, however, McNeilly spent most of the first year consulting with chiefs and associations, but not police boards or the community. This approach was likely based on the knowledge that if the chiefs were not on side or there was not a co-operative relationship with the police, he would not be able to do his job. McNeilly came to the public and police boards much later, after he had built his relationship with the chiefs and the unions. What did he give to get their co-operation?

We are left with an oversight agency that refers the vast majority of complaints to the same people who are being investigated. It was very important that the OIPRD exercise independence as well as oversight in the investigation of more serious matters, but I don't believe this has happened. The OIPRD is known for its comprehensive report on G20 police misconduct, but I believe the study only happened because of public pressure generated through the media. McNeilly would routinely say he was unable to find evidence to back allegations, and the next day that evidence would be published in the *Toronto Star*. His systemic reports are important, but he has no authority to force anything to be implemented. McNeilly's power lies in his ability to direct police to charge one of their own; that power has been used in a limited number of cases.

It is too difficult for ordinary citizens to find out how to file a complaint. Many—likely most—residents of Ontario have never heard of the OIPRD and have no idea where to turn if they have a legitimate complaint after an interaction with a police officer. There should be flyers about it available at universities or in libraries or shopping malls, any place where the public congregates, but the OIPRD does not advertise. There are informational brochures at Toronto police divisions and the desk sergeant might offer you one if you are there and complaining about treatment. If you are on the street and being harassed or if you have been pulled over and believe you have been treated improperly, don't expect the officer to reach into his or her pocket and offer you information on how to complain about their behaviour.

The OCPC has gradually slid into irrelevance. It is supposed to hear appeals of police disciplinary decisions; adjudicate budgetary disputes between municipal councils and police service boards; hear requests from municipalities wishing to reduce, eliminate or amalgamate their police forces; and conduct investigations into the behaviour of chiefs of police, police officers and members of police services boards—or boards as a whole. It is the only oversight body that could have removed me or any other police board chair. It was, in essence, my boss—albeit an absentee one. This slide into irrelevance began under Harris. The OCCPS, predecessor of the current commission, had stronger leadership.

Before my time on the Toronto Police Services Board, I spent three years with the OCCPS, from 1994 to 1997. We would travel anywhere in the province when a police force wanted to disband, amalgamate with the OPP or reduce services. We would ask a lot of questions, tough questions, before we would decide whether to give the green light or not. Then Harris came to power. He replaced the OCCPS membership with people who were police-friendly. He clipped its powers and ultimately dismantled the complaints commission, transferring its function to the civilian police commission, the OCPC.

My first-hand dealings with the present OCPC have demonstrated its irrelevance. After I made comments in 2016 about a couple of cops on a Toronto television station, CP24, Mike McCormack wrote to the OCPC to complain about me. I was no longer chair of the Toronto Police Board. I was a private citizen, and as such the OCPC had no jurisdiction over me. I got legal advice and wrote a letter to McCormack saying I had mixed up two different cases and had erred in my comments. I apologized. I copied this to the OCPC. Within twenty-four hours, a letter went out to McCormack, copied to me, saying I acknowledged my error and the OCPC considered the matter closed. That's how fast they can work if they choose to, even if in this case they were working completely outside their mandate.

A far more important interaction came during 2011–12, when we were working hard to reduce the bloated Toronto police budget by ten percent and actively talking about restructuring the entire police service. Legislation in the province is clear—if you are talking about reducing staff, there are certain steps to be taken and those steps are to be reviewed and approved or rejected by the OCPC. As a precaution, I contacted the OCPC and asked for a meeting with the chair. It might as well not have happened, as the OCPC did not offer a single recommendation. For me, it was remarkable evidence of the OCPC's irrelevance when it comes to the oversight of policing. During this entire discussion of the future of policing, the OCPC was absent from the table.

You would think the OCPC would know how each police service and board across the province was working and would have important insights for us. You would be wrong. When it announced it was probing the Thunder Bay Police Services Board in July 2017, the OCPC was perhaps acknowledging its limitations when, instead of conducting the investigation itself, it appointed Senator Murray Sinclair, former chair of the Truth and Reconciliation Commission, to get to the bottom of the concerning state of civilian police oversight in the northwestern Ontario city.

WE SHOULD DO away with these three institutions. And we should strip the provincial ministry of its responsibility for auditing police boards and police services. Instead, let's create one highly muscular inspectorate with strong powers to investigate public complaints and probe police use of force as well as the conduct of police boards, chiefs and officers. It should have the scope to consider systemic problems with police services. It should also have very strong powers to provide oversight and hold boards, chiefs and officers accountable. And this inspectorate should be an agency of the legislature, not the government, with arm's-length clearance from the government like the Auditor General or the federal parliamentary budget office. Tulloch, in fact, recommended that all three oversight bodies be removed from the *Police Services Act* and that these functions be covered by stand-alone legislation.

The Ontario proposal calls for the appointment of an inspector general, who would oversee police services and boards and would be able to review complaints against board members or chiefs of police. It gives this person the right to appoint inspectors who can receive and act on complaints about policing at all levels.

The inspectorate I propose would have the power and the authority to walk into a police service and have unfettered access to any information or records it needed to get to the bottom of its probe. It would be first on the scene, but with much broader responsibilities than we see now. At the end of an investigation a small portion of information must be covered by privacy, but beyond that the inspectorate would provide full information to the public. Why should the names be confidential? If I were charged with a crime, even if I were wrongfully charged and innocent, my name would be released. And I'm betting I would be a prominent feature in at least one news cycle and likely beyond. One can argue that is unfair too, but the fact remains that there is a double standard in which citizens are named but police officers are not. Police culture starts and ends with secrecy; it will take a huge societal shift to pull the curtain back on this entrenched secrecy.

Citizens have a right to know that their police are held accountable. They have a right to know that police misconduct is being assiduously probed without a nod and a wink and a sit-down with a lawyer so that the officer—rather than the truth—receives paramount protection. The public deserves real oversight that might make officers think twice. The public deserves more than an illusion. The question is whether the public can have anything more than an illusion as long as the present structures and processes—or some variations of them—continue to exist. The history and the track record of these agencies do not inspire confidence.

The track record of the three agencies—the SIU, the OIPRD and the OCPC—shows that they are very busy. They are taking complaints, conducting investigations, holding hearings, writing voluminous reports and supplying the media with stories virtually daily. They provide well-paid and secure employment to scores of civil servants, both civilian and ex-police. Because of these agencies, a large number of lawyers do lucrative business. Thanks to these agencies' work, the government of the day, the mayor of a given municipality, the local police board and the police chief are able to deflect responsibility and avoid taking heat. We've all heard this mantra: "We cannot comment, because Agency X has jurisdiction and this matter is under investigation."

The police associations respond to public questioning of officers' accountability with the drumbeat that they are held more accountable than anyone else by multiple agencies and the chief of police. Associations trumpet the fact that the vast majority of police officers investigated by the SIU are cleared of any criminal wrongdoing; the bulk of public complaints to the OIPRD are dismissed as unsubstantiated, malicious or made in bad faith; and most *Police Services Act* charges laid by police chiefs are concluded with no penalty or a minor one. It all paints a picture that police conduct themselves lawfully and follow the rules. The message is: look at us, we're doing our jobs remarkably well and with great honour.

Don't tell me that most of these charges are unfounded or without merit and that the vast majority of the complainants are lying. It is difficult not to conclude that these elaborate systems of oversight do their work very well. They work hard to assure the public that they hold police accountable in the public interest. At the same time, however, the meagre results of their work make sure that the police interest will not be undermined or compromised. Yes, the illusion is real—and perhaps intended. The public deserves more than this sleight of hand. It will only get this when our leaders are truly committed to a system that is genuinely independent, devoid of vested interests and able to deliver consequences that are good for society, not just good for the police. Tulloch's work is getting us there.

But then the appalling case of nineteen-year-old Dafonte Miller comes along to remind us how far we still have to go. Miller, who is Black, was walking through his neighbourhood in Whitby, Ontario, on the night of December 28, 2016, when he was confronted by a man who identified himself as a police officer. Michael Theriault was off-duty at the time. He is alleged to have beaten Miller so badly with a metal pipe in an apparently senseless attack that the young man was expected to lose an eye.

Yet initially, Miller was the one who was charged. It was only after his lawyer Falconer became involved that the charges against Miller were dropped and charges of aggravated assault, assault with a weapon and public mischief were laid against the off-duty cop. It took four months for the SIU to get involved in the case. Why? The

Durham region police didn't report the attack. Not their job, they claimed, because Theriault was a Toronto cop. Toronto police didn't bother to notify the SIU either. It took the intervention of Miller's lawyer. Blue culture rises again.

What Is the Right Number?

IN FEBRUARY 2010, Bill Blair and I travelled to India on the Indian government's invitation to make connections with senior police authorities there, exchange information about models and methods of policing and observe first-hand how the police dealt with their multiple challenges. Only a few months prior, Mumbai had experienced a serious terrorist attack. And a few months later Delhi was to host a major international event—the Commonwealth Games. We hoped to gain some insights that could be useful in planning for the upcoming G20 summit. When we asked the police commissioner of Delhi about security plans for the Commonwealth Games, he laughed and nonchalantly told us he was not concerned at all. He had some thirty-five thousand officers and they would take care of all eventualities. If necessary, he would have access to more police personnel from other jurisdictions—the right number.

As Mike Del Grande—Toronto city councillor and chair of the city's budget committee—would ask the police services board in 2011, "What is the right number?" As I found out from international representatives over the years from countries like the Netherlands, Norway, Kenya, China and the UK, this was one of the questions exercising the minds of politicians, police governors, police leaders and the public in many parts of the world. The question of size was one of several questions related to the model, methods, organizational structure and cost of policing.

I had attempted a preliminary answer to this question in 2009 at the annual conference of the Canadian Association of Police Boards (CAPB; now the Canadian Association of Police Governance) in Sydney, Nova Scotia. Speaking at the plenary session "Crisis in Policing," I said that our system suffered from several "mismatches" that needed to be tackled. I listed three:

1. between what police are supposed to do and what they actually do;
2. between a community's and the state's needs and demands, and allocation of resources; and
3. between the legislative supports police organizations want and the supports they get.

As the name of the session indicated, governors of local police forces and municipal politicians had begun to realize that policing in Canada was heading into a crisis, if not facing one already. That crisis was primarily deemed to be related to the growing cost of municipal policing and the burden this placed on the local taxpayer. It was in this context that I drew attention to the mismatches.

My point was that an obsolete model of policing based on laws derived from the nineteenth century was failing to meet the needs of the twenty-first century, and that this was contributing to an inefficient system of delivering policing services. We were, in effect, relying on highly paid uniformed police officers trained mainly in the use of force to provide a whole slew of other services. In May 2011, Attorney General and minister of justice for Nova Scotia Ross Landry observed, "The cost of providing policing services, like many other public services, is at a critical juncture. It is at a point where many ask, 'Can the present model of public policing continue without reform? Is it sustainable?'" Landry's question was occupying the minds of cost-conscious politicians in many other parts of Canada as well as in Ottawa.

The Federation of Canadian Municipalities (FCM) had released a national study arguing that the federal government needed to pick up a share of policing costs, since local police forces were performing tasks that came under federal jurisdiction, thus subsidizing federal responsibility through property taxes. On the other hand, the CACP had proposed an integrated model of policing under which the existing separation between federal, provincial and local policing responsibilities would end and those of local police forces would formally include matters like national security, anti-terrorism and cybercrime. To the CACP, the question of who pays for what was of little consequence, on the basis that there is, after all, only one taxpayer.

The Canadian Police Association (CPA) and its provincial member organizations were not convinced that policing costs were too high, arguing that the public was getting value for its money. Consequently, the CPA proposed a comprehensive systemic review to develop the evidence to determine whether costs were in fact too high. The Canadian Association of Police Boards (CAPB) agreed with the FCM that policing was becoming very expensive and that the current funding system for policing in Canada, under which the local municipality picks up the bulk of policing costs, needs to be fixed; it agreed with CACP that we needed an integrated policing model; and it agreed with CPA that a full review would help in making evidence-based decisions. It was in this context that Landry made his comments at a symposium on the future of policing organized by the Canadian Police College (CPC) in Ottawa. Its director general, Cal Corley, had been present during my remarks at the CAPB conference in Sydney and was an early proponent of transforming Canada's model of policing.

An assistant commissioner of the RCMP before taking over the CPC, Corley was the Canadian co-ordinator of Pearls of Policing, an international project of senior police leaders. As part of the project, a group of big-city police chiefs and deputy chiefs as well as senior members of the RCMP, the Ontario Provincial Police (OPP) and the

Sûreté du Québec partnered with their counterparts from Australia, the Netherlands, Hong Kong and the UK to explore the future of policing. In October 2011, participants in the project met in Toronto for the 2011–12 International Pearl Fishers Action Learning Group. Besides having an opportunity to hear about developments in the participants' countries at the meeting, I had been invited to speak about change efforts in Toronto and the issues our civilian police board was attempting to deal with.

A year earlier, from late November to early December of 2010, Corley had organized a study tour of England for ten senior police leaders, the president of the CPA and me as president of the CAPB to observe and learn about changes to policing being made there. During the tour, we learned about and observed some significant changes in policing and police governance made in response to the UK government's demand to reduce its police budget by almost 20 percent over three years. This was a rare opportunity for us to get a first-hand look at what was a radical transformation of the British model of policing. Two years after the study tour, in 2012, Corley hosted a small group of us for three days to consider the future of policing in the context of the global economic crisis.

Between when I raised the issue of mismatches in 2009 and today, considerable discussion has taken place in Canada and around the world about the future of policing. Meanwhile the world has continued to change due to the rise of ISIS, internal security threats caused by terrorist incidents in many parts of Europe and the waves of refugees arriving on the shores of Europe, North America and Australia. These developments provide a critical backdrop for the international debate on the future of policing.

On the night of June 3, 2017, a Saturday, at precisely eight minutes past ten, London police began receiving frantic calls. A white van had veered into a crowd on the iconic London Bridge, hitting five, maybe six people. In the chaos of that night, details were imprecise. Eight minutes later, the three men in the van had been shot and killed by eight armed officers who fired what was said to be an unprecedented forty-six shots at the trio. During those eight minutes of mayhem the three men, armed with thirty-centimetre ceramic knives, slashed and stabbed their way to the Borough Market, killing eight and injuring forty-eight others in a maelstrom of terror. Among the dead was thirty-year-old Christine Archibald from Castlegar, BC, who had worked in a Calgary homeless shelter before moving to Europe to be with her fiancé. Unarmed officers on the street were unable to stop the trio.

If more London police officers were routinely armed, would lives have been saved? This is an ongoing question in England and Wales, home to one of the most lightly armed police forces in the world. It is a question asked with increasing frequency by elected leaders, police officials, rank-and-file police and the public in an age of random attacks in which vehicles, chemicals, knives, machetes and, yes, guns are the weapons of war. It is a question being raised in every major jurisdiction in which officers are not routinely armed, meaning that during the second decade of this century, when many of us are pushing for police reform, there is a powerful counter-push for the American way of policing in places where it has long been resisted.

England endured four major terror attacks in the first half of 2017. On March 22, five people including an unarmed police officer were killed and fifty injured when a man in a rented car drove into pedestrians on Westminster Bridge and then ran toward Parliament, brandishing a knife, before being shot dead. The fatal shot came from an armed protective officer on the Parliament grounds. A May 22 attack by a male suicide bomber killed twenty-two and injured fifty-nine following a Manchester concert by Ariana Grande, a favourite of young girls. The June 3 rampage that began on London Bridge left seven dead and forty-eight injured. On June 9, a van drove into a crowd of Muslim worshippers, killing one and injuring nine.

What's more, England is now experiencing a jump in crime that has some alarmed. The Office for National Statistics reported that for the year ending in March 2017, crime rose by 10 percent across the board in England and Wales. Drilling down into the numbers, it is violent crime that is surging, up 18 percent, with gun and knife crime jumping 20 percent. Police in London were outfitted with one thousand acid-attack kits in their rapid response vehicles during the summer of 2017; in 2016, there were 455 reported crimes in the UK capital in which the weapon or threatened weapon was a corrosive or noxious substance. The rise in acid attacks is believed to be a response by street gangs to a government crackdown on knife and firearm use. Legislation passed in 2015 made a jail term mandatory for anyone found guilty of a second knife offence.[1]

As crime has been rising, the number of police has been declining. There were 123,142 officers in England and Wales by spring 2017, down 924 in one year and down 20,952 since 2010. By the summer of 2017, England and Wales had the fewest number of officers since 1985.[2] The reduction in police levels became a campaign issue in the 2017 British election with Labour leader Jeremy Corbyn promising to raise policing levels by ten thousand if elected and Conservative prime minister Theresa May coming under attack for policing decisions she made when she was home secretary. In her previous role, May had put stock in falling crime rates when she agreed in 2010 to a treasury request to cut policing costs by 18 percent.

Attitudes in the UK began to harden following terror attacks in France. Even though the English counter-terrorism budget was protected and grew at the expense of community policing, alarms were raised about the ability of front-line police to respond to attacks on their streets. Before he resigned after his failed Brexit vote, prime minister David Cameron had committed to reversing the decline in armed officers and had made plans to have troops on standby in case of an assault on English cities. The government also promised transformation—training police to deal with twenty-first-century threats. Still, as he left office, former London police commissioner Bernard Hogan-Howe warned, "The bottom line is there will be less cops. There is only so much you can cut and make efficiencies and then you've got to have less police, and I'm not sure that's wise in this city."[3]

Against this backdrop, in July 2017, officers in England and Wales were asked whether they wanted to be armed with more Tasers, whether more officers should be specially trained in firearms or whether more rank-and-file officers should be armed. Debate over arming English police has periodically flared up over the years, and many of the calls to arms have had nothing to do with terror. It goes as far back as the 1952 killing of unarmed Constable Sidney Miles, who took a bullet to the head and died on the spot during a bungled break-in. The callous slaying in 1966 of three plainclothes officers who pulled over three members of a two-bit gang and paid for it with their lives again sparked debate. Almost forty years later, Constable Sharon Beshenivsky was killed and her partner badly injured by a gunman when the two officers were responding to a 2005 travel-agency robbery.

Yet public opinion—and the opinion of rank-and-file officers—has ebbed and flowed over the years. The summer 2017 canvass was the first time the rank and file had been surveyed on gun use since 2006. At the end of March 2017, according to the Home Office, 5 percent of all English and Welsh police officers were authorized to use a firearm.[4] In the year ending in March 2017, police in England and Wales fired weapons ten times; however, this included six fatal shootings, a twelve-year high. It may look like a spike and perhaps it is. But context is everything. The number of police responses involving officers equipped with firearms steadily declined between 2009 and 2017, from 23,181 incidents in 2009 to 15,705 in 2017. In every year studied from 2009 to 2016, police in England and Wales did not discharge their firearms in more than seven incidents in a given year.[5]

This is evidence of adherence to the cherished British principle of "policing by consent," the basis of modern policing as enshrined by Sir Robert Peel, as opposed to the oppression by the military. It recognizes that police serve only as long as they maintain the consent, approval and respect of the public. That respect can only be secured through the willing co-operation of the public and having the police, in turn, secure observance of those laws. It may sound utopian, but over almost two centuries it has largely worked in England and Wales. The dictums below come from Peel's nine principles of policing, even though it is now believed that the principles were actually crafted by the first commissioners of the London police when they gave their general instructions to the first recruits in 1829.

Contrast some of these principles with the militarized, intimidating, gun-toting, officer-safety-first policing we see in North America. Officers in 1829 were instructed to do the following:

- Recognize that the extent to which the co-operation of the public can be secured diminishes proportionately the necessity of the use of physical force and compulsion for achieving police objectives.
- Seek and preserve public favour not by pandering to public opinion but by constantly demonstrating absolutely impartial service to the law, in complete independence of policy and without regard to the justice or injustice of the substance of individual laws, by the ready offering of individual service and friendship to all members of the public without regard to their wealth or social standing, by the ready exercise of courtesy and friendly good humour; and by the ready offering of individual sacrifice in protecting and preserving life.
- Use physical force only when the exercise of persuasion, advice and warning is found to be insufficient to obtain public co-operation to the extent necessary to secure observance of a law or to restore order, and to use only the minimum degree of physical force that is necessary on any particular occasion for achieving a police objective.
- Recognize that the test of police efficiency is the absence of crime and disorder and not the visible evidence of police action in dealing with them.[6]

We may be living in different times now, but in 2006 more than eight out of ten cops on the streets of England and Wales did not want to be armed. There has been anecdotal polling in the country that shows the public is quite amenable to having its police armed, but there appeared to be no great hue and cry about the issue in the summer of 2017.

Police in London, however, seem to have a problem that plagues police forces the world over–their interaction with racialized minorities. There are other statistics that show that armed or unarmed, London police face some of the same race-based challenges as their North American counterparts. According to data released under a mandatory reporting regimen, in the three months ending in June 2017, 36 percent of 12,605 uses of force by London police were against those who self-identified as Black. Only about 13 percent of the city's population is Black.[7]

When it comes to police carrying firearms, there are two basic questions to answer:

1. Are officers safer (and do they feel safer) with a gun at their side?
2. Is it even possible to begin to disarm police officers in North America, where gun ownership is exponentially higher than it is in the UK?

Let's look at other countries that do not routinely arm their officers. In 2011, following the shooting deaths of two officers, New Zealand adopted an armed response model very similar to the British model. The incoming police commissioner, Peter Marshall, wanted all his officers to have access to firearms in locked safes in their cars, but he didn't want them strapped to his officers' hips. "Nothing...convinces me general arming is going to result in a safer public or indeed safer police officers," he told New Zealand media. "There will be more instances of firearms taken off police and used against them. There would be more inquiries into the conduct of the police as a result. And there would be trust and confidence issues around the police."[8]

Regardless, since the 2011 move, Glock semi-automatic pistols and Bushmaster XM15 M4A3 rifles, as well as ballistic armour, are in front-line vehicles locked in safes. Tasers are also available to front-line officers, similarly locked inside cars. A supervisor's approval is needed for officers to access the weapons. An estimated 5,700 members of the country's 8,100 officers have received training in rifle, pistol and Taser use.[9]

In the summer of 2016, two fatal shootings by police sparked calls to limit officers' access to firearms. New Zealand police, however, do not want to go back to pre-2011 policies. In fact, the New Zealand police association claims that 70 percent of its membership wants the right to carry firearms because more New Zealanders have access to guns. In June 2017 the association published its policy priorities in advance of that autumn's general election: it wants all constables in the force to be armed full-time. The association said there were problems with the lock-box system: "Members regularly report risks associated with the locked box policy, including inaccessibility to the firearms when needed because of the time required to retrieve them, and inaccessibility because the vehicle in which the locked box is stored is out of reach or blocked off during an incident. Members realize the inevitability of an armed police force and want a smooth transition to this position, including a level of training that will assist in avoiding tragedies."[10]

There are many opponents to arming every officer, noted criminologist Greg Newbold among them. Having patrolled with officers in New Zealand and the US, he has seen arrests at gunpoint in America—aggressive takedowns of suspects onto the ground—whereas in New Zealand an arrest usually ends with a request that the suspect get in the car. He told New Zealand media the mere presence of a gun on a cop's hip changed the way the officer thought about people, treated people, even the way the officer walked. The presence of a gun can change a reliable, trustworthy officer into an arrogant, bullying thug, he maintained. Nor would a gun make the officer safer because the presence of a weapon changes the entire dynamic of an officer's interaction with a suspect.[11] —power

Three other nations—Iceland, Ireland and Norway—are also worth examining in this context. Tiny Iceland, with a population of about 334,000, has one of the lowest crime rates in the world, but that does not mean there are no guns in the country. According to the Swiss-based Small Arms Survey, there are thirty guns per one hundred citizens in Iceland. Statistics suggest that Iceland's "violence is the last resort" conflict-resolution policy works far better than America's perceived "a gun is always an option" policy. There are fewer than one thousand police officers in Iceland and although they are trained in firearm use, most are not armed.

Iceland had never had a case of a police officer killing a citizen until 2013. That incident, in which police fired back at a mentally unstable suspect who had shot at police and hit an officer in the helmet with a bullet, traumatized the nation. Police immediately apologized to the man's family and loved ones. That remains the only fatal police shooting in the seventy-three years, since Iceland became an independent republic. By comparison, Stockton, California, a city of comparable size, had three fatal police shootings in the first five months of 2015.[12]

In the summer of 2017, a decision to place armed officers at a large event sparked controversy. Armed members of Iceland's special forces were in attendance at a family-oriented charity fun run, a decision that was not publicized ahead of time. The terror threat in the UK was cited as a reason for the move. Icelandic media reported that the sight of armed police at the event was a shock to many attendees. Police also announced that its special forces unit would be a visible presence at future public events in Iceland. To some, the combination of armed police and the lack of an official rationale was, as chairperson of the Left-Green Movement Katrín Jakobsdóttir put it, "rather unsettling."[13]

Jakobsdóttir is now Iceland's prime minister, heading a coalition government, potentially opening up a new, leftist view of policing for the world to see.

A similar scenario is playing out in Ireland. The national police force, the Garda Síochána na hÉireann (Guardians of the Peace of Ireland), dates back to the eighteenth century and today numbers more than twelve thousand members. The Garda is largely unarmed, with front-line officers predominantly using extendable batons and pepper spray in their day-to-day work. But the Garda has received increased government funding and in December 2016, a new heavily armed, fifty-five-member unit was created, ostensibly to deal with organized crime and gangs. Then in the wake of the London bombings, members were dispatched to Irish streets. The government subsequently announced that because of the London attacks, another twenty members of the Armed Support Unit would be recruited.

During the summer of 2017, their presence became ubiquitous. Armed units were stationed at concerts by Coldplay and U2 following the Manchester attack at the Ariana Grande concert, at a charity cycling event, at local soccer matches and a World Cup qualifying match as well as at the country's Pride parade. But the Garda has been engulfed in controversy, including allegations of inflating the number of breathalyzer tests it administered—an internal probe found it claimed 1.45 million bogus breath tests from 2009 to 2017—inaccurate homicide statistics and financial irregularities at a police training college. It has also come under fire for lack of diversity among its rank and file. In April 2017, the Irish government responded to these complaints by establishing a commission on the future of policing in Ireland.

In Norway, a nation of 5.2 million people, police are now routinely armed following an April 2017 terror attack in Sweden, but this change has been sold as temporary. The possibility of it being temporary is hardly far-fetched in Norway—policy has fluctuated over the years. In reaction to another terror attack in 2014, Norwegian police were armed. That threat abated and fourteen months later they returned their guns. Whether they were routinely armed or not, Norwegian police never fired more than six shots in a single year between 2000 and 2015. They have killed two citizens this century.

Ross Hendy, a former police officer in New Zealand and a researcher at the University of Cambridge, has provided one of the most valuable studies on arming police, comparing the situation in New Zealand with that of Norway and also Sweden, where officers are routinely armed. Based on original evidence and case studies, he found that officers took more risks if routinely armed and that there was greater danger of death and grievous injury to those in mental distress. [14] Hendy found the fact that Norwegian police often have to wait as long as five minutes for permission from a higher authority to use firearms encourages them to peacefully respond to a dangerous situation. The delay helps all concerned. It gives officers time to think.

In most cases, there were double the number of Norwegian officers compared with Swedish officers at the scene, allowing for more tactical safety. One Norwegian officer told Hendy in an interview, "It take[s] me less than a minute to take them [firearms] out and be ready to use them. In my opinion the most sufficient argument is that it gives us time to think instead of getting the sidearm on the hip and just running in to solve a case." Another Norwegian officer told him that if you pull out a gun as the first response, it is difficult to put it away and reverse course.

Of course, there will be a lot less use of firearms by police in a country where there are fewer firearms in the possession of criminals and ordinary citizens. According to the Small Arms Survey, New Zealand has 22.6 guns per 100 citizens. The Canadian rate of gun ownership, it says, is 30.8 per 100, just behind Sweden (31.6 per 100 citizens) and Norway (31.3 per 100). These numbers are not precise and may be dated, but the survey is still the most authoritative gauge of firearm ownership in the world. It doesn't provide figures for Ireland but mentions that there has been a proliferation of guns in the hands of gang members in that country. Iceland has about 30 guns per 100 citizens, England and Wales only six.[15]

Estimates of gun ownership in the United States vary, but all reports indicate that the country is armed to the teeth. The Small Arms Survey says there are 88.6 firearms per 100 citizens, but other estimates indicate there are more guns in the US than people. A congressional study estimated the total number of firearms available to civilians in the United States in 2009 had increased to approximately 310 million: 114 million handguns, 110 million rifles and 86 million shotguns.[16] The US population in 2009 was approximately 305 million.

Regardless of departmental policy when it comes to European police forces, the much lower prevalence of death-by-police may have much to do with the nature and quality of police education and training across Europe. Writing in the *Harvard Political Review*, Nick Danby describes the European commitment to educating police:

> Europeans achieve responsible policing by first centralizing their police standards, which ensures that every police department and academy teaches the same material. In the Netherlands, Norway and Finland, after receiving some form of post-secondary education, the government requires police attend a national police academy for three years to learn this centralized material. In Germany, the process takes at least 130 weeks—more than two full years of preparation. European training is longer because the departments deem it necessary to give officers an all-inclusive and thorough police training to practice communicating with emotionally disturbed individuals and to approach various scenarios through the lens of conflict resolution, rather than one of violence.

> Spanish police, unlike other police forces, always fire a warning shot and aim for non-vital body parts. North American police are trained to shoot to kill. Many forces outside North America require front-line officers to get permission from a superior before shooting, unless their life is in immediate danger.[17]

Clearly, there is no simple answer to the question, "What's the number of uniformed and armed police officers a community needs to be safe?" This is because, as we have seen, the answer has a lot to do with the political and social conditions that exist at any given time, since they have a major impact on public opinion. It would appear there is considerable public anxiety about safety and security in the UK and Europe due largely to national security and terrorism–related concerns. And evidently this condition has worked in the favour of those who support larger, armed police forces.

At the same time, however, the debate about the right number has not affected the significant changes to the model of policing that began to be introduced in places like England and Wales and the Netherlands around 2010. For example, in the Netherlands, there was a consolidation of local policing through amalgamating many small local police forces into a handful of large regional agencies. As well, there was a separation of responsibilities between these amalgamated forces and the national police organization.

England and Wales went even further, as I learned during our 2010 study tour. Different local police forces employed different strategies to achieve the UK government's budget reduction target. Some neighbouring forces adopted a shared service model for their non-policing administrative and business functions. Others handed over certain policing responsibilities, such as court security and prisoner transportation, to private security firms. And yet others created a parallel structure in which they kept responsibility for front-line policing and handed over what they called "middle office" and "back office" functions to private companies. In one instance, we found that a police force had relied on a private IT company to build its disaster-recovery facility. In one large police force, a more businesslike practice of "zero-based budgeting," developed by the accounting firm PricewaterhouseCoopers, was adopted. Under this method, the force required every single policing program to build and justify its annual budget from zero every year.

So the debate over the "right number" notwithstanding, there are far-reaching changes taking place in many parts of the world to how policing is provided, the business model of policing and the methods of service delivery—all for the purpose of either controlling the costs of policing or developing alternative ways to provide policing services. Those in charge of charting the way forward in Canada cannot remain oblivious to these developments.

The Way Forward

SO LET'S GET back to the question this book began with: *What's the matter with police in this country?*

To put it bluntly, it is the use of various types of excessive force, whether brutal, lethal or political. The incidents are widespread and endemic, and there is a sickening pattern. In a majority of the cases, the victims are Black, Indigenous or other racialized people, and they have mental health issues, are poor or are less powerful. The cumulative effect is a picture of hypermasculinity, misogyny, sexism, racism, violence, lack of integrity, collusion and disregard if not contempt for the rule of law and people's rights. This speaks volumes about the dark side of an informal police culture that has an overwhelming influence on policing.

It is a failure of leadership to persist in dismissing these incidents as the conduct of a handful when that so-called handful is so large that it keeps internal systems like professional standards, and external oversight bodies like the SIU and the OIPRD, busy year round, every day. It is an even greater failure of leadership when significant action occurs only when a matter becomes public, communities are outraged, and pressure builds—or when a matter lands before a judge. I have suggested before that our systems of accountability for the most part play a symbolic and not a substantive role. That includes internal as well as external mechanisms.

Incidents of excessive force make it imperative to question the system for recruiting, training, mentoring and supervising police officers. How closely are the educational, moral, ethical and psychological standards of new recruits assessed? How compatible are these standards with contemporary policing and society's needs? At a time when the mission of policing as much as the demographics of our communities have changed so significantly, why is there such a focus during training on shooting a gun? Why is there a persistent absence of a practice of critically reflecting on—and learning from—what worked well in the past and what did not? Why isn't more credence given to developments in law and concerns of the public? Why does it appear that there is a weak system of supervision and accountability based on a wink and a nod, rather than on holding people to the highest standards of professionalism?

An organization that is inward-looking and has the culture of a private club hampers the potential of an individual to be a maverick or an independent thinker. You advance by being a team player. And how do most of those in the top ranks prepare themselves for the task? There is no requirement that a deputy chief or chief must have a degree or training in areas like senior management, human resources, financial management or organizational behaviour. He or she need not demonstrate in-depth knowledge and understanding of the Criminal Code, the *Police Services Act*, the Canadian Charter of Rights and Freedoms or the provincial Human Rights Code. There is no requirement that a person spend a significant amount of time in other types of work environments. They may have been an excellent police officer in one police service, but does that make them excellent executive material—especially when they are so deeply imbued with the culture of that service?

Then there is the police services board, made up of people who are thrown together by happenstance, a combination of local politicians and people supposedly drawn from the community, appointed through provincial and municipal political processes. There are no competencies on which they are assessed and in many cases, their appointment is politically motivated. There is no mandatory training as a condition of remaining on the board. Too often the board is in awe of the police chief, lacks the expertise to deal with the union or doesn't have the courage to hold the chief truly accountable. Too rarely does the board understand its fiduciary responsibility or see itself as the guardian of the public interest.

How can such boards provide truly meaningful, effective and independent governance and oversight? The board's role is further complicated when there is a mayor with a political agenda and the will to dominate. Typically, the board buckles and does this politician's bidding. And the law as it relates to the board as well as the body that oversees the board provide no mechanism to ensure that this does not happen. Consequently, when serious issues arise, the board stays mute or does the bidding of the chief or the mayor. This is not governance in the public interest.

By contrast, the union—the police association—is not at all reluctant to play the heavy. Ontario's *Police Services Act* provides no clear description of the role of the association other than as the bargaining agent for the employees. The law requires that all members of a police service must belong to an association, depending on their rank. Front-line and non-supervisory civilian personnel are members of the police association, while inspectors, staff inspectors, superintendents, staff superintendents and senior civilian managers are part of the senior officers' organization. It is pretty much the same in all provinces.

Over time, using their collective power, unions have greatly expanded their role as bargaining agents by opting for a very broad definition of what constitutes their members' well-being and working conditions. They have used this definition to insert themselves vocally into policy-making and determining the direction a service will take. Their success in gaining this power has been facilitated by compliant boards anxious to avoid conflict, chiefs who see it as in their interest to have the union on their side—and governments who find it advantageous to treat the police unions as partners and stakeholders. The *Police Services Act* reflects the influence of police associations, which have become very powerful, greatly political, well-resourced entities.

But this is only one way in which governments have influenced the direction of policing. As I have discussed earlier, federal and provincial governments have played a critical role in the militarization and securitization of policing on the one hand, and vastly broadening the mission and scope of policing on the other. And having done so, they have demonstrated an inability or unwillingness, so far, to go beyond the duct tape and the Band-Aids that are no longer sufficient answers to the challenges of local policing today.

What, then, is the way forward? The last few years have seen more and more questioning of Canada's model of policing, driven by two considerations: first, concerns about the nature of policing and interactions between police and the public; and second, the perceived high (and growing) cost of policing. The phrase "transformational change" is being bandied about freely by governments and organizations related to policing, and efforts to achieve it are taking place in several provinces and police forces. But moving ahead means navigating many of the roadblocks I have laid out here.

Some of the concerns I have been raising for years have been taken up by others. Events and issues discussed in this book have produced considerable amounts of anger, protest and advocacy in the community, such as the emergence of Black Lives Matter Toronto, the work of Concerned Citizens Against Carding and exposés by journalists like Desmond Cole, Robyn Doolittle, Wendy Gillis, Royson James and Jim Rankin. It would appear that the Ontario government has listened to the demand for modernization of the policing model by overhauling the *Police Services Act*. We have come a long way because, historically, governments have not shown the political will to follow the public interest and create radical change if it is not to the liking of police chiefs and associations. Tulloch's recommendations are very much designed to make the status quo better rather than transform it radically. Nonetheless, he does raise the bar. Ontario's Attorney General accepted all his recommendations and in November 2017 introduced the *Policing Oversight Act 2017* in the provincial legislature.

If the act is fully implemented, Ontario's system of independent police oversight could change significantly. At the same time, the government has also introduced legislation to update the *Police Services Act*, which had remained unchanged for twenty-five years. The two proposed acts are part of an ambitious piece of omnibus legislation called the *Safer Ontario Act 2017*.

All of this is a far cry from the time when, in 2005, Ontario's then–minister of community safety and correctional services, Monte Kwinter, said repeatedly in response to demands and requests that the act would not be opened. He offered small regulatory or administrative tweaks, but said a definite no to any major overhaul.

As Toronto Police Services Board chair, I had compiled a list of reasons to reopen the *Police Services Act*, which had not been reviewed since 1997. The Ontario Association of Police Services Boards shared our view and had begun advocating for legislative change. There was, for example, no provision to extend the probationary period for a police constable. Nor did the act permit suspension without pay for a police officer accused of an egregious offence. Both are outdated and inefficient human resources practices. Without the probationary extension, we lose the opportunity to give someone a little more time and additional training to become a perfectly competent member of our force; we lose our investment in him or her. The suspension policy means we are forced to carry on the payroll, sometimes for years, an officer whose conduct is an affront to community standards. We also need more clarity on where the police board's power ends and the chief's jurisdiction begins. That ambiguity cost us dearly during the G20.

Kwinter simply would not move. Rick Bartolucci and James Bradley, who came after him, did no better. Finally, Madeleine Meilleur, who succeeded Bradley in 2011, agreed to discuss the issue of future of policing with police services boards, police chiefs, the police associations and other stakeholders. By this time, the future of policing and cost of policing had become a national issue and, following the national summit on the economics of policing in 2010, Ontario held its own summit on the future of policing. That was in 2011. And it has taken all these years and two more ministers—Yasir Naqvi and Marie-France Lalonde—for changes to the police act to see the light of day.

The legislation proposes certain significant changes. It seeks to better define the role and responsibilities of the police services boards vis-à-vis those of the chief of police; pays greater attention to issues of diversity and policing of Indigenous communities; calls for mandatory training in diversity, anti-racism and culturally appropriate services; streamlines the duties of police officers by no longer requiring them to enforce municipal by-laws such as traffic enforcement; and gives police services boards greater flexibility in using alternative service delivery methods, including, potentially, private security.

The legislation also sets higher educational standards for entering the police profession, provides for a longer probationary period with the option to extend it (something that I had specifically advocated for) and authorizes police chiefs to suspend officers without pay under certain very serious circumstances.

And, finally, the legislation requires every municipality to develop a community safety and wellness plan with the participation of the health sector, the education sector, the community and social service sector and the police sector.

There are, of course, sceptical voices. Legal scholars like Kent Roach of the University of Toronto have expressed concern about how the new legislation still will not strengthen civilian governance of policing and worry that some of the issues that bedevilled policing before will persist. Others in the community believe that the proof will be in the pudding, as it were, and are waiting to see whether the intent behind the legislation will be truly reflected in the implementation or whether, once again, the organized police voices will prevail. They are very cognizant of the ability of these voices to exert excessive political force, as they have done successfully in the past.

This legislation does no more than offer a modest improvement to the existing model of policing and police governance. It does not lead to a radically new approach to policing. Thus, for instance, while police are required to be involved in the development of a mandatory municipal community safety and wellness plan along with other service providers, the core functions of policing will continue to be about crime and public order. There is no recognition of all of those other functions—mental health, school safety and social issues, for example—that now take up the bulk of police time.

And then there is the Toronto Police Services Board's latest bid to transform policing in this city, "The Way Forward: Modernizing Community Safety in Toronto."[1] It's a glossy document loaded with corporate buzzwords that reads like promo material for a miracle drug—full of glib jargon and breathless claims but short on specifics. It smells a bit like 2011, when the board undertook to reduce the annual police budget by 10 percent over two years, and it includes, once again, a budget reduction of 10 percent by 2019. The transformational task force wants to improve staff scheduling, urges a three-year hiring and promotion freeze and would end the crossing-guard program, reform paid duty and reduce the number of police divisions.

Police association president Mike McCormack immediately sounded the alarm over the safety of our streets and low morale among officers. He released a survey showing—he said—plunging morale among Toronto police, with twenty resignations in the first two months of 2017 and 94 percent of respondents saying the task force had had a negative effect on morale. "The service is bleeding to death," he told Joe Warmington at the *Sun*. "It's a sinking ship. Many officers want to get off." Nothing subtle there. Unsurprisingly, the board caved to the police association on one of its key recommendations: the three-year freeze on hiring.

This is not to say there aren't areas in the transformation report that have potential. I'm thinking of neighbourhood policing, where police focus on calls that need an actual police presence and provide productive, constructive alternatives when an officer is not needed. The report also rightly advocates diverting non-policing calls to other city departments and favours smaller, more efficient police stations. But there is a lot of air between the recommendations and the reality. The report is woefully short on details and it is on a collision course with the two barriers to transformation: police culture and the police union.

The transformation report does not soft-pedal the challenge of culture change. "Culture change in the TPS is complex and will take time to achieve," it says. "That's in part because it's a large operational organization with almost eight thousand members and a diverse range of police and civilian functions. It's also because policing is highly regulated through provincial legislation and by necessity includes a strong emphasis on following procedures and rules. Not everyone sees or experiences this reality in the same way but the words people sometimes use to describe it are variations on a theme: top-down, command-and-control, restrictive, inflexible. Occasionally people even refer to police culture as military or paramilitary."

The report says that a new culture cannot simply be imposed on the police service, but that it must grow and evolve from within. It does, however, provide a laundry list of desired aspects of the new culture, including having a more familiar relationship with neighbourhoods and focusing on community safety while bringing neighbourhood insights and sensitivities to policing operations. The document also talks about collaborating and partnering with communities to focus on solutions and outcomes with a special "sensitivity" toward youth. As well, the report speaks of taking risks, and admitting and learning from mistakes.

However, the report only deals with what I call the formal aspects of police culture. There are informal aspects—the larger, hidden part of the iceberg—that are far more daunting. As I said in my article on informal police culture, "Developed through history, folklore, mythology, symbolic action and memorialization, it has a huge impact on officer behaviour. As the policing research by British academic Jerome Skolnick reveals, informal culture shapes the police officer's 'working personality.'"[2]

Former deputy chief Peter Sloly stated the culture-change goal quite eloquently: "We need the institution of policing to evolve from a thin blue line that separates police from community to a thin blue thread that is interwoven within the fabric of society."[3] I do not believe that the beautiful image of community-oriented policing evoked by Sloly's metaphor can be brought to life by tinkering with the status quo. We need a new vision for policing in general, a new mission for local policing, a new model based on clear identification and articulation of the different needs of governments and communities. We need a new system of governance and oversight that is genuinely independent, has muscle and authority, represents the public interest and is run by those who will not bow to police authority or allow themselves to become beholden to the top brass.

And yes, we need a new formula for the financing of policing that does not stiff the public and make it subsidize the agendas or interests of higher-level governments. It will require political honesty and political guts. It will require that our political masters not look to the police chiefs and police associations for approval, but to the public and the communities they represent. It will require, above all, an intelligent conversation among us, the public. This conversation needs to begin with an informed understanding of what local policing is all about and what it actually does.

The developments so far, whether it is the Tulloch report or the Toronto board's transformational plan, are thus intended to improve the status quo. Despite their positive elements, they are not designed to bring in a new approach to local policing. The same holds true for Ontario's promised changes to the *Police Services Act* even though the province has adopted the term "community safety and wellness" and calls the legislation the *Safer Ontario Act*.

So, where are we headed? As I've outlined before, we have been living with a series of mismatches for years. And as we go forward, we must eliminate them. These mismatches are between what police are supposed to do and what police do, between needs—be they of a community or the state—and the allocation of resources, and between the legislative support police need and the support they get. Another mismatch is the core policing duties expected and the demands and pressures placed on local services by federal and provincial governments.[4]

SO HERE ARE some proposals for a different option. To begin with, there needs to be a clear separation between policing a local community and the policing needs of the federal and provincial governments. Policing related to national security and anti-terrorism is important. It is a federal responsibility, and Ottawa should not be piggybacking on municipal police services to fulfill its responsibility. You shouldn't do it on the cheap and ask the community to subsidize you. Doing that undermines the trust that must exist between the police and all communities as the foundation for true community-based policing. As Christopher Murphy has put it, the demands of national security and anti-terrorism–related policing turn communities at risk into communities *of* risk.

Dealing with major disasters that involve search-and-rescue operations is important too. We have a silly system for it. Ottawa gave one-time funding to five big cities across the country for heavy urban search-and-rescue (HUSAR) teams. There is no regular operational funding for them either from the federal government or the provinces. But Ontario, for example, has a commissioner for community safety who is in charge of this very critical responsibility. The police service that hosts the team ends up holding the bag in more ways than one.

This happened when the Algo Centre Mall collapsed in the northern Ontario town of Elliot Lake in 2012. The HUSAR team based in Toronto had to make the 540-kilometre trip to carry out search and rescue. When public opinion began turning against the McGuinty government, it was a Toronto staff inspector, Bill Neadles (now a superintendent), who faced criticism and Toronto police got the black eye. When McGuinty intervened, he got the credit and the Toronto officer, Staff Inspector Neadles, got the criticism. It was the G20 all over again. The federal and provincial governments must assume full responsibility for these operations.

Finally, we must define precisely what local community policing is all about, separate from the above national and provincial policing responsibilities. Not easy, but it has to be done. As I have said repeatedly in this book, policing is no longer just about what are conventionally considered to be cops' traditional responsibilities, namely protection of person and property; law and order; and enforcing the Criminal Code. These constitute approximately 30 percent of policing. Local community policing today is broadly about safety and wellness—that's 70 percent of what this policing is about.

Much of this is thanks to governments' neoliberal policies and legislation dictated by an obsession with the bottom line that gives priority to balancing the books over providing adequate services in education, health, housing and social services. Social issues have become policing issues because local policing is now expected to pick up after these decisions. Since this is the case, let us find a model that works better than the one we have now.

I believe we need a broader community safety and wellness agency to provide an integrated response to local needs. Dealing with violent crimes and issues of law and order should be a part of the mandate of such an agency, but not its defining feature. This agency should be required to invest at least as much in prevention and promotion of safety and wellness as in reactive enforcement.

Its approach to community safety must be outcome-based. At this time, the work of police on creating a safe community is measured in terms of input and output. That is, we spent x amount of money, deployed y amount of resources and had z results by way of the number of arrests, charges laid, break and enters investigated, et cetera. But how did these things enhance a community's feeling or experience of safety and wellness? Safety and wellness are measured not by the statistical absence of crime but by the presence of a sense of ownership of public spaces, of neighbourliness, of belonging, of mutual respect and trust, of equality, inclusivity and cohesion. An integrated approach to community safety and wellness must be based on these kinds of outcomes.

The armed, uniformed police officer must not be the sole provider of this agency's services. It should be a multi-disciplinary agency composed of many types of specialists. Like a spider's web, it should be a network of expertise. We need specialists who deal with people with mental health challenges. We need specialists who deal with safety in our schools. We need specialists who deal primarily with domestic violence. We should have those specialists in integrated units, ready to deal with those matters, rather than having generalists trained in ballistics and dealing with violent crime responding to all calls. We should have specialists who deal with financial crimes and cybersecurity, particularly the safety of the elderly, who are often duped by scammers.

How many officers do we hire who are auditors, IT specialists, economists or financial analysts? Who carries out these functions? In Toronto, we probably don't have half a dozen officers with the level of expertise those specialties require. It would take a huge overhaul of recruitment and training. We would be looking for non-uniformed, unarmed men and women who are computer savvy, not people who have shoot-to-kill expertise. In today's police world, we are using highly trained master mechanics to change the oil. And we are using oil changers as master mechanics. These practices don't make sense.

We are deploying uniformed and armed police officers to carry out functions that can be better performed by special constables and other trained civilians. Why do we use uniformed police officers to catch speeders? Offences like speeding or noise complaints are provincial offences. The main job of the uniformed police officer should be to enforce the Criminal Code, and a provincial offence is not a crime. We've seen how this can lead to problems. Officers pull over a driver who is Black for speeding and emotions are running high. There is a costly mess. Police may ramp it up by trying to provoke a confrontation, planting drugs or manufacturing a charge of resisting arrest.

If you need someone to simply hold a radar gun, why isn't that person a special constable who deals with just that? A lot of the officers who make huge sums of money each year on overtime pad their bottom line by giving out speeding tickets. The armed, uniformed police officer should be one component of a reimagined community safety and wellness agency surrounded by mediators, social workers and mental health workers. This agency need not even be headed by a uniformed officer, though there would be senior police officers and a police leader would be part of the top management team.

My point is that we need to slice the organization and its functions in several ways. And as we do this, we cannot ignore the reality of tiered policing in our communities. We already have housing police, campus police, transit police, security protecting our nuclear plants—to name some. And we have private police. Many condominium buildings have a guard who lets you in and checks your credentials. You cannot go to a shopping mall without encountering teams of grim-looking security guards dressed and equipped to resemble police. You cannot walk the streets without seeing numerous white vehicles, similar to police patrol cars, with the word SECURITY in large letters on the side.

This is our first line of oil changers. They, too, must be taken into account as we develop a full understanding of what constitutes conventional policing. Thus, we need to define a policing function in the conventional sense and a wellness function. And we need to decide who can best provide these functions.

This kind of far-reaching change will not come from within because police agencies are conservative institutions that are resistant to change, comfortable with the way they have always functioned. It will take political will, and it will take a new legislative framework. The securitization of the police and turning them into agents of the surveillance state are consequences of this lack of political will.

In England, political will got things done. Police boards were scrapped. A policing and safety commissioner elected by the public was created as a position. Chiefs were made accountable to the commissioner, who sets the portion of the tax rate for policing and has the power to hire and fire them. The idea here is not that we follow the UK model, but that we institute effective governance accountable to the community. Our police boards are largely weak institutions composed of people who may be well-meaning but are not—and are not trained to be—up to the task.

Furthermore, police services boards have their hands tied by legislation, the political power of police chiefs and police associations, and quite often, strong-willed mayors and/or councillors. And of course, police culture. If we are to move to a new type of community safety and wellness agency, we have to rethink governance. Such an agency would require a model of governance that has the competence, leadership and resources to oversee all the safety and wellness functions and all the policing functions—whether performed by public police or private police, whether in a public housing community, on a university campus or at a shopping mall.

So let us turn to the policing component of a community safety and wellness agency. First of all, the personnel selected to perform this function must be individuals with an inclusive outlook toward the community they serve. Their working personalities should be free from suspicion of the "other" that is a prevailing feature of the informal and hidden police culture.[5]

The uniformed police officers employed by this reimagined provider of community safety and wellness must be people with broad educational backgrounds that extend beyond high school (a certificate or diploma in a police foundations course from a college should not be treated as post-secondary education). They should be assessed rigorously for their social, moral and ethical values as well as the emotional and psychological dimensions of their personality. As employees, they must be subject to the same system of accountability for their conduct as in most other occupations: prompt discipline by management, including the ability to suspend and terminate, subject to grievance and arbitration.

And they should receive training that is consistent with the needs and reality of today's policing, training that develops the different types of knowledge, understanding and skills necessary for providing a wide range of services. Further, there needs to be a culture of officers engaging in continuous learning—professional development through education in a wide variety of areas at the college and university level. If these highly paid people are to be regarded as professionals, they should be enabled and supported to act like them.

In my vision, the programs and services of this new agency should be located near the community it serves. Right now, we have police divisions but we do not have neighbourhood-based community safety programs. The highly trained and heavily armed specialists assigned to areas such as guns and gangs, undercover operations and drug detail can be stationed in larger facilities distributed across the city. Everyone else should be deployed in smaller units in neighbourhoods.

Then there is the fundamental question of whether every uniformed police officer should be armed with lethal force options. This is so sacrosanct that when I first suggested that perhaps all police officers should not be carrying guns, the police association mocked me on the cover of its in-house magazine. The illustration showed a criminal applauding me. But I look to the United Kingdom, where the bulk of London officers do not carry guns. Guns are carried only by highly trained police officers, members of a unit about one thousand strong. Despite the current anxiety about security and safety in places like London, there is no push for arming every single cop on the street.

Britain is rightly lauded for its neighbourhood policing strategy. When I study the data out of London, which has thirty-five thousand police officers, the rate of injury or death of officers is tiny. It's a culture thing. People in London are not shot at by police because in order to shoot, constables would have to summon a highly trained officer with a gun. When he was that city's mayor, Boris Johnson decided to increase the number of police officers who had Tasers, but he limited this to the officers who were already permitted to carry weapons. The increase gave London no more than 700 Tasers for a uniformed force of 35,000, whereas Toronto at the time had around 450 Tasers for a uniformed force of 5,400.

When there is any move in the direction of disarmament here, the police association brings officer safety to the fore. It has managed to shut down any conversation. But the conversation needs to happen, and politicians cannot shy away from it if they are serious about change. That raises the question of leadership. In our system of single-entry recruitment, police leaders are people who entered at the bottom and worked their way up. I have expressed earlier my misgivings regarding the effect of this pattern on independent, strong leadership without fear or favour. We need to consider having at least two entry points: one for those who wish to do front-line work and another for those who aspire to be senior officers.

We do this in civilian jobs and it is the norm in most other occupations, including the military. The duties, responsibilities, expertise and expectations are different for front-line work versus management. Why shouldn't the system of entry, educational requirements, skills, abilities, qualities, et cetera, also be different? Why not deliberately develop a cadre of leaders who will bring a different mindset, world view and outlook and who will not be embedded in the social world of the front line from years spent in those ranks?

That brings us to the issue of the top leadership. I have come to the firm conclusion that in our present system, where our top leaders have risen through the ranks of the same organization—with all those consequences that I have mentioned earlier—very few turn out to be independent, innovative change leaders capable of fresh thinking. They are too attached to the service they joined at a young age, its culture, traditions, conventions and social world. This is inevitable. They are rewarded with these promotions for their excellence in policing, when an entirely different set of skills and abilities is needed for leading a complex organization, such as questioning current practices.

Those chosen to serve at the top must have an extensive academic background, a broad education in areas of management, the capacity for independent thinking, openness to new ideas—and they must be unencumbered by emotional attachment to the agency's social networks. There are some options for disrupting emotional attachment. One, obviously, is to end the practice of promoting from within, which is common in Canada. Another is to require that people aspiring to one of the top jobs spend a period of time away from the agency, ideally working in a senior management capacity in a different type of organization altogether. This would expose them to a different culture, different approaches and different thinking. Policing needs a fresh kind of leadership to deal with contemporary challenges and a complex environment. Same old, same old, just will not do.

And finally, there is the question of accountability and oversight. In Ontario, it is fractured, scattered and ineffective. In the UK, there is Her Majesty's Inspectorate of Constabulary (HMIC). A few years ago, a civilian named Tom Winsor was named its head. This was historic because until then, the position had been filled by an ex–police commissioner. HMIC has the power to conduct inspections of core policing functions in all forty-three police forces in England and Wales. We don't have to copy this practice holus-bolus, but we should keep in mind that real reform takes a gigantic effort, with real power given to would-be reformers. Otherwise, the status quo is never dislodged and we tinker, time and again.

We can't afford any more tinkering. One of the tenets of Sir Robert Peel's principles of policing is "The ability of the police to perform their duties is dependent upon *public approval* of police existence, actions, behaviour and the ability of the police to secure and maintain *public respect* [my emphasis]." The "public approval" and "public respect" Peel refers to will not be obtained through symbolic actions, but through meaningful, substantive measures. The alternative is more public cynicism and more public mistrust. It will take political will and political guts to get there. And it must happen now.

Endnotes

Introduction

1. "Young black men again faced highest rate of US police killings in 2016," *The Guardian*, Jan. 8, 2017, www.theguardian.com/us-news/2017/jan/08/the-counted-police-killings-2016-young-black-men.

2. "Fatal shootings by police remain relatively unchanged after two years," *The Washington Post*, Dec. 30, 2016, www.washingtonpost.com/investigations/fatal-shootings-by-police-remain-relatively-unchanged-after-two-years/2016/12/30/fc807596-c3ca-11e6-9578-0054287507db_story.html.

3. Dr. Lorne Foster, Dr. Les Jacobs, Dr. Bobby Siu, *Race Data and Traffic Stops in Ottawa, 2013–2015: A Report on Ottawa and the Police Districts*, October 2016, www.ottawapolice.ca/en/about-us/resources/.TSRDCP_York_Research_Report.pdf.

4. "RCMP head tells indigenous chiefs there are 'racists' on his force," *Toronto Star*, Dec. 9, 2015, www.thestar.com/news/insight/2015/12/09/rcmp-head-tells-indigenous-chiefs-there-are-racists-on-his-force.html.

5. "SIU concerns 'regularly ignored,' critics say," *Toronto Star*, Mar. 13, 2017, www.thestar.com/news/crime/2017/03/12/siu-allegations-regularly-ignored-by-police-critics-say.html.

6. Christopher Murphy, *Securitizing Canadian Policing: A New Policing Paradigm for the Post 9/11 Security State*, 2007.

Chapter 1

None.

Chapter 2

1. "Singled Out," *Toronto Star*, Oct. 19, 2002.
2. "Police stop more blacks, Ont. study finds," CBC, May 26, 2005, www.cbc.ca /news/canada/police-stop-more-blacks-ont-study-finds-1.565724.
3. "Racial profiling exists; promises of internal probe fell flat," *Toronto Star*, March 31, 2005.
4. "New chief, new hope: Blair offers an honest take," *Toronto Star*, April 8, 2005.
5. Human Rights Tribunal, *Phipps v. Toronto Police Services Board*, June 18, 2009, www.yorku.ca/lfoster/2017-18/RESP%204052/miscellaneous_files /Phipps_HRTO.pdf.
6. "Race matters: blacks documented by police at high rate," *Toronto Star*, Feb. 6, 2010, www.thestar.com/news/gta/raceandcrime.html.
7. *Known to police: Toronto police stop and document black and brown people far more than whites*, *Toronto Star*, March 9, 2012, www.thestar.com/news/insight /2012/03/09/known_to_police_toronto_police_stop_and_document _black_and_brown_people_far_more_than_whites.html.
8. Toronto Police Service, *The Police and Community Engagement Review* (*The PACER Report*). Toronto: Toronto Police Service, n.d., 34. http://tpsb.ca /component/jdownloads/send/30-community-engagements/458-the -pacer-report.
9. "Toronto police chief Mark Saunders's secret carding report." *Toronto Star*, May 26, 2015, www.thestar.com/news/gta/2015/05/26/toronto-police -chief-mark-saunders-secret-carding-report.html.

Chapter 3

1. "WTO riots in Seattle: 15 years ago," *Seattle PI*, www.seattlepi.com/local/ article/WTO-riots-in-Seattle-15-years-ago-5915088.php#photo-797476.
2. Honourable John W. Morden, *Independent Civilian Review into Matters Relating to the G20 Summit*. Toronto, June 2012, tpsb.ca/items-of-interest/ send/29-items-of-interest/460-g20-summit-independent-civilian-review.
3. Ibid.
4. Office of the Independent Police Review Director, *Policing the Right to Protest*, May 2012, p. 205.
5. Ibid., p. 206.
6. Ibid., p. 227.
7. Ibid., p. 237.
8. Ibid., p. 98.
9. Ibid., p. 100.
10. Ibid., pp. 97–8.

Chapter 4

1. Sentencing of James Forcillo by Justice Edward Then, July 28, 2016, www. scribd.com/document/319568957/Reasons-for-the-sentence-of-James -Forcillo.
2. Testimony from James Forcillo, Nov. 26, 2015.
3. "Outdated '21-foot rule' for police shootings finally bites the dust," *Toronto Star*, March 21, 2016, www.thestar.com/news/crime/2016/03/21/please -dont-post-online-separately-add-to-the-bottom-of-one-of-the-other-pieces. html.
4. Testimony from Dan Pravica, Dec. 15, 2015.
5. "Sammy Yatim: Dennis O'Connor resigns from Chief Blair's police review in wake of streetcar shooting," *Toronto Star*, Aug. 28, 2013, www.thestar.com/ news/crime/2013/08/28/sammy_yatim_dennis_oconnor_resigns_from _toronto_police_chief_bill_blairs_police_review_in_wake_of_streetcar _shooting.html.
6. "Judge acquits Toronto cook, ruling police used excessive force," *Toronto Star*, March 13, 2013, www.thestar.com/news/crime/2013/03/13/judge _acquits_toronto_cook_ruling_police_used_excessive_force.html.
7. Sentencing of James Forcillo by Justice Edward Then, July 28, 2016.
8. "Under Pressure From Protesters, NYPD Chief Resigns," *ThinkProgress*, Aug. 2, 2016, thinkprogress.org/under-pressure-from-protesters-nypd-chief -resigns.

Chapter 5

1. Paul Dubé, *A Matter of Life and Death*, Ontario Ombudsman, June 2016, www.ombudsman.on.ca/Files/sitemedia/Documents/OntarioOmbuds manDeescalationEN_1.pdf.
2. Ibid.
3. Ibid.
4. "Coroner's jury calls for better de-escalation training for police," *Toronto Star*, Aug. 2, 2017, www.thestar.com/news/gta/2017/08/02/coroners-jury -recommends-more-mental-health-training-for-police.html.
5. Honourable Frank Iacobucci, *Police Encounters with People in Crisis*, July 2014, www.torontopolice.on.ca/publications/files/reports/police_encounters _with_people_in_crisis_2014.pdf.
6. "Black men perceived as more threatening, expert tells Andrew Loku in-quest," *Toronto Star*, June 12, 2017, www.thestar.com/news/gta/2017/06/12 /black-men-perceived-as-more-threatening-expert-tells-andrew-loku -inquest.html.

7. "People see black men as larger and stronger than white men—even when they're not, study says," *Washington Post*, March 14, 2017, www .washingtonpost.com/news/morning-mix/wp/2017/03/14/psycho logists-we-see-Black-men-as-larger-and-stronger-than-white-men-even -when-theyre-not.

8. "Stand Down," *The Walrus*, July 16, 2014, thewalrus.ca/stand-down/.

9. This so-called condition was very much in vogue in policing circles at one time and, in Ontario, was promoted most prominently by a former deputy chief coroner, Dr. James Cairns. Coroner's inquests were routinely re-turning verdicts that an individual's death was caused by excited delirium. It took a considerable amount of advocacy on the part of some of us who were members of a provincial advisory committee on policing standards to convince the Ministry of Community Safety that this was not a medical condition but could be the symptom of one.

10. Testimony of Const. Andrew Doyle, coroner's inquest, Oct. 31, 2013.

11. Testimony of Const. Henry Tang, coroner's inquest, June 13, 2017.

12. Testimony of Const. John Tanner, coroner's inquest, Sept. 20, 2010.

13. "Canadian study to examine scope of PTSD among public-safety workers," *The Globe and Mail*, July 28, 2016, www.theglobeandmail.com/news/politics /canadian-study-to-examine-scope-of-ptsd-among-public-safety-workers /article31174013/.

Chapter 6

1. Toronto Auditor General's Office, Appendix 1, *Police Paid Duty: Balancing Cost Effectiveness and Public Safety*, December 1, 2010.

Chapter 7

1. "John Tory plans to smooth Toronto Police relationship with watchdog," *The Globe and Mail*, November 27, 2014, www.theglobeandmail.com/news /toronto/john-tory-plans-to-smooth-toronto-police-relationship-with -watchdog/article21822648/.

2. "Relationship between police, citizens concerns Tory," *Toronto Sun*, November 27, 2014, www.torontosun.com/2014/11/27/relationship -between-police-citizens-concerns-tory.

3. "Race takes centre stage at Toronto mayoral debate," Global News, Oct. 11, 2014, globalnews.ca/news/1610153/race-takes-centre-stage-at-toronto -mayoral-debate/.

Chapter 8

1. "Chief Blair on Mukherjee: 'I'll leave that up to the public,'" *Toronto Sun*, Dec. 8, 2014, www.torontosun.com/2014/12/08/chief-blair-on-mukherjee -ill-leave-that-up-to-the-public.

2. "PBA President: Police Officers 'Thrown Under the Bus' by de Blasio in Wake of Eric Garner Grand Jury Decision," CBS New York, Dec. 4, 2014, newyork.cbslocal.com/2014/12/04/pba-president-police-officers-thrown -under-the-bus-by-de-blasio-in-wake-of-eric-garner-grand-jury-decision/.

3. "Keep Alok Mukherjee as chair at the Toronto Police Services: #NoResignationMukherjee," Change.org, Dec. 5, 2014, www.change .org/p/kathleen-wynne-keep-alok-mukherjee-as-chair-at-the-toronto -police-services-noresignationmukherjee.

4. "Facebook post seeming to make light of spousal abuse has police services board chairman under fire again," *National Post*, Dec. 10, 2014, news .nationalpost.com/toronto/facebook-post-seeming-to-make-light-of- spousal-abuse-has-police-services-board-chairman-under-fire-again.

5. "Respect police while criticizing them," *London Free Press*, Dec. 22, 2014, www.lfpress.com/2014/12/22/respect-police-while-criticizing-them.

Chapter 9

1. "Indigenous women nearly 10 times more likely to be street checked by Edmonton police, new data shows," CBC, June 27, 2017, www.cbc.ca/news /canada/edmonton/street-checks-edmonton-police-aboriginal-Black -carding-1.4178843.

2. "York Regional Police now investigating Thunder Bay Indigenous teen deaths," *Toronto Star*, June 23, 2017, www.thestar.com/news/canada /2017/06/23/york-regional-police-now-investigating-thunder-bay -indigenous-teen-deaths.html.

3. Dr. Lorne Foster, Dr. Les Jacobs and Dr. Bobby Siu, *Race Data and Traffic Stops in Ottawa, 2013–2015: A Report on Ottawa and the Police Districts*, October 2016, www.ottawapolice.ca/en/about-us/resources/.TSRDCP _York_Research_Report_Summary.pdf.

4. "Toronto marijuana arrests reveal 'startling' racial divide," *Toronto Star*, July 6, 2017, www.thestar.com/news/insight/2017/07/06/toronto-marijuana -arrests-reveal-startling-racial-divide.html.

5. The province has recently appointed Ontario Court of Appeal Justice Michael H. Tulloch to conduct this review.

6. I am thinking here of the likes of Audrey Campbell, the steady hand as the community co-chair of Toronto's PACER advisory committee, and her po-

lice co-chair, Stacy Clarke, the courageous police sergeant who, as a Black woman, believed deeply that carding was an injustice. At considerable risk to her own future prospects, Clarke joined hands with Campbell in order to stay at the table with Chief Saunders and convince him to do the right thing. As well, I commend the many community members of the PACER advisory committee, who would not give up. Meeting after meeting they came, overcame their frustration with police obduracy and kept asking the hard questions. Such was their impact that Tory, Pringle and their new colleague on the police board, city councillor Shelley Carroll, began attending the meetings themselves. The lawyers, like Howard Morton, Paul Copeland, Clayton Ruby and Peter Rosenthal, who appeared before the board time after countless time, urging the board on, providing critique of half measures and advice on how the board should exercise the authority given to it. The tireless champion of civil liberties Noa Mendelsohn Aviv, a lawyer from the Canadian Civil Liberties Association, who had mastered the ability to offer powerful analysis and legal advice and who also helped us write a strong joint submission to the provincial government. Knia Singh, who transformed his personal experience of repeated carding into energy for action. Through the Osgoode Society Against Institutional Injustice, an organization that he had formed as a law student at the Osgoode Hall Law School, he made countless appearances before the board, wrote numerous submissions and advocated constantly through the media. Anthony Morgan, a lawyer at that time with the African Canadian Legal Clinic, was factual, analytical and unperturbable; he articulated the experience and impact of anti-Black racism powerfully. Kingsley Gilliam of the Black Action Defence Committee, who remembered and reminded the board of the history of a legacy that needed to be eradicated. The heads and staff of agencies like the Ontario Human Rights Commission, the office of the Information and Privacy Commissioner of Ontario and the Office of the Independent Police Review Director, the provincial entity that deals with public complaints against the police, who provided important support to the community's struggle. I am thinking of Black Lives Matter Toronto, a dynamic arrival on the scene. Led by young Black and other racialized people, BLM injected new energy into the fight with its articulation of the issues and its blunt yet innovative interventions. I am thinking of my Ryerson colleagues—professors Akua Benjamin, Winnie Ng, Anne-Marie Singh and Idil Abdillahi—who, combining a passion for social justice with academic rigour, played an invaluable role in making the community's case to the government.

7. "'We are at risk of turning into a surveillance society': Alok Mukherjee," *Toronto Star*, June 5, 2015, www.thestar.com/opinion/commentary/2015/06/05/we-are-at-risk-of-turning-into-a-surveillance-society-alok-mukherjee.html.

8. *War Comes Home*, American Civil Liberties Union, www.aclu.org/feature/war-comes-home.

9. "BEARCAT in Keene Mocked by John Oliver on HBO," Aug. 28, 2014, www.shirelibertynews.com/bearcat-in-keene-mocked-by-john-oliver-on-hbo/.

10. "'Militarizing police': Winnipeg buys $343K armoured vehicle for officers," CBC, Dec, 9, 2015, www.cbc.ca/news/canada/manitoba/militarizing-police-winnipeg-buys-343k-armoured-vehicle-for-officers-1.3357289.

11. "RCMP commissioner worried about police militarization," *Maclean's*, Feb. 6, 2017, www.macleans.ca/news/canada/rcmp-commissioner-worried-about-police-militarization.

Chapter 10

1. "The life and bloody death of Andrew Loku: Toronto police officer's face 'went white as a ghost' after shooting," *National Post*, July 17, 2015, nationalpost.com/news/toronto/the-life-and-bloody-death-of-andrew-loku/wcm/eb1e9b5c-f403-47be-8845-f6fd621d6d77.

2. "Attorney General has yet to read SIU report on Loku shooting—let alone make it public," *Toronto Star*, April 19, 2016, www.thestar.com/news/crime/2016/04/19/attorney-general-has-yet-to-read-siu-report-on-loku-shooting-let-alone-make-it-public.html.

3. Honourable Michael H. Tulloch, *Report of the Independent Police Oversight Review*, April 2017, p. 50.

4. *Special Investigations Unit Annual Report 2016–2017*, www.siu.on.ca/pdfs/siu_ar_2016-17_eng_online_f.pdf.

5. "Are these cops above the law?" *Toronto Star*, Oct. 28, 2010, www.thestar.com/news/gta/2010/10/28/are_these_cops_above_the_law.html.

6. *Report of the Independent Police Oversight Review*, p. 5.

7. Ibid., p. 26.

8. Ibid., p. 26.

9. Ibid., p. 260.

10. "Officers and the SIU," *The Back-Up: Hamilton Police Association Newsletter* 4:2 (Summer 2009), p.25.

11. Ian D. Scott, *Issues in Civilian Oversight of Policing in Canada*, Canada Law Books, 2014, p. 274.

12. Ibid., pp. 274–75.

13. "Toronto police failed to co-operate with SIU, letters from former director Ian Scott allege," *Toronto Star*, Dec. 12, 2013, www.thestar.com/news/crime /2013/12/12/toronto_police_failed_to_cooperate_with_siu_letters _from_former_director_ian_scott_allege.html.

14. "Addressing Police Excessive Use of Force: A Proposal to Amend the Mandate of the Special Investigations Unit," 2004, www.cacole.ca/resource %20library/conferences/2004%20Conference/2004%20Conference%20 Presentations/Scott,%20I.%202004.pdf.

15. Scott, *Issues in Civilian Oversight of Policing in Canada*, p. 282.

16. *Wood v. Schaeffer*, SCOC, Dec. 19, 2013, scc-csc.lexum.com/scc-csc/scc-csc/en /item/13388/index.do.

Chapter 11

1. "London police given 1,000 acid response kits after surge in attacks," *Guardian*, July 24, 2017, www.theguardian.com/uk-news/2017/jul/24 /london-acid-attacks-police-given-1000-emergency-response-kits.

2. "Crime rise is biggest in a decade, ONS figures show," *The Guardian*, July 20, 2017, www.theguardian.com/uk-news/2017/jul/20/official-figures-show -biggest-rise-crime-in-a-decade.

3. "Met police chief says cuts will lead to fewer officers in London," *The Guardian*, Feb. 3, 2017, www.theguardian.com/uk-news/2017/feb/03/met -police-chief-bernard-hogan-howe-policing-numbers-london.

4. "Police use of firearms statistics," www.gov.uk/government/collections/ police-use-of-firearms-statistics.

5. "Police use of firearms statistics, England and Wales: April 2015 to March 2016," www.gov.uk/government/statistics/police-use-of-firearms-statistics -england-and-wales-april-2015-to-march-2016.

6. "Definition of policing by consent," www.gov.uk/government/publications /policing-by-consent/definition-of-policing-by-consent.

7. "Met using force against disproportionately large number of Black people," *The Guardian*, Aug. 1, 2017, www.theguardian.com/uk-news/2017 /aug/01/met-police-using-force-against-disproportionately-large-number -of-black-people.

8. "No routine arming of police: Commissioner," April 5, 2011, www.stuff.co.nz /national/politics/4851590/No-routine-arming-of-police-Commissioner.

9. *Police Weapons: New Zealand*, www.loc.gov/law/help/police-weapons/new -zealand.php.

10. New Zealand Police Association, *Toward a Safer New Zealand*, June 22, 2017, www.policeassn.org.nz/newsroom/publications/other-publications/2017-new-zealand-police-association-policy-document.

11. "Two police shootings in a week renew calls to limit officers' access to firearms," July 14, 2016, www.stuff.co.nz/national/crime/82120503/almost-one-dead-every-year-from-police-shootings-in-last-decade.

12. "By the numbers: US police kill more in days than other countries do in years," *The Guardian*, June 9, 2015, www.theguardian.com/us-news/2015/jun/09/the-counted-police-killings-us-vs-other-countries.

13. "Armed Police Raise Concerns," *Iceland Review*, June 12, 2017, icelandreview.com/news/2017/06/12/armed-police-raise-concerns.

14. Ross Hendy, *Routinely Armed and Unarmed Police: What Can the Scandinavian Experience Teach Us?* Institute of Criminology, University of Cambridge, April 2014, www.academia.edu/6290307/Routinely_armed_and_unarmed_police_what_can_the_Scandinavian_experience_teach_us.

15. "New Armed Actors Research Note: Estimating Civilian Owned Firearms," Small Arms Survey, www.smallarmssurvey.org/about-us/highlights/highlight-research-note-9-estimating-civilian-owned-firearms.html.

16. William J. Krouse, *Gun Control Legislation*, Congressional Research Service, November 14, 2012, fas.org/sgp/crs/misc/RL32842.pdf.

17. Nick Danby, "Lessons from Inspector Clouseau: What America's Police Can Learn from Europe," *Harvard Political Review*, March 17, 2017, harvardpolitics.com/online/lessons-inspector-clouseau-americas-police-can-learn-european-nations/.

Chapter 12

1. Toronto Police Service Transformational Task Force, *The Way Forward: Modernizing Community Safety in Toronto*, January 2017, www.torontopolice.on.ca/TheWayForward/files/action-plan.pdf.

2. "How an 'informal,' veiled culture affects policing," *Toronto Star*, May 25, 2017, www.thestar.com/opinion/commentary/2017/05/25/how-an-informal-veiled-culture-affects-policing-mukherjee.html.

3. "There is a problem with our policing," *Globe and Mail*, July 23, 2016, www.theglobeandmail.com/news/toronto/todays-policing-model-fails-to-serve-and-protect-public-and-officers/article31090245/.

4. Alok Mukherjee, "Let's Tackle the Mismatches!" Canadian Association of Police Boards Annual Conference, Sydney, NS, August 14, 2009.

5. Mukherjee, "How an 'informal,' veiled culture affects policing."

Index